DOMESTIC VIOLENCE AND SEXUALITY

What's love got to do with it?

Catherine Donovan and Marianne Hester

First published in Great Britain in 2014 by

Policy Press
University of Bristol
6th Floor
Howard House
Queen's Avenue
Clifton
Bristol BS8 1SD
UK
t: +44 (0)117 331 5020
f: +44 (0)117 331 5367
pp-info@bristol.ac.uk
www.policypress.co.uk

North America office:
Policy Press
c/o The University of Chicago Press
1427 East 60th Street
Chicago, IL 60637, USA
t: +1 773 702 7700
f: +1 773-702-9756
sales@press.uchicago.edu
www.press.uchicago.edu

British Library Cataloguing in Publication Data
A catalogue record for this book is available from the British Library

Library of Congress Cataloging-in-Publication Data
A catalog record for this book has been requested

ISBN 978 1 44730 743 3 hardcover

Cover design by Qube Design Associates, Bristol
Front cover: istockphoto.com
Printed and bound in Great Britain by CPI Group (UK) Ltd,
Croydon, CR0 4YY
Policy Press uses environmentally responsible print partners

FSC
www.fsc.org
MIX
Paper from
responsible sources
FSC® C013604

Contents

List of figures and tables   iv
About the authors   v
Acknowledgements   vii

one   What is the problem?   1

two   How we did the research: the COHSAR research approach   35

three   Setting the context: sexuality matters   57

four   Identifying and experiencing domestic violence and abuse   89

five   What's love got to do with it?   121

six   Barriers to help-seeking: the gap of trust   157

seven   Key findings and implications for practice   195

References   217
Index   235

List of figures and tables

Figures

4.1   Modelling the relationship between the incidence and   113
      impact of domestic violence and abuse: a worked example
      with emotional abuse
7.1   Duluth Power and Control Wheel   202
7.2   Power and Control Wheel for lesbian, gay, bisexual and   203
      trans relationships
7.3   COHSAR Power and Control Wheel   205

Tables

4.1   Emotional, physical and sexual behaviours from same   98
      sex partners (%, N=746)
4.2   The impact of emotional, physical and sexual behaviours   107
      from same sex partners – ever (%, N=731)
4.3   Domestic abuse group memberships and proportions   115
      within groups self reporting DVA and 'combined abused'
      (last 12 months)
4.4   Emotional, physical and sexual behaviours used by   117
      respondent to partner (%)
4.5   Relationship type by abuse scale (last 12 months)   118
7.1   Indicative behaviours in the COHSAR Power and   206
      Control Wheel

About the authors

Catherine Donovan is Professor of Social Relations at the University of Sunderland, UK, and leader of CASS, the Centre for Applied Social Sciences. She has conducted (mainly qualitative) research in lesbian, gay, bisexual and, latterly, trans (LGBT) communities for over twenty years. With Jeffrey Weeks and Brian Heaphy she conducted the first comprehensive study of families of choice in the UK (*Same sex intimacies: Families of choice and other life experiments*, 2001, Routledge). Her current research, in collaboration with Rebecca Barnes, focuses on those who have behaved in ways that could be labelled abusive. Catherine is on the board of Broken Rainbow, the charity providing support for victims and survivors of LGBT domestic abuse, and on the steering group of NEDAP (North East Domestic Abuse Project), a regional development project promoting best practice for LGB and/ or T people experiencing domestic violence and abuse. She has also worked with the Northumbria Probation Service to develop their Solo Enhanced one-to-one module for abusive LGB and/or T partners. Catherine has also conducted research with John Clayton and Jacqui Merchant on the impact of austerity in the North East of England, specifically the ways in which the rhetoric of localism and the big society are experienced in reality in the voluntary sector and the emotional impact of austerity on practitioners and volunteers.

Marianne Hester is Professor of Gender, Violence and International Policy at the University of Bristol, UK, and heads the Centre for Gender and Violence Research. She is a leading researcher of gender-based violence and has directed ground-breaking research in the UK, Europe, China and Scandinavia (using a range of methods) including historical and theoretical work (*Lewd women and wicked witches*, 1992, Routledge) and, with Lorraine Radford, the first major study in the UK on child contact and domestic violence (*Mothering through domestic violence*, 2006, Jessica Kingsley). Current research projects include: male domestic violence victims and perpetrators accessing the health service; rape and the criminal justice system; and domestic violence perpetrator programmes across Europe. She has worked closely with government departments and non-governmental organisations, as expert advisor to the NICE (National Institute for Health and Care Excellence) Programme Development Group on preventing and reducing domestic violence, as Research Director to the Department of Health and National Institute for Mental Health, as specialist advisor to the

Home Affairs Select Committee and as NSPCC (National Society for the Prevention of Cruelty to Children) Professor of Child Sexual Exploitation. She was awarded an OBE in 2012 in recognition of her research and prevention of domestic violence. She is patron of Devon Rape Crisis and South Tyneside Women's Aid.

Acknowledgements

The research was funded by the Economic and Social Research Council grant RES-000-23-0650. It was informed by an advisory group consisting of representatives from Broken Rainbow, the Northern Rock Foundation, Northumbria Probation Service, University of Portsmouth Equalities Unit, Central Manchester Women's Aid, Glasgow Women's Library, Scottish Equality Network, Stonewall Cymru, and Devon and Cornwall Police.

We want to thank all who worked on the research project, and in particular Jonathan Holmes and Melanie McCarry who carried out much of the fieldwork, Eldin Fahmy who did the statistical analysis for Chapter Four, our many project administrators but most especially, Jennifer Sewell and Jo Tyler; and latterly to Paula Willerton for her work on the bibliography and proofreading. The research would not have been possible without the active support of the many LGBTQ organisations and equalities networks across the UK who helped to distribute the survey via their members and websites and to develop the interview sample.

Catherine would like to thank Melissa Girling for her love and support during the research and writing of the book. Marianne would like to thank Rosemary Schonfeld for all her love, support and useful insights throughout the writing of this book and during the research on which the book is based.

We want to dedicate the book to all of those lesbians, gay men, bisexual and/or queer women, trans people, and heterosexual women and men who took part in the research and who shared their experiences with us.

ONE

What is the problem?

This book

In this book we provide the most detailed discussion so far in the UK of domestic violence and abuse (DVA) in same sex relationships, based on a large-scale study involving a national survey, interviews and focus groups. Given the lack of research on DVA in same sex relationships we set out to develop a study which also allowed comparison of the experiences of such behaviour across heterosexual and same sex relationships. As the book is largely about experiences of individuals in same sex relationships, the focus is mainly on those identifying as lesbian and gay men. However, we are also able to move beyond the limitations of looking only at lesbian, gay male or heterosexual experiences of DVA to make comparisons between these groups. Where possible we also refer to experiences of bisexual or transgendered individuals, a small number of whom took part in our research. When we discuss the social networks and/or communities that those living in same sex relationships are connected with or belong to we refer to lesbian, gay, bisexual, trans and queer (LGBTQ) communities. Finally, we use the term 'same sex', while acknowledging that more recently, especially in North America this term has been superseded by the term 'same gender'. We use 'same sex' partly because this is the language we adopted in the research and partly because it is still the term most often used in the UK context.

The book tackles a number of key questions:

- What is domestic violence and abuse in the context of same sex relationships?
- Are the domestic violence and abuse experiences of those in same sex relationships similar and/or different to those in heterosexual relationships?
- What about gender if individuals are the same sex?
- What has love got to do with it?

As authors we began this project from different research backgrounds. Marianne had already been researching DVA over many years, exploring experiences of both adults and children, victimised and perpetrators, in largely heterosexual contexts. By contrast, Catherine had been researching intimacy and family in same sex contexts. It made sense to combine our knowledge and research experience, allowing us to explore in greater depth the issue of DVA in both same sex and heterosexual relationship contexts, and looking at how relationships supposedly built around love can also be very abusive. We were especially interested in the question of 'What's love got to do with it?' because we had found time and again women victimised by male partners attributing their minimising of the violence and abuse or difficulties in leaving the relationship to notions of love – 'but I love(d) him' being a frequent refrain, and our work on same sex couple-headed families and relationships appeared to echo something similar.

Background

An extensive literature and research on heterosexual DVA now exists in both the UK and internationally developed from research and practice since the late 1960s. DVA in heterosexual relationships began to be re-identified from that time, with the UK 'second wave' women's movement at the forefront of developing support and services. In contrast, research on DVA by intimate partners in same sex relationships has a much more recent history. During the 1980s and 1990s there was some initial discussion, in the UK and elsewhere, about DVA in lesbian relationships, and to a lesser extent gay male relationships (for example, Lobel, 1986; Kelly, 1991; Hall, 1992; Taylor and Chandler, 1995). The early literature and studies on same sex domestic violence (as it was termed then) was focused mainly on lesbians, partly because lesbians were becoming visible as a domestic violence 'group' by beginning to access domestic violence and rape support services ostensibly set up for heterosexual women or seeking help via therapy or lesbian or gay community organisations (Lobel, 1986). As Lockhart, White, Causby and Isaac in the US (1994) explain 'Until the 1980s, much of what was known about lesbian battering was based upon clinical and/or practice observation and reports from the battered lesbian' (Lockhart et al, 1994, 469). Studies on DVA in gay male relationships have emerged more recently, building on concerns about and studies on gay men's health arising from work on HIV/AIDS (for example, Island and Letellier, 1991; Greenwood et al, 2002; Henderson, 2003; Stanley et al, 2006).

During the 1980s there was some discussion in lesbian communities in the US and UK about DVA in lesbian relationships and how such behaviour might be tackled. For instance a conference was held on

'Violence in the Lesbian Community' in Washington DC in September 1983. At the same time, there were strong tendencies to minimise, hide and deny the existence of such abuse. There were a number of reasons for this. Some feminists were arguing that lesbian relationships are a 'utopic' alternative to oppressive heterosexual relationships – that lesbian relationships are believed likely to be egalitarian compared to the inevitability of male/female inequality in heterosexual relationships (see Hester, 1992). Other feminists argued that women are 'naturally' less aggressive or violent than men, thus making it difficult to talk about DVA by women against other women (see Ristock, 2002a). Speaking out about experiences of abuse thus forced 'an uncomfortable recognition in relation to women's use of violence' (Radford et al, 1996, 6). Other reasons given for minimising DVA in lesbian relationships have focused on the assumptions that violence and abuse from women is less serious or severe than that from men; while in gay male relationships, because it is two men, who are assumed to be able to be violent, it is assumed that the violence and abuse experienced will be part of a 'fair fight' (for example, Tesch et al, 2010).

The political and policy context also played an important part in stopping open discussion of same sex DVA. In the 1980s right wing governments in both the US and UK were instigating a backlash against 'liberal' ideas about family and relationships and attempting to re-impose 'traditional family values'. This included presenting HIV/ AIDS as a 'gay male' disease, and the Conservative government in the UK specifically targeting lesbian and gay communities through Section 28 by stopping 'promotion' of lesbian and gay relationships as 'pretend families' in schools and more generally. Part of the Local Government Act 1988, Section 28 stated that

> A local authority shall not (a) intentionally promote homosexuality or publish material with the intent of promoting homosexuality (b) promote the teaching in any maintained school of the acceptability of homosexuality as a pretended family relationship by the publication of such material or otherwise. (1988 Local Government Act, Section 28)

Although the legal implications of the law have been unclear it provided a clearly negative message about lesbian and gay relationships and communities and Section 28 was not repealed in England and Wales until 2003 (2003 Local Government Act) (see Chapter Three for more discussion of this). For these various reasons it is therefore not surprising that research into same sex domestic violence and abuse (SSDVA) has lagged behind that on heterosexual DVA.

We are writing this book in a climate of much greater openness and acceptance of LGBTQ communities in the UK. While the Conservative party in government in the 1980s were enacting Section 28, a Conservative prime minister has now, in the 2010s strongly promoted gay marriage. Moreover, it is increasingly recognised in both policy and practice that DVA occurs across all population groups including those involving lesbian, gay male, bisexual or transgendered individuals (Povey et al, 2008; Home Office Affairs Select Committee, 2008). Since 2007, the availability of civil protection in the form of non-molestation and occupation orders have also been extended to same sex couples (2004 Domestic Violence Crimes and Victims Act, Part 1, section 3). Yet the context of heterosexism and homophobia that still prevails in many respects, and with which many individuals defining as LGBTQ have grown up, also have profound impacts on the nature and experiences of DVA in same sex relationships. We explore further these contextual issues and their implications in Chapter Three.

The policy context and definition of DVA

Knowledge and understanding of DVA has been conceptualised and defined in a variety of ways and from different perspectives including the needs of government and/or professional groups in relation to identification and measurement (Hester, 2004). As knowledge about DVA has developed, so has its definition and the terminology used to describe it. 'Wife battering' is no longer used, in recognition that cohabiting and/or dating heterosexual women can be subject to DVA. It is now recognised that DVA can be experienced in same sex relationships, by men, both within and beyond the lifetime of a relationship and with the active collusion and violence of extended family members.

Building on previous Labour government initiatives, the UK Conservative–Liberal Democrat coalition government that came into power in 2010 developed a new Strategy on Violence Against Women and Girls (Home Office, 2010) and for the first time adopted a definition of DVA as gender-based, using the United Nations (UN) Declaration (1993) on the elimination of violence against women to underpin the Strategy:

> The declaration enshrines women's rights to live without
> the fear of violence and abuse and the United Kingdom's

ratification of the UN Convention on the Elimination of all Forms of Discrimination against Women (CEDAW) upholds this principle. (Home Office, 2010, 4)

This is an important step in recognition of the predominance of gender-based violence and gender inequality, which however excludes SSDVA from this particular policy approach, although the related Action Plan does acknowledge that 'sexual orientation' also 'plays a role' (Home Office, 2011, 6). In addition, DVA as a potential feature in same sex relationships is included in the more focused, and largely gender-neutral, Home Office definition.

Until recently the Home Office used the term 'domestic violence', emphasising the criminal justice aspects of such behaviour. However, increasingly, victims/survivors' support agencies have called for the phenomenon to be called domestic abuse both to de-emphasise physical violence and to include the possibilities of other kinds of violence, such as emotional, financial and sexual. Following public consultation, the Home Office thus adopted the term 'domestic violence and abuse' from March 2013 and expanded their previous definition beyond an emphasis on individual incidents, to include the portrayal of DVA as involving a pattern of controlling, coercive or threatening behaviour. The definition of domestic violence and abuse now states that it is:

> Any incident or pattern of incidents of controlling, coercive or threatening behaviour, violence or abuse between those aged 16 or over who are or have been intimate partners or family members regardless of gender or sexuality. This can encompass, but is not limited to, the following types of abuse: psychological, physical, sexual, financial and emotional. (www.homeoffice.gov.uk/crime/violence-against-women-girls/domestic-violence/)

With further qualification as follows:

> Controlling behaviour is: a range of acts designed to make a person subordinate and/or dependent by isolating them from sources of support, exploiting their resources and capacities for personal gain, depriving them of the means needed for independence, resistance and escape and regulating their everyday behaviour.

> Coercive behaviour is: an act or a pattern of acts of assault, threats, humiliation and intimidation or other abuse that is used to harm, punish, or frighten their victim. (www. homeoffice.gov.uk/crime/violence-against-women-girls/ domestic-violence/)

The definition includes so called 'honour' based violence, female genital mutilation (FGM) and forced marriage. The Home Office website points out that this is not a legal definition, in that the behaviours may in themselves not constitute a crime, and also stresses that it 'is clear that victims are not confined to one gender or ethnic group'. (www. homeoffice.gov.uk/crime/violence-against-women-girls/domestic-violence/)

While we, in some respects, prefer the term 'domestic violence', as it emphasises the impact of the experiences and keeps in mind the extremity of fear and risk with which many victims/survivors live, in this book we adopt the Home Office term 'domestic violence and abuse', at times using the abbreviation DVA.[1]

In the last 17 years the UK government has developed specific strategies for addressing violence against women. Initiated by the New Labour governments between 1997 and 2010, a National Domestic Violence Strategy has promoted a Coordinated Community Response (CCR) (Home Office, 2007) in England, Wales and Northern Ireland based on three principles: prevention and early intervention, protection and perpetrator accountability – primarily through the criminal justice system – and support for survivors and their children. These principles underpinning *A Place of Safety* (2007), the Government's consultation paper were adopted from the Scottish Executive's *Domestic Abuse: National Strategy for Scotland,* written by the Scottish Partnership on Domestic Violence established in 1998 (Robinson, 2006). In England, Wales and Northern Ireland, the 2004 Domestic Violence, Crime and Victims Act led to a broader awareness that DVA can occur across sexuality, gender and relationship status by making provision to extend non-molestation orders and occupation orders to same sex couples either cohabiting or in civil partnerships; and to victims/ survivors regardless of whether they cohabit with their abusive partner. In Scotland many of the same legal remedies have also been made available. The 2001 Protection from Abuse (Scotland) Act attached powers of arrest to common law interdicts granted to protect anybody from abuse from another person. There is no distinction made about what kind of relationship exists. In addition the 2003 Criminal Justice (Scotland) Act granted similar powers of arrest for breaches of non-harassment orders as were included in the 2004 Domestic Violence, Crime and Victims Act in the rest of the UK.

The CCR is crystalised in a triumvirate of interventions provided with ring-fenced government funding: specialist domestic violence courts (SDVC), Multi-agency Risk Assessment Conferences (MARACs), Independent Domestic Violence Advisers (IDVAs) and, since 2006, (Robinson, 2009), Independent Sexual Violence Advisers (ISVAs). MARACs and IDVAs taken together as a model of intervention in domestic violence and abuse have been characterised as best practice in homicide prevention (CAADA, 2012a).

The national organisation, Coordinated Action Against Domestic Abuse (CAADA) provides protocol and policy templates and accredited training for MARACs and IDVAs across the UK including a risk assessment protocol, the CAADA–DASH (domestic abuse, stalking and honour-based violence) Risk Assessment Tool. The risk assessment undertaken by practitioners from partner agencies of the MARAC is used to calculate the risk perpetrators present to victims/survivors and their children. Those at the highest risk are referred to the MARAC where safety planning and support can be coordinated by IDVAs as well as identifying how the perpetrator can be made accountable. There have been various critiques of this approach (for example, Coy and Kelly, 2011; Walklate and Mythen, 2011) based on concerns about what and how risk is assessed, whether it is assessed correctly and what the implications are for those who are not assessed as being at the highest risk. There is some evidence that, as a result of the UK Coalition Government Spending Review, risk assessments are being used more broadly as a tool to ration services (Walklate and Mythen, 2011) and there are some concerns that this is also occurring within the DVA field (Towers and Walby, 2012). Given the evidence that DVA has high levels of repeat victimisation there is also a strong argument to suggest that responding to a victim/survivor at low and/or medium risk, that is, early intervention, could act as an important preventative tool for victims/survivors. Indeed earlier studies indicated that this is the case (Hanmer et al, 1999; Donovan et al, 2010). Nonetheless there is also some evidence that the CCR has had some success in reducing the risks that heterosexual female victims/survivors and their children face (Howarth et al, 2009; Steel et al, 2011), although Coy and Kelly (2011) argue that this is because of the work of IDVAs rather than the rest of the CCR (see also CAADA, 2012a).

There is also, however, some evidence that the CCR is failing to respond appropriately to the needs of LGBTQ victims/survivors, including those who are at the highest risk. Less than 1 per cent of those referred to the MARACs are identified as LGBTQ (Donovan and Rowlands, 2011; CAADA, 2013) which is widely recognised as disproportionately under-representative. Donovan and Rowlands (2011) identified four aspects of the MARAC process whereby LGBTQ victims/survivors might drop out: through an inappropriate use of the CAADA risk assessment checklist with victims/survivors, the criteria used to make referrals to MARACs, the agencies making referrals to the MARAC and the agencies that sit on the MARAC. Their conclusions suggest that the reasons for the disproportionately small numbers of LGBTQ victims/survivors being referred to MARACs are that the MARACs are dominated by police referrals and decisions about referrals are weighted by numbers of previous reports to the police. As our and other's research shows, victims/survivors from same sex relationships are very unlikely to report their DVA experiences to the police (Donovan et al, 2006; Tesch et al, 2010; LGBT DAF and Stonewall Housing, 2013) and this necessarily results in few opportunities for them to be referred to the MARACs. Research on police records has also found that few lesbians and gay men report to the police and that they are not recorded as repeat victims. Of the nine cases of same sex DVA (seven involving gay men and two involving lesbians) out of 692 cases tracked over three years (Hester and Westmarland, 2006) all showed up only once. In addition, Donovan and Rowlands (2011) concluded that practitioners utilising the risk assessment checklist do not always consider the particular circumstances of those in same sex relationships that could enable them to risk assess more appropriately; there is a lack of LGBTQ specialist agencies involved with the MARACs; and there is a lack of agencies represented on the MARACs who might be used by LGBTQ victims/survivors. Finally there is also evidence that DVA risk itself is constructed in ways that reflect the heterosexual assumption and prevents the correct identification of DVA and risk levels in those whose DVA experiences do not match the public story about DVA (see later in this chapter) (Robinson and Rowlands, 2009; Donovan, 2013). While legislation pertaining to, and cross-government definitions of, DVA acknowledge that DVA can occur in same sex relationships, practice is still influenced by the public story and/or based on evidence from the experiences of heterosexual women. This can act to prevent a consideration of the particular circumstances of same sex relationships and how DVA might operate within them.

Public stories: physical violence and victims

Despite the increasingly wide definition used by government, in the popular imagination domestic violence and abuse often conjures up a particular public story related to the heterosexual experience that also emphasises physical violence. Jamieson (1998, 11) has argued that it is important to understand who the tellers are of public stories and their pervasive nature:

> Cumulatively, pervasive stories are inevitably consequential for both private and public life. They become representations that people cannot avoid working with at both a deep and surface level. Pervasive stories are a stock of narratives that anyone can draw on or distance themselves from when telling their own story...Stories also feed into both public and private lives when they coalesce into official views shaping public policies, laws and the distribution of resources. (Jamieson, 1998, 11)

Typically, argues Jamieson, pervasive public stories originate with people in powerful positions within powerful institutions. In relation to the public story about DVA, however, its origin has not been from within any powerful institutions, but the result of feminist activism and scholarship over several decades and, more recently, the coincidence of this with a generation of feminists and/or sympathisers within government. The outcomes have been both a story of success and a story of exclusion. The public story about DVA locates the phenomenon inside heterosexual relationships within a gendered victim/perpetrator dynamic (the stronger/bigger man controlling the weaker/smaller woman), and forefronts the physical nature of the violence. Ristock (2002a) has argued that such dichotomous understandings of DVA prevent both discussions about those experiences that lie outside the defining binaries and also recognition of and support for those living with those experiences. Certainly, among those in same sex relationships, the pervasive public story has prevented many from recognising their experiences of DVA (for example, Ristock, 2002a; Donovan et al, 2006; Barnes, 2008; Donovan and Hester, 2010). In addition, as we discuss in Chapter Six, the public story also has an impact on how SSDVA is responded to by mainstream and specialist DVA services.

Another aspect of the public story about DVA constructs the victim in particular ways that, we argue, also act to prevent recognition of domestic violence and abuse, particularly in same sex relationships. Others have pointed out how problematic the term 'victim' is in relation to heterosexual women who have experienced DVA, and the work of Campbell and colleagues (1998), and Campbell and Soeken (1999), and our previous work (Hester, 2012; 2013) have provided accounts of how heterosexual women often act with agency to address, resist, prevent and otherwise cope with the violence of their partners. Baker (2008) argues that the construction of victim as weak and resonant with femininity has an impact on heterosexual women who have experienced domestic violence and abuse to the extent that it influences their sense of self. Certainly, in the current research, respondents have talked of how they 'hate the word "victim"' (Donovan and Hester, 2010) and how they felt the term 'victim' held negative connotations for them as individuals in same sex relationships.

Kwong-Lai Poon (2011) explains how the literature on gay male DVA, similarly to that on heterosexual DVA, has used an individualising and pathologising model of victims and perpetrators as binary constructs with 'good' or 'pure' victims and 'evil' or 'pure' perpetrators, and argues for 'a language that accounts for the diverse experiences of abuse' (Kwong-Lai Poon, 2011, 123). We suggest that the term 'victim' is held by many – both women and men – to be a label that jars with their self perception. They resist the notion that they have been weak or passive. Elsewhere we have used the term 'victimised' to convey the sense that the person experiencing domestic violence and abuse is subject to the power and control of their partner but is able to and does exert agency within the relationship (Hester, 2006). Here we use the term 'victim/survivor' to convey a similar notion, while mindful that the term 'victim' has tended to be linked to a criminal justice context and discourse.

Understanding domestic violence and abuse

Perspectives explaining domestic violence and abuse have ranged from seeing the phenomenon as an individual or psychological problem linked, for instance, to (over)consumption of alcohol, through it being perceived as a learnt behaviour, to the more holistic feminist understanding of domestic violence and abuse as men's power over and control of women, and further feminist approaches that de-centre the heterosexual experience, focusing instead on intersectionality.

In this book we will use two main approaches to understanding DVA and their application to heterosexual and same sex DVA. The first draws on the feminist notion of power and control, looked at through the lenses of positionality and intersectionality (Hester, 2010). The second draws from the work on intimacy and involves practices of love (Donovan and Hester, 2011), which, we argue, provide important means of actively constructing power over and control of intimate partners.

Power and control, positionality and intersectionality

Feminist scholarship in particular has developed heterosexually oriented 'gender and power' analyses of DVA that problematise the social construction of masculinity as embodied in heterosexual men, explaining DVA as the exertion of power and control by men over women in intimate relationships within contexts of gender inequality (Hester, 2004). We would argue that what is the central feature in this model is the exertion of power and control, while the forms this takes are related to and arise out of the context. Although the feminist power and control model has been criticised as inherently heterosexist, this is not necessarily the case. In what follows, we look at some of the debates about understanding DVA, ending up with a closer look at both 'positionality' and 'intersectionality', which we argue are key to such understanding. We use a model where DVA is about exertion of power and control, and where the forms this takes and the resulting experiences are mediated by intersections of, for instance, gender, sexuality, 'race', ethnicity, age and class. We see intersectionality as a structural phenomenon that positions individuals and their experiences in different ways. Bograd outlines this very well. Although talking about the experience of marginalised women in the US, her description also applies more widely to the experiences of LGBTQ communities in our research:

> While discussion of intersectionality may seem abstract, it relates to real and life-threatening consequences, as the ramifications of social location reverberate through psyche, family relations, community support, and institutional response. (Bograd, 2005, 31)

Merrill (1996), in one of the earliest volumes on SSDVA argues that domestic violence and abuse is not about gender but about power and control:

> The phenomenon of same sex domestic violence illustrates that routine, intentional intimidation through abusive acts

and words is not a gender issue, but a power issue. A certain number of people, given the opportunity to get away with abusing their partners, will do so because they hunger for control over some part of their lives. This perceived lack of power allows abusers to escape from responsibility for their actions. (Merrill, 1996, 3)

Stark (2007), in contrast, argues that coercive control is a specifically heterosexual phenomenon. While DVA is a pattern of behaviours on the part of the perpetrator, the aim of which is to exert power and control over the victim/survivor and thereby to situate the abuser as dominant in the relationship, what is particularly important is the relationship-specific features of coercive control (Stark, 2007). Thus it is not merely the type of violence used but the effect to which it is put that is important, and that this takes place within a gender unequal context. His argument thus reinforces feminist approaches that have identified power and control rather than physical violence as being the defining features of DVA. It also facilitates an understanding of DVA as a cumulative pattern of behaviours by perpetrators and their impacts that may also transcend boundaries drawn by sexuality and gender. However, Stark's argument that his version of coercive control is intrinsically gendered and therefore specifically about heterosexism/ sexual inequality leads him to expressing concerns that the model cannot be applied to SSDVA. He contends that we do not yet know enough to do that. As we will explore in greater detail in later chapters, our work on same sex domestic violence and abuse suggests that there are indeed features of the model that are applicable more widely even if they have developed from the heterosexual/heterosexist context.

Johnson (2006) identifies four patterns of DVA, related to different contexts. 'Intimate terrorism' is the 'archetypal' DVA that we may expect to see reported to the police. Such 'intimate terrorism' will usually involve one partner exerting power and control, being violent, involve frequent abuse, and is likely to escalate and to result in serious injury. Other patterns identified by Johnson are 'mutual violent control', 'violent resistance' and 'situational' or 'common couple' violence. 'Mutual violent control', although rare, is akin to 'intimate terrorism' as both partners are violent and vying for control. 'Violent resistance' is when the victimised partner uses violence in retaliation or self-defence, often resulting in injury. This is sometimes seen where women in fear of severe violence or threat of death from their male partner use a weapon to protect themselves and/or their children (see Hester, 2012). 'Situational' or 'common couple' violence is where both partners may use violence in specific situations, but where this is of relatively low frequency, unconnected to control, and unlikely to escalate or to involve serious injury. Johnson developed his typologies for categorising data on heterosexual DVA. In earlier work he argues that where violence in same sex relationships is concerned, this can be characterised typically by bi-directional 'common couple' or 'situational' violence, by contrast to heterosexual relationships where uni-directional 'patriarchal or intimate terrorism' is more prominent (Johnson, 2006). His rationale was that lesbian or gay violence and abuse does not take on patriarchal family values. Yet, as we will discuss in Chapters Three and Five, the societal context of the heterosexual family, and associated 'patriarchal' and heteronormative values, do indeed form a backdrop for, and are also likely to infuse LGBTQ relationships in some way and be evident in SSDVA.

Not surprisingly, there has been an ongoing debate about the applicability of the so-called heterosexual or heterosexist (Hassouneh and Glass, 2008) model of DVA to same sex relationship contexts. In particular, the feminist understanding of domestic violence and abuse as a pattern of coercively controlling behaviours that draws on, constructs and re-constructs gender inequality has been deemed too steeped in heterosexual experiences and constructs. Renzetti (1992), for instance, in research on DVA in lesbian relationships, argues that a gender and power analysis can be applied, but needs to be expanded to take into account the different experiences, meanings and interventions related to DVA that 'intersectionality' provides. That is, not just gender, but also the effects of location and discrimination linked to sexuality, 'race', and ethnicity. Renzetti's (1992) study on violence and abuse within lesbian relationships, was one of the first to explore issues regarding gender and power in a same sex context. Despite a lack of pre-existing gendered roles to constrain them, she found that power and power relations were still an extremely significant aspect of the relationships of the lesbians she surveyed in terms of who perpetrated the violence and abuse. Not only did she find a link between power imbalances and propensity to be the abusive partner, but also that the greater the disparity of power, the more severe the physical and psychological abuse (Renzetti, 1992). Moreover, 'the factor that in this study was most strongly associated with abuse was partners' relative dependency on one another' (Renzetti, 1992, 116).

Ristock (2002a) is more critical of the gender and power framework. She argues that in lesbian relationships experiences of domestic violence are heterogeneous and social context is particularly important, with a lack of binary categories such as 'victim' and 'perpetrator'.

Using detailed interviews with 102 mostly lesbian women she suggests her work moves beyond surveys that provide limited and often heterosexually-defined factors that appear to correlate with lesbian abuse or provide typologies of abuse. Instead, she was able to consider 'a range of contextual factors that surround abusive relationships' (Ristock, 2002a, 57), including contexts of invisibility and of normalisation. She explains that 'each of these contextual factors may increase the probability of experiencing or committing violence; however, this does not mean that they cause violence or that individual women in such contexts make risky partners' (Ristock, 2002a, 57). She found the abuse women experienced from female partners was very heterogeneous, involving a variety of emotional, physical and sexual abuses within different contexts, although also loosely fitting around patterns of 'patriarchal terrorism' and 'common couple violence'.

Going even further in their critique of the feminist approach, Island and Letellier (1991), focusing on gay men, argue that a 'gender and power' model does not apply at all to SSDVA and instead suggest that gender-neutral and individual, psychological models should be applied. In a similar vein, Stanley et al (2006) argue from their study on gay men that '[d]ifficulties in conflict resolution and attachment fears appeared to better explain the occurrence of violence than did the intent to control one's partner' (Stanley et al, 2006, 31). Kwong-Lai Poon (2011, 124), from research about gay men, argues in a similar vein that we should 'move away from the abstract, but fixed notions of victims and perpetrators while allowing us to see multiple and sometimes contradictory aspects of their personality'.

An important question is whether these authors are comparing similar groups of people. For instance, as Ristock asks: 'is the psychological and social meaning of "violence" in a relationship the same for lesbians and heterosexuals, gay men and lesbians? Are we counting the same things?' (Ristock, 2002a, 12). In Ristock's study the interviews and focus groups with 102 lesbian women were sampled conveniently via adverts about lesbian relationship violence. The sample included women 'who defined as victims, and as perpetrators, and those who felt they fit neither category' (Ristock, 2002a, 30). In contrast, Stanley et al (2006) included 69 gay and bisexual men, 'chosen from a randomly selected community sample, who reported at least 1 violent episode in an interview exploring their intimate relationships' (Stanley et al, 2006, 31). As we discuss further in Chapter Four, there may be considerable differences where individuals self-define as experiencing DVA (as in Ristock's sample) but also where they report one, or more, 'violent episodes' or behaviours that may be construed by researchers as DVA.

As we discuss in the following chapters, our research indicates both similarities and differences across experiences of SSDVA in relationships. For instance there were many similarities in the range of abusive behaviours experienced across gender and the impacts of such behaviour, but also important differences that appear to reflect wider processes of gendering and gendered norms (Hester and Donovan, 2009). Moreover there were important features where the form of the DVA was linked specifically to a social and cultural context of inequality for lesbian and gays as gender and sexual minorities (Donovan and Hester, 2008). Consequently, in this book we build an understanding of domestic violence and abuse that draws on the feminist model, using ideas of 'power over' and 'control', and combined with understandings of social and cultural contexts that can incorporate social positioning and intersectional identities especially as linked to gender and sexuality, but also incorporating dimensions such as age, motherhood, income status and education. We are less able to forefront the importance of 'race' and ethnicity in the experiences of SSDVA as a consequence of the particular sample recruited to this research. Nevertheless where appropriate we draw on other research to provide further insights into SSDVA.

Also, we argue that domestic violence and abuse is both 'discursive' and experienced materially and bodily (Hester, 1992). Definitions often incorporate behaviours or acts without much consideration of the impact of those behaviours. Yet the impact and effects of domestic violence and abuse are precisely what makes it problematic and abusive, and with material, social, emotional and bodily consequences. Impact is a key feature in the definition and understanding of domestic violence and abuse that we apply in this book, and (as we will outline in greater detail in the next chapter) has also led us to develop a new generation of survey methodology. The impact of domestic violence and abuse may vary between individuals due to their location in particular sets of social relations and different contexts. For instance, the impact of domestic violence and abuse on heterosexual men may be less severe than the impact on heterosexual women (Walby and Allen, 2004), while the experiences of lesbians living in abusive relationships may be more heterogeneous than those of heterosexual women (Ristock, 2002a).

This brings us to ideas about positionality and intersectionality. As Cockburn (2007) explains, we need the concept of 'positionality' because this allows us to see and speak of the way individuals and groups are placed in relation to each other in terms of significant dimensions of social difference that include gender and sexuality, let alone social class, 'race' and so on. 'Intersectionality' is related to positionality in that it 'is a term that highlights the way dimensions of positionality cross-cut each other, so that any individual or collectivity experiences several simultaneously' (Cockburn, 2007, 6). In this sense we are drawing in particular on Crenshaw's ideas about 'structural intersectionality', (Crenshaw, 1994, 95) which she developed to help analyse and understand the influence of social location and experiences for different women. This is in contrast to the more fluid 'anti-categorical' approaches drawing to a greater extent on post-structural concerns (see McCall, 2005), which we do not see as adequately describing or explaining the similarities and differences in our data. Crenshaw developed her ideas about intersectionality in response to problems in addressing violence against black women ('women of color') in the US, although building on ideas she had heard from Southall Black Sisters in the UK who had for a long time been addressing the specific problems faced by black and South Asian women experiencing partner violence. Crenshaw's concern was to understand how black women's experiences were qualitatively different from those of white women due to the former's experiences of racism as well as sexism. The issue is one of individuals having complex multiple identities, and not merely one of 'adding' together a list of oppressions. This complexity influences:

> the ways in which the location of women of color at the
> intersection of race and gender makes our actual experience
> of domestic violence, rape and remedial reform qualitatively
> different from that of white women. (Crenshaw, 1994, 95)

Walby et al (2012) further develop the concept of intersectionality, at the same time critically suggesting that the work of writers such as Crenshaw provides too much focus on victims, and thus obscures perpetration as well as power relations. As Walby and her colleagues explain, '[t]he analysis of intersectionality has often focused on the actions of the disadvantaged groups…this obscures the role of the powerful within sets of social relations' (Walby et al, 2012, 230). At the same time, they are keen to move beyond the current tension in the debates, especially the extent to which the intersecting categories are deemed as fluid or as stable. Arguing against the use of 'categories', and arguing in favour of an approach that systematically addresses the ontological depth of inequalities, they suggest that:

> The way forward is to recognise the historically constructed nature of social inequalities and their sedimentation in social institutions…At any one moment in time, these relations of inequality have some stability as a consequence of their institionalisation, but over a period of time they do change. (Walby et al, 2012, 231)

Drawing on complexity theory, Walby and colleagues also argue that the intersection of inequalities does not provide 'mutual constitution' but 'mutual shaping':

> 'Mutual shaping' is a better concept than 'mutual constitution' since it enables the retention of naming of each relevant inequality or project while simultaneously recognising that it is affected by engagement with the others. It acknowledges the way that the systems of social relations change each other at the point of intersection, but do not become something totally different. (Walby et al, 2012, 235)

In the chapters that follow, we draw on such a notion of structural intersectionality, which allows analysis of experiences and perpetration of DVA situated in complex yet definable contexts of inequalities and discrimination.

The concept of intersectionality thus helps us understand:

- inequality (unequal power relations)
- the impacts of inequality (differential power and access to resources)
- the use and impact of DVA in contexts of gender and sexuality
- access to resources and responses by professionals.

In other words, we see intersectional frameworks as 'a way of thinking about power, thinking about who is excluded and why, who has access to resources and why' (Morris and Bunjun, 2007, 2).

Understanding how gender and sexuality, age, class, income and so on intersect with regard to how individuals may use, experience, respond to and/or address and embody violence and abuse enables us to compare similarities and differences across abusive female and male same sex or heterosexual relationships, and to consider possibly different experiences and different needs for these groups of individuals with regard to help-seeking and interventions (Hester, 2010; Bograd, 2005). We need to take into account the unequal positioning of lesbians and gay men within our society, as this has an effect on the forms of violence and abuse used within same sex relationships, and also has an impact on the extent to which, and ways in which, lesbians, gay men, bisexual and trans people seek help. At the same time, the processes of gender have an impact on the way violence and abuse 'work' in same sex relationships, and on the resulting experiences and outcomes. Age is also important here because DVA prevalence surveys and crime surveys indicate that age intersects with both gender and sexuality such that the use of and impacts of violence and abuse appear to be more intense for younger age groups, especially those aged under 25 (Walby and Allen, 2004; Hester and Donovan, 2009). These are issues we explore further in Chapters Three and Four.

Love and emotion work

A further question that we presented rhetorically at the beginning of this chapter is 'what has love got to do with it'. We would suggest that relationships that involve DVA, regardless of the gender or sexuality of partners, probably start out consensually and are motivated by love or, including in the case of arranged marriages, positive feelings and hopes for love between partners. We therefore decided to unpack how love is understood and enacted when DVA is present in order to explore this dimension of adult intimacy, and in particular how practices associated with love and emotion work in intimate relationships might provide further insights into the experiences of DVA. Thus, in Chapter Five we investigate how practices of love in adult relationships can constitute forms of controlling behaviours that facilitate the embedding of relationship rules in favour of the abusive partner and position the survivor as responsible for the abusive partner and the relationship.

Love was a focus of this study because, in western societies, a public story about adult intimacy is that it is increasingly founded on love. Love in this context is constructed in such a way as to assume notions of choice and consent as being central to the rationales for entering and remaining in adult relationships. Others have written about the ways in which the rise of industrial capitalism and consumer culture have led to individualisation or 'liquid love' (for example, see Beck and Beck-Gernsheim, 1995; Bauman, 2003). In these arguments, the fragmentation of families, and subsequently society, has resulted from the belief that self-fulfilment through the free choice of a love partner is the ultimate aim of human existence. Those who argue that society and family is, as a result of individualisation, less connected, caring and cohesive and more selfish, self-interested, uncaring and greedy see the evidence and consequences in increased crime, youth disaffection, anti-social behaviour and neglect of society's most vulnerable people (who would, they argue, have once been cared for by their families). For some of those who support this view, feminism has been a destructive influence, encouraging women to abandon their obligations to traditional motherhood, family and the civilisation of men through marriage (for example, Dennis and Erdos, 1992; Murray, 1996a, 1996b). Others are more optimistic about the social changes that have occurred in the private sphere. They credit the influence of feminisms and investment in welfare principles, along with the impact of social movements (for example, the trade union and suffrage movements, the disability rights movement and the gay liberation movement), in successfully challenging oppressive social structures, institutions and the authority embedded in them. Consequently, and particularly with the financial and material support of welfare benefits and social housing, spaces have opened up for members of these groups to become financially independent of social institutions and structures and engage in 'experiments in living' and loving (Williams, 2004; Weeks et al, 2001; Beck, 1992).

Thus, the argument goes, has love become increasingly important for understanding the organisation of western societies. Yet the common sense presentation of love as a set of feelings over which humans have no control has obscured the ways in which love is shaped through dominant understandings of the heterosexual assumption (Weeks et al, 2001): the law, political ideologies and cultural mores, rules, values and expectations about how gender and sexuality are enacted give the lie to essentialist beliefs about love. Adult relationships based on love can be understood sociologically and their initiation, enactment, regulation and expression are socially constructed (Jackson, 1993; Fraser, 2008; Lloyd and Emery, 2000). Love, however, cannot be understood without exploring its relation to gender and sexuality. Dominant understandings of love in contemporary society construct love as heterosexual and feminised, yet with a trend towards the belief in equality between the sexes (for example, Lloyd and Emery, 2000; Donovan and Hester, 2011; Illouz, 2011). Cancian (1990) argues that the feminisation of love is evidenced in the increasing emphasis placed on sharing feelings, expressions of love and emotionally supportive talk – the 'disclosing intimacy' of Jamieson (1998) – which are all associated with femininity. Cancian (1990) also demonstrates how this feminised love has become embedded in traditional gender roles such that women expect to find fulfilment from falling in love and becoming financially and emotionally dependent on a man.

Masculinity has become predominantly constructed through characteristics such as being the provider, materially and financially, for the family, contributing practical aspects of care and understanding sex as a measure of intimacy (Duncombe and Marsden 1995; Jamieson 1998). Most of the work done on how households are maintained and emotions experienced in heterosexual relationships and families points to men being able to set the terms in those relationships, hold the household power over key decisions, and organise their leisure time to suit themselves (for example, Vogler and Pahl, 1999). Women on the other hand are brought up to understand and enact a femininity that prioritises feelings, care work and emotion work (Hochschild, 1979) in relation to those around them and to prioritise the needs of others, especially male others, above their own (for example, Duncombe and Marsden, 1993). Aggression and violence are not only seen to be illustrative of masculinity but are seen to be unwomanly. While, for a girl to be perceived as 'like a boy', a tomboy, can be a badge of esteem while young, being 'like a man' is to be avoided especially when this might call a woman's sexuality into question.

Disclosing intimacy, care and emotion work have not been given the same value in the construction and expression of masculinity, and have been identified as a key source of conflict and/or dissatisfaction in heterosexual relationships (Duncombe and Marsden, 1995). The result of these inequalities is that many heterosexual women come to realise that their needs are secondary to those of their male partners (Wilcox, 2006). Heterosexual men often perceive their relationship as a base from which to engage with the world, expecting that their partners will look after that base in ways that provide a haven for men to return to for servicing (see also, for example, Morris, 1999; Vogler and Pahl, 1999; Jamieson, 1998; Wilcox, 2006). In return, many men understand their role to be primarily as the provider and, because this often involves being the main earner, being the key decision-maker, especially about finances.

Such analyses about how love is lived in heterosexual relationships are very different from Giddens' (1992) treatise on the transformation of intimacy. Giddens (1992) argues that the nature of love is changing away from romantic love, as the dominant model of love, to what he calls confluent love. For Giddens, confluent love in the pure relationship is predicated upon sharing emotional needs and desires, the mutual negotiation of the terms of the relationship and contingency: that adults stay together until they no longer feel their needs are being met. He argues that personal fulfilment within adult intimacy has become a central feature and expectation of intimacy. Feminism has empowered women to have higher expectations in their intimate lives in favour of an egalitarian negotiation of equals to fulfil both of their needs. Giddens holds up lesbians as the pioneers of the pure relationship: living outside the heterosexual assumption, influenced by feminism to aspire to egalitarianism, negotiation and a mutual meeting of needs has, he argues resulted in lesbians 'showcasing' the pure relationship with confluent love.

Jamieson (1998) among others (for example, Wight, 1994) critique Giddens, pointing to the lack of empirical evidence for the pure relationship and highlighting the continuing material limits to contingency, negotiation and egalitarianism – not least of which is the presence of children but also, as we have discussed above, includes the inequalities around resources and emotion work that remain in many heterosexual relationships. Jamieson also argues that though 'disclosing intimacy' may be aspired to as an ideal more so than in previous eras, it is difficult to conclude that it is the most important aspect of intimacy. She argues that other aspects of relationships such as practical care have been ignored in this emphasis on emotional support and disclosure. Thus those behaviours that might be more associated with men are not included in the debates about how love is practised.

In their work on families of choice, Weeks et al (2001) found evidence of what they called the egalitarian ideal among same sex relationships. This reflexive commitment to finding ways of doing relationships that aspired to egalitarianism was coupled with an understanding from many that living outside heterosexuality provided an opportunity to pursue this ideal in a way that was not as easy to achieve in heterosexual relationships because of gendered expectations about how relationships can be practised. However, not all of the respondents in their study had achieved the ideal and many were aware that power dynamics existed in their relationships. Some also talked about previous relationships that had been abusive but many were aware that power was certainly an issue they had to attend to and compensate for in their negotiations of the egalitarian ideal (Heaphy et al, 1999).

In order to discuss the ways in which love is implicated in experiences of DVA, we use the concept of 'relationship practices' (Morgan, 1999) to focus on the many behaviours that constitute an adult intimate relationship and distinguish it from other kinds of relationships such as friendships, parental or acquaintance relationships. They include those behaviours that are required to keep a household or households (depending on whether the adults in the relationship are cohabiting) running, the organisation of finances, the organisation of and participation in leisure activities either alone, together and/or with children, parental activities and the organisation of and participation in wider family (of choice) activities alone, together and/or with children. Within these relationship practices we identify a subgroup that we call practices of love. These are the disclosing of intimacy, caring and emotion work and sexual behaviours. We acknowledge that the other relationship practices, including when and how they are enacted, construct a relationship context in which feelings of love and intimacy are also communicated or not, but the communication that results from these practices of love can be crucial to how a relationship characterised by DVA is understood and made sense of. The focus on practices of love provide a bridge from our discussion of positionality and intersectionality to the practices of power and control in action. As we discuss further in Chapter Five, the doing of emotion work situates individuals as victimised and perpetrators through the practice and embodiment of emotional support in the relationship. Practices of love, by creating a seemingly 'gendered' context, reflected in heteronormative relationship practices and practices of love, feed into the complex intersectionality and positioning of individuals.

As part of our approach, Lloyd and Emery's (2000) explanatory frameworks for aggression in heterosexual courtship provide the basis for a broader discussion about how dominant constructions of heterosexuality, masculinity and femininity underpin and map onto ideas about love and romance. In reality of course depictions of gender are less static, fixed and impermeable to change. Many men are able to be caring and empathetic without feeling this to be a slur on their manhood, although this often becomes easier with age. Young men experience enormous pressure to exhibit local norms of masculinity which typically involves shows of physical strength, aggression or toughness, being interested in sport and uninterested in education and those who are unable or unwilling to do so are often victimised and bullied. The research on homophobic bullying suggests that, rather than the motive for bullying being the sexuality of the target, it is their non-conformity to localised gender roles which are taken as a sign of sexuality which may not always be accurate. It is perhaps these patterns of expectations about masculinity in young men that underpins the high levels of DVA for young heterosexual women in their dating relationships (for example, Barter et al, 2009). On the other hand it is increasingly evident that women are able to be aggressive, violent and abusive to strangers and those they know. It is important, however, that in analysing women and girls' violence account is taken of the different motives for and meanings of violence and its impact (Irwin and Chesney-Lind, 2008).

As well as gender norms shaping and influencing the perimeters and substance of what it is to be a girl and a woman, a boy and man, there are also norms about heterosexuality. While heterosexuality can be seen in some ways to map onto norms of gender it is important that we understand sexuality and gender to be separately constituted (for example, see Richardson, 2007). Heterosexuality is not just a sexual identity but a set of expectations about a certain kind of life and a particular kind of intimacy. This is notwithstanding that in the UK and many other western countries, Civil Partnerships or same sex marriage licences are now available and provide a normative framework, based on heterosexual marriage, prioritising the legal and formal structuring of intimacy over biology, social or emotional relationships.

The way in which heterosexuality might be lived therefore involves particular constructions, not only of heterosexual male sexuality and heterosexual female sexuality, but also an explanation about how and why any heterosexual woman and man might come together to form a relationship and/or a family. Thus we are led onto social and cultural constructions of what on the one hand we might call heterosexual courtship – the behaviours that are expected of heterosexual women and men as they begin their trajectory to adult heterosexuality – and on the other what we might call heterosexual love – the feelings that are said to be produced that act as both a glue and as a lubricant between heterosexual men and women in relationships and families. The legal contract of marriage is then expected to create a binding web of legal and financial responsibilities and rights between women and men and adults and their legal and/or biological children. At one and the same time love is presented as the lubricant that facilitates the institution of heterosexuality, and heterosexuality is presented as the road map of and to love. Dominant constructions of love are embedded in relationship practices and provide a set of expectations about how adult intimacy might work. The road map is itself also based on institutionalised hierarchies and inequalities based not only on gender and sexuality but also 'race' and ethnicity, social class, faith and disability, the dynamics of which are played out both in individual relationships and in society between different social groups and in the relationship between the state and those living in it. The social context in which and by which love is constructed and lived is itself socially constructed by wider factors such as economics, labour markets and politics.

Yet we also know that what we are calling relationship practices and practices of love are also motivated by expectations and assumptions about what a relationship might consist of other than those resulting from the socially prescribed gender roles outlined above. In short, then, love is understood to be a set of expectations about emotions and values that underpin relationship practices and practices of love which are heteronormative, articulated through individuals and their relationships but also reflected in societal and cultural mores, rules and regulations. The heteronormative construction of love does, however, raise questions for those desiring same sex love and relationships. Can they love? Do they love in different ways? As Hart (1986) argues, those who are not heterosexual grow up in the same society as those who are heterosexual. They are schooled in gender, heterosexuality and love as a matter of course because they are assumed to be gendered in ways that reflect their sexed body, and heterosexual. In Chapter Three we discuss the impact of the heterosexual assumption. In its benign form this preferentially promotes heterosexuality. In its more malign form this promotes the view that anything other than heteronormative gender roles and heterosexuality are deviancies that present a threat to 'normal', that is, heterosexual relationships, love and family life, and to children and young people. Increasingly, as we explain in Chapter Three, there is acceptance of same sex relationships and families that are headed by lesbians and gay men who parent children. There are, however, consequences for those who are not heterosexual and/or those who do not conform to gender norms of behaviours. On the one hand it would seem that love is a universal human emotion that everybody regardless of gender and sexuality can experience. On the other hand there are debates about whether those in same sex relationships can really 'do' love because it is understood as a heterosexual set of behaviours – hence the outcry against same sex marriage. In addition, those in same sex relationships have talked about being able to do relationships differently because of being freed up from heteronormative expectations (see Weeks et al, 2001). Yet we might ask how easy it is to resist dominant heteronormative constructions of what love is and how practices of love might be enacted, especially when there is a universal construction of love being a basic human emotion that everybody can feel. Gender norms might be more visible to resist as inappropriate or to re-define in same sex relationships yet, embedded in the dominant construction of love as they are, it becomes possible to see that anybody, regardless of gender or sexuality could imagine that love involves one partner being in charge and the other being the follower; that one is outward facing while the other is inward facing, that one enacts emotion work and takes responsibility for their partner and the relationship while the other becomes the partner who makes most of the key decisions and becomes more powerful in setting the terms of the relationship. How such practices can be acted out in a manner that creates a shift from merely 'power' to 'power over' is discussed further in Chapter Five.

DVA in same sex relationships: previous research

As indicated above, previous research, policy and practice in the UK concerning domestic and sexual violence have tended to focus on heterosexual women who are victimised by male partners, family members, or other men. This is not surprising, as heterosexual women constitute the largest victim group (Smith et al, 2010). It is increasingly recognised in both policy and practice, however, that domestic and sexual violence and abuse occurs across all population groups. Gay and bisexual men, lesbian or bisexual women and transgendered individuals have also been identified in policy debates and government statistics to experience domestic and sexual violence and abuse (Home Office Affairs Select Committee, 2008; Smith et al, 2010; Roch et al, 2010). In the UK specifically, there is a small, if growing, number of local and national surveys and qualitative studies exploring SSDVA (Henderson, 2003; Stovold et al, 2005; Hunt and Fish, 2008; Hewitt and Macredie, 2012). Studies on DVA in lesbian relationships in the UK have tended to be qualitative, involving small purposive samples. Same sex surveys, aimed mainly at gay men, have generally included very limited questions regarding DVA and have omitted exploration of contextual factors.

One of the earliest studies of SSDVA in the UK using a survey approach was commissioned by Stonewall in 1995. Taking a wide definition of DVA that included both intimate partners and other family members, the study found that '38 per cent of LGBT people aged under 18 years experienced homophobic domestic violence and abuse from parents and family members' (cited in Broken Rainbow, 2002, 18). The Sigma surveys (Henderson, 2003), which included a section on DVA in a gay men's health survey and questions about DVA in a separate questionnaire to lesbian women distributed through Gay Pride events, found that 22 per cent of lesbians and 29 per cent of gay men had experienced physical, mental or sexual abuse or violence from a regular same sex partner at some point. A further survey from Stonewall, on lesbian and bisexual women's health (Hunt and Fish, 2008) and involving 6,178 respondents, also included questions about

DVA. It found that one in four of respondents had experienced DVA at some time, a third of these with male perpetrators, and DVA from female partners was mainly emotional and physical. None of these surveys, however, took into account the impact of the violent and abusive acts on those concerned, making it difficult to understand the meaning of the 'prevalence' data.

Researching domestic (or sexual) violence and abuse in same sex relationships presents particular methodological problems with regard to obtaining representative samples. The 'hidden' nature of the LGBTQ population means that it is impossible to recruit a random or representative sample involving merely LGBTQ groups, and none of the surveys above are therefore representative. The main prevalence data on domestic violence and abuse in the UK is derived from the Crime Survey for England and Wales (CSEW)[2] interpersonal violence module (Walby and Allan, 2004; Povey et al, 2008). The CSEW asks respondents to record their sexuality, although as the numbers identifying as gay male or lesbian have been small the data has therefore not tended to be published, and the survey may generally be perceived as a 'heterosexual' sample. In 2010, however, data from 500 of the 25,000 CSEW IPV module respondents in each of the years 2007/08 and 2008/09 who identified as gay, lesbian or bisexual, were amalgamated to produce a larger sample for analysis (Smith et al, 2010). Overall, the majority of victims aged 16 to 59 answering the CSEW IPV module (94 per cent) identified themselves as heterosexual/straight, 2 per cent as lesbian/gay and it is noteworthy that 4 per cent said 'don't know or do not want to say'. People who identified as lesbian or gay were more likely to have experienced any domestic violence and abuse than those who reported they were heterosexual/straight (13 per cent compared with 5 per cent). Lesbians or bisexual women (12 per cent) and 6 per cent of gay or bisexual men reported experiencing one or more instances of non-physical abuse, threats or force (but not including sexual assault) in the past year. These figures are higher than those reported by heterosexual women (4 per cent) or men (3 per cent) (Smith et al, 2010). The authors of the CSEW report suggest that the higher levels of abuse in the CSEW data 'may be due, at least in part, to the younger age profile of individuals identifying themselves as in this group' who are at greater risk of partner abuse (Smith et al, 2010, 62). While nearly two-fifths (37 per cent) of LGB respondents were aged 16–24, this was the case for only about one fifth (21 per cent) of heterosexual respondents. With regard to sexual assault from any perpetrators, the CSEW found that lesbian women again reported the highest prevalence, followed by gay or bisexual men (Smith et al,

2010). The gender of the perpetrators is not made apparent, however, nor is their relationship to those victimised. Thus we cannot tell if the lesbians were abused by female partners or (probably more likely) a former male partner or other male. Who the perpetrator may be is a crucial factor to take into account when determining and comparing 'prevalence' across lesbian, gay male and heterosexual groups, and is thus a serious omission in the CSEW data.

Ristock (2011) outlines a similar problem to the CSEW data with the Statistics Canada research on violence and victimisation. Sensational newspaper headlines indicated that in Canada 'Domestic violence is more widespread among same-sex couples than straights', with figures indicating that 15 per cent of lesbians and gay men and 28 per cent of bisexuals reported abuse by a partner in the past five years compared to only 7 per cent of heterosexuals. Questions had not been asked, however, about whether the abuse actually occurred in a same sex relationship (Ristock, 2011, 1–2).

The somewhat older representative prevalence data from the US is perhaps more informative. The national US Violence Against Women survey (NVAW) (Tjaden et al, 1999; Tjaden and Thoennes, 2000), included a small sub-sample of individuals identifying as gay or lesbian, and is one of the only representative studies to compare heterosexual and same sex samples. It found that in same sex relationships, male respondents were more likely than women to report violence from intimate partners; and that women in heterosexual relationships were the most likely to report violence (Tjaden et al, 1999). Of women living with a female intimate partner, slightly more than 11 per cent reported being raped, physically assaulted, and/or stalked by a female cohabitant compared to 30.4 per cent of the women who had married or lived with a man as part of a couple and who reported such violence by a husband or male cohabitant. Approximately 15 per cent of the men who had lived with a man as a couple reported being raped, physically assaulted, and/or stalked by a male cohabitant, compared with 7.7 per cent of the men who reported such violence by a wife or female cohabitant. Unfortunately, again no measures of impact were explored regarding same sex relationships. The authors suggest that while more research is needed to support or refute whether these findings indicate that there is more DVA in heterosexual contexts, the evidence does indicate that intimate partner violence is generally perpetrated by men, whether against male or female intimate partners. They conclude as a consequence, that 'strategies for preventing intimate partner violence should focus on risks posed by men' (Tjaden and Thoennes, 2000: v).

The more recent National Intimate Partner and Sexual Violence survey (NISVS) data from the United States (Walters et al, 2013) echo the NVAW data in showing that most perpetrators of intimate partner and sexual violence are male. In contrast to the NVAW survey, but similarly to the Canadian survey, the NISVS suggests that individuals identifying as lesbian, bisexual and gay male experienced more physical, sexual and emotional abuse from intimate partners than those identifying as heterosexual. The lifetime prevalence of rape, physical violence, and/or stalking by an intimate partner as reported in the NISVS was: for lesbians 43.8 per cent, bisexual women 61.1 per cent, heterosexual women 35.0 per cent, gay men 26.0 per cent, bisexual men 37.3 per cent and heterosexual men 29.0 per cent. However, the NISVS survey also includes data on perpetrators, showing that sexual violence to lesbian, gay male, bisexuals or heterosexual women was experienced mainly from male perpetrators, and that intimate partner violence experienced by bisexual women was also largely from male perpetrators. Thus, the higher levels of intimate partner violence for lesbians and bisexual women were not necessarily within same sex relationships. The NISVS data survey also provides data on the impact of intimate partner violence (non-sexual) and on sexual violence and stalking, indicating the particularly harmful impact of intimate partner violence on women, and on bisexual women in particular.

> More than half of bisexual women (57.4 per cent), a third of lesbian women (33.5 per cent), and more than a fourth of heterosexual women (28.2 per cent) who experienced rape, physical violence, and/or stalking by an intimate partner in their lifetime reported at least one negative impact (for example, missed at least one day of school or work, were fearful, were concerned for their safety, experienced at least one post-traumatic stress disorder symptom). (Walters et al, 2013, 2)

(McClennen, 2005) has argued that studies from the US have increasingly indicated that prevalence of DVA may be similar across same sex and heterosexual relationships, but what differs are help-seeking behaviours, but as our discussion above suggests, comparison can be difficult and problematic. This is compounded where studies on SSDVA use a variety of methodologies and samples, and apply varying definitions of violence and abuse. Apart from the CSEW, NVAW and NISVS surveys, samples have often reflected only the experiences of white, middle-class, lesbians and gay men who are between the ages of 25 and 35 years and who are 'out' enough to engage with venues that carry and support the surveys being done. What are presented as 'prevalence' studies may in actual fact be based on limited population samples, from a clinical setting such as the health sector, and are not representative but convenience samples. As a consequence, rates of incidence and prevalence have varied enormously across studies. The study by Greenwood et al (2002) in the US, of 'battering victimisation' among men who have sex with men, is one of the only studies that appears to have achieved something approaching a randomised approach, using a probability-based sample of 2881 men. However, it would not currently be possible to construct similar samples in the UK, and the methodology has not been attempted with regard to female–female relationships. The definition of DVA also varies across studies, with some focusing on sexual or physical abuse only, others incorporating psychological abuse, and others exploring 'acts of aggression'. Across the various studies, some show more violence and abuse in lesbian than in gay male relationships, while others show less. Elliot (1996), for instance, found that studies in the US of abuse in lesbian relationships showed a prevalence of 22–46 per cent physical violence and 73–6 per cent emotional violence, while in a study of gay men 17 per cent had been in a physically violent relationship. The review of American literature by Turell (2000) showed a prevalence of between 8 per cent and 60 per cent with regard to physical violence and 65–90 per cent prevalence of emotional violence in lesbian relationships, while in gay male relationships prevalence rates of physical violence were within a narrower band of 11–47 per cent. A more recent overview of prevalence of intimate partner DVA, primarily looking at men's experiences, found an even wider range of prevalence rates across studies, attributing such variation to 'type of IPV included, whether the reference period includes the past 12 months, or lifetime experience, and the method used to assess IPV' (Nowinski and Bowen, 2012, 36). Waldner-Haugrud et al (1997), in the US, found higher rates of physical violence in lesbian relationships (47.5 per cent) than in gay male relationships (27.9 per cent), and Greenwood et al (2002) found similar levels of male–male physical violence (22 per cent) based on the previous five years. By contrast, in the UK, one of the few existing surveys (Henderson, 2003) reports lower levels of abuse for lesbians than for gay men, with 22 per cent of lesbians and 29 per cent of gay men having experienced physical, mental or sexual abuse or violence from a regular same sex partner at some time. This is quite a different picture to that suggested by the recent survey data from the US referred to earlier (NISVS – Walters et al, 2013).

There are also intrinsic problems with the approaches used by many surveys. Much of the research on heterosexual DVA and the surveys on same sex DVA have emphasised prevalence without context or impact being considered, and have in the main been based on the Conflict Tactics Scale. In an attempt to provide replicable data on the incidence and prevalence of interpersonal violence, Straus et al (1980) developed the Conflict Tactics Scales (CTS) as a measure to quantify the amount and type of violence used in interpersonal relationships to resolve conflict. In its original format the CTS monitored how many times a man or woman had been violent towards their partner in the previous 12 months and how often the partner had been violent towards them in the same time period. Only one half of the couple were asked to fill in the scale and the total sample was split equally between female and male. The measurements on the scale ranged from 'verbal reasoning' to 'verbal aggression' and 'physical aggression'. The outcome of using this methodology led the researchers to conclude that heterosexual women and men were equally violent and that this type of interpersonal violence could be conceptualised as 'mutual combat' (Straus, 1999).

There have been many criticisms of the CTS approach. Initially it addressed only physical violence without including emotional abuse (Dobash and Dobash, 1992). There was no consideration of the impact of the violence on the victim/survivor, for instance no differentiation between a push and severe physical violence leading to hospitalisation. In response to this, Straus and colleagues developed the CTS2, in which they added questions relating to sexual violence and created differential 'levels' of violence, particularly in relation to any injuries sustained (Straus, 1999). The questions on impact are still limited, however, and thus differential experiences of victimisation by men and women in relation to physical acts, let alone in relation to a wider range of potentially abusive behaviours cannot be established. Archer (2002), based on a meta-analysis of 58 studies using the CTS, agrees that the CTS approach has limitations and creates difficulties in determining the actual impact of an act of physical aggression, specifically 'the extent to which they represent innocuous actions akin to symbolic violence, or whether they are likely to cause injuries' (Archer, 2000, 338). He suggests as a consequence that 'severity of impact ratings' should be incorporated in future CTS based studies.

The SIGMA and Stonewall research in the UK (Henderson, 2003; Hunt and Fish, 2008), mentioned above, used a CTS type approach, and without questions on impact or intentions related to the abuse. As a result it is not possible to differentiate between hitting someone as part of wider controlling behaviours, that is, as a part of ongoing domestic violence and abuse, or hitting as a means to prevent being assaulted, that is, as an act of self-defence. In the UK the CTS approach has also been used in the CSEW module to assess frequency of domestic violence and abuse, although with increasing recognition that 'the CTS concentrates on the perpetrator's actions to the exclusion of the impact and consequences' and 'tends to generate a spurious gender symmetry that vanishes if and when the impact of the act is brought into focus' (Walby and Allen, 2004, 37). By taking such contextual factors into consideration, the CSEW concludes that prevalence data provides a very partial picture of experience of domestic violence and abuse. (Heterosexual) men and women actually experience very different levels of severity and of impact of domestic violence and abuse, with women experiencing the greater severity and impact (Walby and Allen, 2004).

Evidence from qualitative research with women and men in heterosexual relationships indicates that answers to questions about abuse are gendered, with women tending to overstate their violence against their partners and men tending to underestimate (Hearn, 1996b). Qualitative evidence from heterosexual relationships also suggests that women are rarely the initiators of violence and are more likely to be acting in self-defence (Dobash and Dobash, 2000; Hester, 2009). These critiques also raise questions about whether individuals in same sex relationships may answer questions in different ways, or whether self-defence is a gender or sexuality-related issue. These significant questions have not previously been explored with survey samples and this was something we felt was important to achieve (see Hester and Donovan, 2009).

Our research

We wanted to move beyond the shortcomings of the previous work, and to compare more directly lesbian, gay male and heterosexual reports of domestically violent and abusive behaviours. In order to do so, our research used a combination of a national survey of same sex relationships, focus groups with lesbian, gay male and heterosexual women and men and interviews with LGBTQ and heterosexual women and men. We used an approach that was rooted in understandings of experience of DVA, including experiences and intersections related to gender and sexuality. This 'feminist epistemological approach' informed all our work. It allowed us to develop a detailed survey approach that took into account a range of abusive behaviours as well as impact, context and abuse of partners in intimate relationships. It led us to take a detailed look in interviews at how individuals perceived their best and worst relationship experiences. Drawing on our previous research findings regarding DVA and love, and on the literature about intimacy, we also explored how constructions of love featured in relationship descriptions involving worst and abusive experiences.

The discussion in this book indicates the importance of such an approach and how it contributes further to our analysis of how and to what extent such behaviours are experienced similarly or differently by individuals depending on sexuality, gender or age. The approach takes us a step further in analysis of domestic violence and abuse by moving beyond the generally heteronormative approaches of most surveys while also taking into account lesbian, gay male and heterosexual experiences and positionality.

Summary

- The discussion of domestic violence and abuse in same sex relationships has been relatively recent compared to that of DVA in heterosexual relationships, largely due to a context of homophobia.

- The research on which this book is based was conducted, and the book itself has been written, against a background of increasing openness about same sex relationships, also reflected in policy and legislation on DVA.

- Despite the increasingly wide definition of DVA used by government, in the popular imagination domestic violence and abuse often conjures up a particular *public story* focused on the heterosexual experience and emphasising physical violence, with implications for identifying and recognising DVA in same sex relationships both by victims/survivors and practitioners/professionals.

- We explore two main approaches to understanding DVA and their application to heterosexual and same sex DVA:
  - The first draws on the feminist notion of power and control, looked at through the lenses of *positionality* and *intersectionality* particularly focusing on gender, sexuality and age.
  - The second draws from the work on intimacy and involves *practices of love*, which provide means of actively constructing power over and control of intimate partners.

- Previous research on DVA focused mainly on heterosexual relationships. The more limited research on same sex DVA has often focused on one group (either lesbians or gay males) and with either survey or interview approaches. There are an increasing number of representative surveys involving both heterosexual and same sex identities, but they do not always make clear whether the DVA took place in heterosexual or in same sex relationships.

- Our research set out to enable comparison across both gender and sexuality (comparing experiences of men and women in same sex relationships, and between same sex and heterosexual relationships), using both survey and in-depth interviews.

- Previous survey research on DVA has been limited by lack of attention to the context of the abuse. Our research developed a sophisticated measure of impact to overcome this problem.

Notes

[1] DVA is, however, a bit of a mouthful and therefore the title of this book refers to Domestic Violence.

[2] The Crime Survey England and Wales was formerly the British Crime Survey. The change in name is to reflect more accurately its geographical remit and to acknowledge that there is a Scottish Crime Survey. Although this change came about during the writing of this book we use the Crime Survey England and Wales (CSEW) throughout as this is more accurate and to reflect the change made.

TWO

How we did the research: the COHSAR research approach

It was important that we adopted a research approach and developed methods that could deal with issues of gender, power and sexuality, let alone other differences. We used a feminist epistemological approach as this would help us to construct research instruments (survey, interviews) geared to exploring how processes of gendering and power might operate in similar or different ways in abusive female and male same sex and heterosexual relationships. Following our analysis of existing research (see Chapter One), the survey instrument also needed to provide data regarding a range of domestically violent and abusive behaviour while taking into account both context and impact, and to include questions about experiences of abuse from partners and use of such behaviour against partners. Some of these issues were further explored in the interviews, which also looked at links between love and violence. In this chapter we explain the rationale for our research approach, discuss the survey and interview methods that resulted, and outline the basis for our analysis. The overall approach is called COHSAR (COmparing Heterosexual and Same sex Abuse in Relationships)

Framing the research

Methods are situated historically (Hester et al, 2010). They not only reflect the socio-economic context and concerns of different eras, but develop and change over time as different interest groups and needs emerge (Savage and Burrows, 2007). Different research traditions have consequently developed in different parts of the world and at different times, and different methods have also achieved differential degrees of credibility and impact. The often critical stance of feminists regarding quantitative methods have to be seen in this light. Quantitative methods, and survey approaches in particular, have tended to be used for policy research, often in ways that have not been sensitive to gender or women's experiences and concerns (Skinner et al, 2005). The (western) feminist academic project has been to uncover the positioning of 'women' and gendered beings in the social world. In that respect the feminist project has always been about 'deconstruction' in some way and about the uncovering of meaning. It is therefore not surprising that feminists have often argued that qualitative approaches are more appropriate to the feminist project as these provide rich data that allow the application of a variety of textual and deconstructive techniques, allowing us to uncover how gender is construed, perceived and so on in a myriad of contexts. We would, however, agree with Ann Oakley (2000) for the need to move beyond and indeed to close the 'paradigm war' that has existed between quantitative and qualitative approaches, as it stops us using the most appropriate methods for the job or producing the best research possible. As Oakley argues:

> Qualitative research is not more authentically female or feminine than 'quantitative' research…It is not necessarily more ethical either…There is no such thing as 'simply' recording or publishing data. There must always be selection; the critical issue is whether this is made according to the kinds of open and systematic criteria which other people can inspect, or not…The more appropriate goal is…the continuation of systematic enquiry. (Oakley, 2000, 296–97)

The key issue is therefore to obtain 'a more critical, and ethical, approach to all kinds of methods' (Oakley, 2000, 302). Echoing Oakley we would suggest that drawing on the lessons from feminist approaches is an important means of achieving this (Hester et al, 2010).

To think epistemologically is to ask questions about what can be known, and the interrelationship between knowledge, experience and 'reality' (Skinner et al, 2005). How knowledge, experience and reality might interrelate, however, is an area of contestation within feminist debates (Ramazanoğlu with Holland, 2002). There can be different epistemologies and they lead to different knowledge about the social world. For us, the importance of adopting a feminist epistemological approach is that such approaches have a questioning of power, gender and sexuality as a central focus. The relationship between gender and power is, of course, something that is not straightforward, and different approaches have been adopted, for instance, 'standpoint' or 'postmodern' approaches with distinctions between how to understand reality and who the knowers are. 'Standpoint' approaches seek to understand the experience of oppression from the positioning as subordinated, where women or lesbians and gay men may all be constituted as the 'ruled' (Smith, 1988). Postmodern approaches instead attempt to understand the many 'realities' and subjugated knowledges discoursively produced at different times and locations, tending also to a rejection of 'static' identity positions such as 'women', 'lesbians' and 'gay men'. In these approaches, moreover, conceptualisations of power and control have been increasingly neutralised in many respects. For instance the Foucauldian project has created understandings of power and control as fluid concepts created through interactions between individuals, but largely without structured power. The identification and understanding of structural inequalities, and in particular what Stark (2007) calls 'sexual inequality' (male–female inequality) has also largely been lost from the application of 'power and control' models, at least in the US. This is what Stark takes issue with and why he is reluctant to use the model of power and control. He sees the use of 'coercive control' as a way of putting sexual inequality back into the equation.

Our research approach draws to some extent from both standpoint and postmodern perspectives, but (as outlined in Chapter One) with an emphasis on the material and on the constructions and experiences related to structural inequalities and oppressions. We build on the knowledge of situated power from standpoint approaches and the recognition of difference from postmodern approaches. This allows us to take into account the intersection of inequalities and difference such as those associated with gender, sexuality, 'race', ethnicity, age, disability, class, income and education (Crenshaw, 1989; Bograd, 2005; and see Chapter One). Understanding how gender and sexuality intersect with regard to how individuals may use, experience and embody domestic violence and abuse (DVA) is crucial to our project of comparing similarities and differences across abusive LGBTQ or heterosexual relationships. That provides only a very partial picture, however. Incorporating intersections and mutual shaping with regard to our participants' experiences and locations as they relate to ethnicity, age, disability, class, income and education is also crucial and further enhances our understanding of DVA use, experience, embodiment and help-seeking. Linked to this, we see knowledge about DVA – what it is, what it does – as rooted in the accounts of victims/survivors, and to a lesser extent in the accounts of perpetrators of DVA and witnesses (Hester et al, 2007). The use of 'experience' in feminist research is of course an area of contestation (Ramazanoğlu with Holland, 2002). We do not see experience as providing 'truth', rather, accounts of experiences are 'stories' that may vary in their telling over time and to different audiences. Nonetheless, how individuals report experience does help us to begin to understand similarities and differences across heterosexual and LGBTQ lives, to develop our understanding of the questions that need to be asked, and thus to construct better research instruments that reflect situated knowledge. As Ramazanoğlu with Holland (2002) point out '[d]espite the problematic status of accounts of experience, they provide knowledge that otherwise does not exist' (p 127).

The COHSAR survey

We wanted to apply a feminist epistemological approach in the development of a questionnaire survey that would reach a much wider sample of individuals in same sex relationships, and which could be used to compare data on DVA among individuals identifying as LGBTQ with those identifying as heterosexual. We therefore set out to develop a questionnaire that would not only draw on existing surveys of DVA, such as the Crime Survey for England and Wales (CSEW), but would incorporate questions that might reflect to a greater extent 'how we know' about such violence and abuse in same sex as well as in heterosexual relationships. In other words, to reflect what previous research on 'experience' of DVA tells us about the possible features and dynamics of such abuse, while at the same time allowing new knowledge to emerge. It can, however, be difficult using questionnaires to capture 'patterns over time', to identify what individuals may experience as 'coercive control' or 'situational' violence, let alone to take into account different contexts for the abuse. In what follows we discuss some of the ways in which we attempted to address these issues in constructing the COHSAR questionnaire.

Much of the debate about the use of surveys in researching DVA has focused on measures and approaches used in heterosexual surveys. Similar measures have, however, increasingly been used for same sex DVA surveys, and also need to be examined if comparison is to be made across heterosexual and same sex relationships (Hester et al, 2010). Consequently, many of the critiques in relation to heterosexual surveys are also of relevance to the development of a survey approach for SSDVA.

Obtaining the COHSAR survey sample

Ideally, the survey should have used a representative sample, but this was not possible in the UK, as there was no national dataset in existence with information about sexual identity and contact details or location of the individuals concerned. Indeed, the difficulty in obtaining representative samples within LGBTQ communities has generally been seen by researchers of same sex DVA as 'the greatest challenge facing researchers in this area…and a true random sampling strategy probably is…impossible to achieve' (Murray and Mobley, 2009, 377). Although sexual identity was added as a question in the UK Integrated Household Survey from 2009, this was not available when we carried out the COHSAR survey. Instead, we decided to carry out a large UK-wide 'community' survey with a convenience sample as the most wide reaching and ethical alternative to a representative sample (McCarry et al, 2008). To maximise the sample we developed an extensive network of contacts (over 220) with LGBTQ and DVA organisations across Scotland, Northern Ireland, Wales, North-East England, North-West England, Central England, South-West England and South-East England including London using internet searches, LGBTQ literature, national helplines, the media and personal contacts.

A total sample of 800 responses was obtained, from which 54 cases were removed because: their sexuality was unknown; or they had not had a same sex relationship; or they identified as heterosexual *and* had never had a same sex relationship (some individuals who define as 'heterosexual' may have had a same sex relationship in the past). This resulted in a final data set of 746 individuals who had been or were in a same sex relationship.

The questionnaire included sections on: personal demographic information; decision making and conflict resolution in own relationship; own experience of negative emotional/physical/sexual behaviours including impact; own use of negative emotional/physical/sexual against partner including motives, help-seeking; and a final section asking whether respondents had experienced DVA plus other questions eliciting views and opinions (for a detailed outline of the contents and sampling, see McCarry et al, 2008).

To name or not to name something as DVA

In developing the questionnaire we were immediately faced with an important question – whether or not to name as 'domestic violence and abuse' the phenomenon we were ostensibly studying (Hester and Donovan, 2009). Should we be up-front in stating that this was a questionnaire about DVA? Or develop a questionnaire about something less obviously defined such as 'problems in relationships'? Previous research has indicated the difficulties (even greater than in heterosexual relationships) involved in naming as 'domestic violence and abuse' harmful or abusive behaviours or experiences within LGBTQ relationships (for example, Giorgio, 2002). We also acknowledged the difficulties some individuals might have in perceiving anything other than physical violence as 'domestic violence and abuse'. Ethics are an important feature in feminist research (Skinner et al, 2005) and the ethics involved in using a covert or an overt approach therefore also had to be considered.

We decided to carry out an extensive consultation exercise, with representatives from a range of LGBTQ groups, to test which approach to use and why. Two alternative cover sheets were produced, both introducing the research as 'Same sex relationships: when things go wrong'. One used the following sentence as part of the more detailed description for the research: 'Recently, in the UK, there has been a growing concern to make services more relevant, appropriate and accessible to people in same sex relationships who might need help or advice because of domestic abuse', while the other, using mostly the same sentence, omitted the last part: 'because of domestic abuse'. The majority of those consulted said they would prefer the latter, framing the questionnaire in terms of relationships generally, rather than explicitly stating a focus on DVA:

> 'Personally, I think you should go covert as people who may be suffering domestic abuse might be put off filling it in. In addition, people who think that they aren't suffering domestic abuse but whose partners are exhibiting some of the behaviours listed might be more 'honest' about their answers if the questionnaire is not marketed as a domestic abuse questionnaire.' (Critical reviewer)

It was also apparent from the interviews, carried out once the questionnaire survey had been completed, that this approach helped to elicit a wider range of responses. For instance, one lesbian interviewee talked about controlling experiences she had had, not being able to get her partner to leave the house, being continually questioned about everything she did and about whom she was with. She had wondered if this was adequate as the basis for saying on the questionnaire that she had experienced domestic abuse:

> 'And...when I was filling out the questionnaire...I did think, "Well actually, is this really going to count,"...but it does fall into it, I think.' (Kay, a white lesbian, aged 35–9 at interview, 32 years old when DVA relationship began)

Individuals such as Kay might not as readily have responded to a survey explicitly about DVA. With regard to ethics, taking a more covert approach thus seemed justifiable in that it allowed a wider range of individuals to talk about potentially abusive relationship experiences.

Following extensive piloting, the survey was thus described to potential respondents as examining 'when things go wrong' in same sex relationships and the term 'domestic violence and abuse' was deliberately not used in the survey until the last page (Hester and Donovan, 2009). The sample, however, still had a larger proportion of respondents who had experienced potentially abusive behaviours from a partner than the more general health surveys carried out within LGBTQ communities (Hunt and Fish, 2008; Guasp, 2012; Henderson, 2003; and see Chapter Four).

Comparison with previous surveys

To achieve comparison between male and female same sex relationships, and with heterosexual relationship experiences, the survey replicated some of the CSEW self-report module on domestic violence. Areas for replication included time periods and violence/abuse types. Relevant US studies were also drawn on for development of same sex specific questions relating to types of abuse, as well as items on decision-making and conflict resolution (Renzetti, 1992; Turell, 2000), which allowed the questionnaire to move beyond the 'heteronormative' approach of the CSEW and to allow comparison across sexuality and gender (McCarry et al, 2008; Hester and Donovan, 2009).

While the CSEW refers to both intimate partner and non-partner violence (Povey et al, 2008), we wanted to focus only on intimate partner violence. From our previous research (for example, Radford and Hester, 2006) we were aware that questions regarding experiences of DVA needed to be both detailed and nuanced. Consequently a wide range of questions pertaining to respondents' experience of emotional abuse (27 items), physical abuse (13 items), and sexual abuse (nine items) both within the last 12 months and earlier, were asked. In each case respondents were asked whether they had 'never', 'sometimes' or 'often' experienced the behaviour in question. Many of the questions on emotional behaviour reflected those used in the CSEW including questions about being isolated and about financial control. We also included questions that were directly targeted towards the same sex community about being 'outed' and having sexuality used as forms of abuse. We replicated questions from surveys with gay men that particularly related to HIV related abuse, for example, withdrawing medicines, while recognising that this kind of abusive behaviour could be used in relation to any health condition where medication is used.

In addition we also asked questions about other identity abuses, for example, whether respondents had ever had their 'race', social class, disability and so on used against them or used their partner's identities in these regards against them.

The CSEW questions on rape and sexual assault accommodate the 2003 Sexual Offences Act definitions of rape. According to the Act, while both a woman and a man can be a victim of rape, it remains that only a man can commit rape. In order to incorporate the experiences of women who felt they had been raped in a lesbian relationship, however, our questions needed to be open enough so that women could define their own experiences and not be excluded because of legally prescribed gendered definitions. Also, while both heterosexual and LGBTQ individuals may participate in sado-masochistic sexual activities, there has been much more debate about issues of consensual and non-consensual behaviour in this regard and in relation to HIV and sexual experiences more widely in LGBTQ communities. Questions about breaches of requests for safer sex and safe words were thus included, and were deemed important in discussions with the LGBTQ community during the pilot phase. This is a key area that differentiates our questionnaire from the CSEW and again, moves beyond the heteronormative.

In addition, respondents were asked to identify whether their responses related to the behaviour of a current partner, to a previous partner, or to both. To determine validity and reliability of the items relating to potentially abusive experiences both separate and combined scales were developed. Three separate scales relating to emotional, physical and sexual abuse behaviours were created, as well as a combined scale including the three items. All were found to be reliable (Cronbach's Alpha 0.865, 0.895, 0.807, 0.915 respectively). In Chapter Four we outline the findings from the survey and discuss some of the issues and meanings by also incorporating findings from the interviews.

In order to check whether respondents who had answered affirmatively to experiencing any of the potentially abusive behaviours might also consider that their experiences constituted 'domestic violence and abuse', we included a further question towards the end of the questionnaire that explicitly asked if the respondent had ever experienced domestic violence or abuse in a same sex relationship.

Incorporating impact

As indicated in our discussion of the previous studies on SSDVA, we would argue strongly that surveys looking at prevalence of seemingly DVA behaviours should also look at the impact of these behaviours (Hester et al, 2010). Without including questions about impact it is not possible to differentiate between individual behaviours that may create the kinds of changes and feelings in victims/survivors associated with experiencing the power over and control of DVA, and those that do not. Other surveys have tended to use narrow measures of such impact, via severity (using number of times something happened) and whether or not there is physical injury. For instance in research based on the Conflict Tactics Scale (CTS), severity is determined by frequency of incidents and rating tactics used. It is difficult to assess whether or not this is commensurate with the actual impact on the individuals concerned, however. We wanted to go beyond these approaches and thus constructed a much more detailed and sophisticated set of questions. It is generally assumed that higher levels of abuse should be associated with a greater impact upon respondents (Walby and Allen, 2004). We were able to test whether the relationship between the frequency of incidents of abuse and its impact on respondents' lives reflected this assumption. As detailed further below and in Chapter Four, we found strong association between frequency of incidents and greater impact, which was especially marked where individuals experienced combinations of physical, sexual and emotionally abusive behaviours.

In order to explore the impact that abusive behaviours may have had on the respondent, each of the three sub-sections on potentially abusive behaviours (physical, emotional and sexual) also included questions about impact related to those behaviours. To move beyond the limitations of previous surveys we included a wide range of questions that might allow us to understand the nature and severity of impact, and which we devised from previous research. The result was a multi-response survey item listing 26 possible outcomes and inviting respondents to tick all that applied in relation to emotional, physical and sexual abuse separately. The questions included physical and psychological impacts, effects on relationship quality and partner interactions, as well as questions regarding acts that may be seen as self-defence or retaliation. There was also the possibility of answering that there was no impact. The result was three scales with a high degree of Alpha reliability measuring the impacts of emotional, physical and sexual abuse (Cronbach's Alpha 0.933, 0.959, 0.951 respectively).

With regard to the assumption that higher levels of abuse should be associated with a greater impact upon respondents, this was also reflected in the relationship between the frequency of incidents of abuse and its impact on respondents' lives. Overall the empirical (Spearman's rank) correlation between scores on the impact scales and potential abuse scales relating to the previous 12 months supported this assertion with strong correlations evident between impact and emotional behaviour (0.503, $p<0.001$), physical behaviour (0.463, $p<0.001$) and sexual behaviour (0.432, $p<0.001$) (Hester et al, 2010). We discuss the findings related to the intersection of the abuse and impact scales in Chapter Four.

In relation to those respondents who had disclosed that they had used some of these abusive behaviours against their partner/s, we asked respondents to explain 'why' they had abused their partners and they were given a choice of 21 closed responses from which to choose (they could opt for as many as applicable). It should also be noted that this question was only relevant to those who had identified that they had used potentially emotionally, physically or sexually abusive behaviours against any of their ex/partners. This question was important in differentiating between behaviour carried out by partners with the intention of harming or controlling their ex/partners and those behaviours used in self-defence for example. This is a significant point of departure between our survey and some other surveys that are unable to differentiate between mutual abuse, aggressive abuse and actions carried out in self-defence. The consequence of not doing so leads in other surveys to data that may misrepresent some actions as actively DVA when instead it constitutes defensive behaviour. The findings regarding use of potentially abusive behaviour against partners are discussed in Chapter Four.

The COHSAR survey participants

The COHSAR survey included a wide range of demographic questions. Murray and Mobley (2009) recommend that where representative sampling is not feasible, researchers should report in great detail the demographic characteristics of the sample, and report at least:

> age, gender, ethnic background, self-reported sexual orientation, income level, education level, employment status, current relationship status, the length of the relationship and the partner's demographic characteristics. (Murray and Mobley, 2009, 378)

In what follows, we outline all such details for our sample, apart from employment status and partner's demographic characteristics. In addition, we report on respondents' parenting of children and about disability, as these are issues that have previously been found to make individuals vulnerable to DVA (Radford and Hester, 2006; Thiara et al, 2011).

The ages of respondents to the COHSAR survey ranged from 16 years to individuals in their late 60s, although most were in their 20s and 30s. This is a wider age group than in most other surveys on DVA in the LGBTQ community in the UK (see for example, Henderson, 2003; Hunt and Fish, 2008). The average age of our respondents was 35.37. Female respondents tended to be a bit older than the men (for women mean age 35.77, median 37; for men mean age 34.48, median 32). The age distribution for the transgender individuals, just four people, was older, with one in the 20–24 age group, and the rest aged between 40 and 59 years.

When age is looked at in relation to sexuality, there were slight differences in age by self-identified sexuality groups. For instance older women were more likely to call themselves lesbian and younger women were more likely to use the term 'queer'. Overall the oldest individuals were lesbians (mean age 37.11, median 37). The second oldest group were gay men (mean age 34.90, median 37), followed by homosexuals – who were mainly men (mean age 34.62, median 32), then gay women (mean age 34.48, median 32), and queer – who were mostly women (mean age 32.50, median 32). The youngest were individuals identifying as bisexuals (mean age 30.95, median 27).

Gender was apparent for 736 of the 746 individuals in the sample. Nearly two thirds identified as women (61 per cent), and more than a third as men (38 per cent). There were also four individuals identifying as transgender (0.5 per cent), and one individual identifying as queer (0.1 per cent). Women were most likely to identify as 'lesbian' and over two-thirds of women (70 per cent) defined themselves in this way. The second largest category among women was 'gay woman' (16 per cent). Men mainly identified as 'gay man', with more than three-quarters of the men identifying in this way (76 per cent). The second largest category among the male respondents was homosexual (18 per cent). Other self-identifications used were bisexual and queer. More women than men defined themselves as bisexual (10 per cent compared to 4 per cent of men) or as queer (3 per cent compared to 1 per cent of men). Very few women (1 per cent) identified as homosexual. One individual identified as queer in relation to both gender and sexuality. The four transgendered individuals identified themselves in four separate ways: as bisexual, gay woman, lesbian and queer. Of the ten individuals whose gender was unknown, half identified as homosexual (50 per cent), and the rest as bisexual (30 per cent) or queer (20 per cent).

The question about ethnicity used mostly the same categorisation as the 2001 Census, and our findings echoed those in the general population where that was the case. Most respondents identified as white (95 per cent compared to 92 per cent in Census). The proportions identifying as mixed or Chinese were similar to those in the Census, but we had considerably smaller proportions of Asian or black respondents, possibly because the COHSAR survey did not subdivide the categories of Asian or black, which was the case in the Census. In particular the 'other' category, which was more than four times as large in our survey than in the Census, may have contained what the census termed 'other Asian' and 'black other'. Individuals identifying as homosexual were most likely to be white (98 per cent), with bisexuals most likely to be represented among individuals of mixed, Asian, black or other ethnic backgrounds (92 per cent).

The income level for the COHSAR respondents was slightly higher than the population generally at the time of the research. The average (mean) income for all the respondents was £22,432.43, rising to £23,569.67 if only those aged 20 and over were taken into account (with a median, 'midpoint', income of £25,500 – compared to general population median for full-time men of £25,000 in 2005, and for full-time women £19,400 (National Statistics, 2006)). Even so, one in five earned less than £10,000, and nearly half earned less than £20,000. As may be expected, there was a tendency for income to increase with age until 60 years and decrease again thereafter at retirement age. Those earning over £40,000 were clustered between 30–55 years. The income distribution also reflected the wider income inequality between men and women in the UK population at that time. The largest group of men were earning £21–30,000, compared to only £11–20,000 for the largest group of women. These gendered 'norms' become especially important in discussion about the apparent vulnerability to DVA for lower income groups, and this is explored further in Chapter Four.

The educational attainment of the survey respondents was generally much higher than that of the UK population. Half of the respondents (51 per cent) were educated to at least degree level compared to 27 per cent in England and Wales generally (2011 census), and nearly one in five of our respondents (19 per cent) had at least an 'A' level qualification. Just over a quarter of respondents (28 per cent) had attained GCSE, NVQ or vocational level qualifications. Very few respondents (3 per cent or less) had no qualifications, compared to 23 per cent in England and Wales (2011 Census).

The vast majority of respondents (87 per cent) had been in a same sex relationship during the past 12 months, with more than two-thirds currently in such a relationship (71 per cent). For about one in seven it was their first same sex relationship (15 per cent). This was similar for both women and men, but there were significant differences between men and women in terms of length of relationships (Chi-square=15.503, p=0.03). Men predominated in shorter relationships, lasting up to one year, but also in relationships lasting two to five years or more than 20 years. Women were generally more likely to have longer relationships, lasting between one and 20 years. This also reflected what happened regarding staying or leaving a DVA relationship: men were more likely to leave a DVA relationship more rapidly than were women.

Out of 713 individuals who answered the question 'Do you have a disability?', more than one in ten said they did (11 per cent). By comparison, in the 2001 Census, a greater number of respondents answered the broader question asking whether they had a long-term illness, health problems or disability that limited their ability to work or their daily activities (18 per cent). Slightly more of the women (12 per cent) than the men in our survey (10 per cent) said they had a disability. Half of those individuals indentifying as transgendered said they had a disability (50 per cent, although the numbers are very small). If sexuality is taken into consideration, the largest proportion of individuals with a stated disability was among those identifying as queer (22 per cent, although small numbers). One in six bisexuals (17 per cent) and just over one in ten lesbians (11 per cent) had a disability, while less than one in ten gay women, gay men, or homosexuals said that they had a disability.

One in six of the survey respondents (16 per cent) parented children. The majority of parents – more than two-thirds (71 per cent) – had all or some of these children living with them. This included most of the school age and teenage children, and a few of the adult children. Not surprisingly, women were almost three times as likely as the men to be parents. One in five women parented children (22 per cent) compared to less than one in ten men (7 per cent). Individuals identifying as transgendered were most likely to be parents, although the numbers are very small (33 per cent). This gender pattern also meant that women identifying as lesbians were most likely to parent children, and nearly a quarter said they were parents (24 per cent). Other, largely female, groups such as bisexuals (19 per cent), gay women (14 per cent) and queers (10 per cent), were more likely to parent than those comprising largely men, that is, homosexuals (9 per cent) and gay men (8 per cent).

The COHSAR interviews

Given the lack of detailed data on SSDVA, especially in the UK, the obvious approach would be to develop knowledge of intimate relationships that might be abusive, via in-depth interviews with a range of LGBTQ individuals and heterosexuals. We did indeed adopt an interview approach, which included a follow-up sample from the survey and further participants. As explained earlier, in a departure from most other research in this area, our research was not labelled as being about DVA. Instead we encouraged participation from anybody with experiences of relationships that had 'gone wrong'. In this way we intended to forestall pre-conceptions on the part of participants about what kinds of relationship experiences 'counted'. In addition, other researchers have been concerned that, in framing their research in terms of an exploration of DVA in heterosexual, same sex or LGBTQ relationships, they have 'primed' participants to give a particular account of DVA reflecting dominant binaries of perpetrator and victim with particular constructions of what perpetrators and victims 'are like' (for example, see Ristock, 2002a). The expected account coincides with the public story of DVA, that is, that it should be heteronormative, based in a long-term monogamous relationship and predominantly experienced through physical violence (for example, Aguinaldo, 2004). Because we did not approach the research in this way, it is possible that we were able to facilitate a range of different DVA stories to be told (notwithstanding the caveats outlined above regarding participants intersecting identities and access to resources) in relationships which were short (sometimes only a matter a months) and long (up to 20 years), predominantly emotionally abusive (as typically the accounts of women in same sex relationships were) in relationships living apart as well as together, with children and without; and with accounts from victims/survivors that not only challenge their construction as passive victims but overturn them insofar as they understood themselves to be the (emotionally) stronger person in the relationship (see Chapter Six).

The interview schedule reinforced our intention to provide spaces for participants to reflect on how love can be understood in relationships that go wrong as well as those that go right. The development of the interview schedule was informed by both the survey and four focus groups (8 heterosexual women, 6 heterosexual men, 3 lesbians, and 2 gay men). Questions were based around an exploration of two accounts: a best and a worst relationship experience and from beginning to end or current situation. For some respondents their best relationship was also their worst and for others they had only had one relationship so we were led by respondents in how they wanted to respond. Questions then asked about how they had met the partner in their best relationship, whether they loved that partner and how they knew that they did, whether their partner loved them and how they knew that, what the best and the worst things were about their relationship, how they organised their relationship (including how household tasks were distributed, decisions made, bills paid, holidays organised, interior design decided on in shared homes, parenting and so on), how they resolved/accommodated disagreements and differences and, if appropriate, how the relationship had ended. They were then asked the same set of questions about a worst relationship experience. At the end we asked more general questions about respondents' views of love and DVA in same sex and heterosexual relationships, whether they had experienced domestic violence and abuse and how they defined this. For those respondents who were recruited to the interviews through the survey it is entirely possible that they might have expected to talk about abuse given the tenor of the survey questions; that not every participant did so suggests that our recruitment strategy was successful in its aims to be inclusive of a range of relationship experiences. It is perhaps another measure of the success of our approach that several participants were ambivalent about whether their experience could be named DVA, especially if it had not involved physical violence, but also precisely because it did not seem to fit what they understood to constitute DVA from the public story. On the other hand it is also of some concern that some participants apparently normalised experiences that were by any standards emotionally abusive and were concerned to explain away the behaviours of their ex-partners with reference to a mental health or other crisis the ex-partner had been experiencing at the time.

Analysis of the interview data was thematic. That is, interview transcripts were read and re-read to identify and code themes that emerged from the data in relation to the key research questions: what kinds of differences and similarities occur in the abusive experiences of lesbians, gay men, heterosexual women and heterosexual men; what, if any, narratives of love are drawn on to make sense of abusive experiences and whether these differ across gender and sexuality. The analysis was underpinned by a reading of the sociological literature on love and intimacy to aid the identification of behaviours that have, in that literature, been gendered, for example, caring relationship practices, disclosing intimacy, emotion work, decision-making, setting the terms of relationships (Duncombe and Marsden, 1993, 1995, 1996; Jamieson, 1998; Hochschild, 2003; Cancian; 1990; Giddens, 1992). This was to both interrogate how these relationships practices are understood and lived in same sex relationships as well as to consider whether and how they are enacted differently or in similar ways when the relationship is abusive and regardless of gender and sexuality. NVivo7 was used to aid coding of the themes. Codes were tested and collapsed to identify three key features of abusive relationships: types of abuse; relationship practices and spheres of power and control; and narratives of love. A separate reading of whole transcripts was also carried out in relation to individuals who took part in the questionnaire survey, which highlighted that individuals were more likely to focus on a previous relationship (before the previous 12 months) when talking about abusive experiences (see also Lie and Gentlewarrier, 1991; Turell 2000).

As discussed above, we do not claim that the interview accounts given were the 'truth'. They were in any case dependent on respondents' memories and their tendency to tell relationship stories that were necessarily selective and put together with hindsight and from their own perspective. Participants, however, also made active choices to take part in the research, about which relationships they wished to give accounts of and about what to tell about those relationships. As Gabb (2008, 52) argues: 'the selection of a particular story, the details that are emphasised and the manner in which the story is told all signify and represent choices made by the participant'. Thus we can suggest that while memories and hindsight might provide particular lenses on relationship experiences that make those experiences unstable as (absolutely) factual or truthful, it might also be the case that particular experiences because of their shocking or harmful impacts (or alternatively their kind, loving impacts), remain 'alive' in people's memories and act as 'critical moments' that can be selected as authentically representative of a relationship experience. Given the topic we were exploring we also encountered respondents for whom the interview acted as a cathartic experience insofar as in the telling of a relationship story in the context of our study they understood for the first time that they had experienced abuse which resulted in some distress (see also Kelly, 1988; Ristock, 2002b).

Thus, the interview data collected was the result not just of participants' accounts but also the result of an interaction with us as interviewers asking particular questions and so shaping the stories that were told (Duncombe and Marsden, 1996). Nonetheless, we present them as stories that have validity in that they provide accounts that are 'a necessary element of knowledge of gendered lives and actual power relations' (Ramazanoğlu with Holland, 2002, 127) and thus provide insights into the ways in which relationships can be understood. One of our key intentions with this research project was to enable new stories to be told (Plummer, 1995) about DVA in the UK context. While, as we have said in Chapter One, there have been some pioneers raising their heads above the parapet to signify that DVA is an issue in lesbian relationships (Hall, 1992; Taylor and Chandler, 1995), it is also the case that there has been silence about this issue across LGBTQ communities. Because of this we approached participants as willing audiences for their abusive relationship stories and conveyed our willingness to believe and honour their accounts as authentic and our intention to use the research and endeavour to make changes in wider society so that others might benefit. In this way we further sought to enact the feminist principles underpinning the work (for example, Ristock, 2002c; Harrison et al, 2001).

In total, 68 interviews were conducted with 20 lesbians (including one who identified as a trans woman), 19 gay men, 14 heterosexual women, nine heterosexual men, three bisexual women and three queer women. Of the lesbians, bisexual, queer and heterosexual women, 19 gave accounts of female same sex DVA relationships and 13 gave accounts of heterosexual DVA relationships. Just over a half of the gay men and a third of heterosexual men said that they had experienced abusive behaviours in their same or opposite sex intimate relationships.

Respondents' ages ranged from 19 to 64 years of age. Lesbians, bisexuals and queer women's ages ranged from 19 to 54 years, gay men from 20 to 64 years, heterosexual women from 20 to 59 years and heterosexual men from 20 to 59 years. Most were between the ages of 20 and 59 years old. The overwhelming majority of participants identified as white (with one identifying as white French) or white British. One lesbian identified as black British and one identified as African. Although the survey sample indicates that we were able to recruit a profile that reflects that of the UK population in terms of 'race' and ethnicity, we were singularly unsuccessful through the survey at recruiting black and minority ethnic people to the interviews (only one lesbian volunteered through this route). We then pursued several different routes to recruiting participants from these groups, including placing adverts in mainstream newspapers read by particular groups; contacting websites that targeted members of these groups and snowballing through personal and professional networks. At the end of this process we were only successful in recruiting one African lesbian.

Our status as a research group that was all white will undoubtedly have had an impact on our recruitment in this area. The need remains for work to be done in the UK with LGBTQ people from black and minority ethnic groups on DVA (see Hester et al, 2012 for some initial work in this area).

Five respondents identified as having a disability. In general, the sample was educated with incomes at or above the average. Incomes ranged from under £10,000 to over £60,000. In parallel with the profile of those who completed the survey, most men earned £21–30,000 with the highest earner being a heterosexual man while most women earned £11–20,000. Most respondents were educated to degree or above with women slightly more likely to have higher educational qualifications. However, women were also more likely to only have GCSE or A levels. It is interesting to note that while women as a group were as likely to be educated as men their incomes did not reflect this.

It is important to reflect on the knowledge that can be ascertained about DVA from a sample that is for the most part, white, and, at least at the time of the interview, relatively well resourced in terms of education and income. Clearly the accounts of DVA will not be inclusive of the experiences of those who are not white, nor who are less well resourced. That the men were, on the whole more resourced than the women will no doubt have provided more choices about their response to their experiences, for example that they might have found it easier to leave an abusive relationship (see also Aguinaldo, 2004). Yet a complicating other factor in this approach to acknowledging the positionality of respondents who said they had experienced DVA is that of the age they had been when they had done so. Only one person we interviewed was still in the relationship they described as abusive. The African lesbian, Zoe, explained how she believed that she had made changes in her relationship such that it was no longer abusive. Everybody else who described abusive relationships was talking about experiences in the past, some of which had occurred several decades in the past. As will be discussed more fully in the following chapters, age is an important factor in understanding experiences of abuse, particularly but not exclusively in same sex relationships. Acknowledging how age and resources (or 'social capital'), defined here in terms of education and income, might intersect in ways such that the former dictates the extent of the latter must be done to make sense of their accounts. It might be that their youthful age and corresponding lack of relationship experience had more salience in shaping experiences of abuse than resources, for example.

Other differences in gender might have also influenced participants' ability to respond to an abusive relationship. Typically, the women, regardless of sexuality had lived with their abusive partner and had longer abusive relationships while the gay men typically did not live with a partner (only three out of nine interview accounts of abusive relationships were in cohabiting relationships) and had shorter abusive relationships. Living together (nine of those in female same sex relationships), being married (eight of those giving accounts of abuse in heterosexual relationships), and parenting children, (seven of those who were married and seven of those giving accounts of female same sex relationships) will have been factors making it more difficult to leave an abusive relationship. Here, it is possible that structured dependency, more associated with heterofemininity yet also evidenced in these lesbian, and female bisexual and queer relationships played a crucial role in these women remaining in abusive relationships for longer than men.

Postscript

The COHSAR survey has provided the basis for a new generation of research and created much interest among researchers of DVA in the UK, US, Sweden and Australia. In the UK the COHSAR survey has been used as the basis for an important national study of teen relationship violence (Barter et al, 2009), and to inform cross sectional surveys regarding DVA of men accessing GP surgeries and sexual health clinics (PROVIDE, www.bris.ac.uk/social-community-medicine/projects/provide/).

Summary

- We used a feminist epistemological approach as this enabled us to construct survey and interview schedules geared to exploring how processes of gendering and power might operate in similar or different ways in abusive same sex or heterosexual relationships.

- Our research approach emphasised the constructions and experiences related to structural inequalities and oppressions. This allowed us to take into account the intersecting of potential inequalities or differences such as those associated with gender, sexuality, 'race', ethnicity, age, disability, class, income and education.

- We developed a questionnaire that drew on existing national surveys of DVA, such as the Crime Survey for England and Wales, and incorporated further questions that might reflect to a greater extent than previous surveys 'how we know' about such violence and abuse in same sex as well as in heterosexual relationships. In addition, in order to move beyond the heteronormative, we drew on existing North American surveys that include questions specific to those in same sex relationships, such as the use of sexuality, access to medication and/or agreements around safer sex and sadomasochism to control a partner.

- Ideally, the survey should have used a representative sample, but this was not possible in the UK, as there was no national dataset in existence with information about sexual identity and contact details or location of the individuals concerned. Instead, we carried out a large UK-wide 'community' survey as the most wide reaching and ethical alternative.

- The survey questionnaire included sections on: personal demographic information; decision making and conflict resolution in own relationship; own experience of negative emotional/physical/sexual behaviours including impact; own use of negative emotional/physical/sexual against partner including why s/he did this, help-seeking; and a final section asking whether respondent had experienced domestic abuse plus other questions eliciting views and opinions.

- The survey, about 'problems in relationships', resulted in a final data set of 746 respondents who had been or were in a same sex relationship. The sample had a larger proportion of respondents who had experienced potentially abusive behaviours from a partner than the more general health surveys carried out within LGBTQ communities in the UK.

- To explore the impact that abusive behaviours may have had on the respondent, the sub-sections on potentially physical, emotional and sexual abusive behaviours also included questions about impact related to the experience of those behaviours. This included physical and psychological impacts, effects on relationship quality and partner interactions, and whether acts may be seen as self-defence or retaliation.

- The ages of survey respondents ranged from 16 years to late 60s. Nearly two thirds identified as women, and more than a third as men, with a further four identifying as transgender, and one as queer. More than two-thirds of women identified as 'lesbian' and more than three-quarters of men identified as gay.

- Sixty-eight interviews were conducted with 20 lesbians (including one who identified as a trans woman), 19 gay men, 14 heterosexual women, nine heterosexual men, three bisexual women and three queer women. The sample was majority white women, most of whom had experienced domestic abuse. All but one of the lesbian, gay, bisexual and queer respondents also took part in the survey. All the heterosexual interviewees were recruited separately.

- The interview schedule provided an opportunity for respondents to talk about how love can be understood in relationships that go wrong as well as those that go right. The interview schedule was based around an exploration of a best and a worst relationship experience.

THREE

Setting the context: sexuality matters

A look at the legislative landscape of the UK and many neo-liberal, western democracies across the world at the beginning of the twenty-first century would suggest that a fundamental shift has occurred in how lesbian, gay, bisexual and trans people and their intimate and familial relationships are perceived. From living lives that were considered not only deviant but dangerous and a threat to society and its core institutions such as 'the family' and its children, laws have been passed that legitimate their lives and relationships and provide many of the same protections, rights and obligations as heterosexual women and men (see Weeks, 2007). Simultaneously, however, there is also evidence that in the living of their everyday lives, intimate and familial relationships, LGBTQ people still face enormous challenges, discrimination, hostility and violence. It would seem that at the same time as arguments have been won that human rights are universal, regardless of sexuality, perceptions about those living outside heterosexuality position them as different. The differences seem to fall into two categories, both of which find their origins in the centrality of heterosexuality to the organisation of society and the location of social power. The first is that sexual minorities are perceived as outside society and therefore that they pose threats to society. This is most often applied to gay men who are still associated with being a threat to children and young people because of a particular, erroneous, perception of their sexuality that confuses it with paedophilia. The second category of differences relate to an apparent inability to comprehend how same sex intimate or same sex parental relationships work: the central dilemma here focuses on whether they are the same as heterosexual relationships or, because of essentialised assumptions about gender, different. Such debates have been countered from within LGBTQ communities in opposing ways. Those arguing that 'we are all the same', insist that 'we all want the same things' and seek to reassure the heterosexual majority that there is no threat to society's institutions by including LGBTQ people in them. Those arguing that 'we are different' are interested in challenging society's institutions to change them for everybody to address social inequalities and oppressive power structures.

These opposing perceptions and arguments have profound impacts on the everyday lives of those living outside heterosexuality and are exacerbated by the additional inequalities that result from being young, disabled, working class, or from within trans and/or black and minority ethnic communities. These inequalities mean that on the one hand positionality has an impact on the multiple ways in which an individual comes to understand their sense of self and how others perceive them as a member of the multiple social groups to which they belong. On the other hand, an intersectional exploration of their experiences reveals how their multiple identities, positioned unequally in social and cultural hierarchies, has an impact on their potential and actual access to material and socio-cultural resources available in, and treatment by, the social groups, networks, localities, regions and broader society in which they live. For example, alongside the exclusionary experiences those identifying as LGBTQ recount from broader, mainstream society are the exclusionary experiences they recount from within LGBTQ communities because of their 'race' and ethnicity, their social class, their faith, their age and/or their disability.

In this chapter, while remaining aware of the multiple identities of LGBTQ people within society we unpack those pertaining to the differences perceived about LGBTQ people and heterosexual people more generally to understand how these might have an impact particularly on how DVA is experienced and understood by those living in same sex relationships. The centrality of heterosexuality, not only as an ascription of identity but as an organising framework in society, along with associated assumptions about gender, should not be underestimated because, as we argue, perceptions of how adult intimacy might work have profound implications both for how survivors of DVA might understand their own experiences as well as how those who might provide support may understand them.

We also wish to counter the current emphasis in the literature exploring the experiences of DVA in same sex relationships which focuses on psychological and individualistic approaches and instead to foreground the importance of the social and cultural contexts in which those in same sex relationships come out and engage in intimate, familial and parental relationships. We do not disagree that individuals' cognitive and psychological potentials will have an impact on how they react and respond to the heterosexism and homophobia they face in carving out a life as a lesbian, gay woman or man, a bisexual, a queer and/or a trans person. We also want to make the case, however, that how individuals make sense of their sexuality and/or gender identity, along with their other multiple identities is shaped and influenced by social and cultural norms constructed through material, structural and institutional processes that are profound in their impact.

To talk about the ways in which the institution of heterosexuality is central to understanding how DVA is understood in both heterosexual and same sex relationships we use Weeks et al (2001) concept of the 'heterosexual assumption'. Similarly to Rich's (1980) 'compulsory heterosexuality' and Blassius' (1994) 'heterosexual panorama' this provides us with a way of describing and analysing a society organised and constructed as if all of its citizens are heterosexual and aspiring to heterosexual goals for personal and intimate lives. Not only are individuals assumed to be heterosexual but society's institutions, infrastructure, legislation and policy also have embedded in them dominant ideas about how heterosexuality should be lived, for example, in provision for welfare, families, health, security, employment, and so on. The heterosexual assumption or heterosexual hegemony, is based on 'the naturalistic fallacy [and] gender and sexual binarism and their hierarchical positioning' (Weeks et al, 2001, 42) and facilitates a nuanced exploration not just of the obvious and explicit but also the implicit and covert ways that heterosexuality is expected, normalised and privileged in neo-liberal, western societies in private as well as in public lives. Such a take allows us to acknowledge the apparent gains achieved by LGBTQ people in countries across the western world and some developing countries while being able to point to the myriad ways in which the heterosexual assumption persists and has a negative impact on individuals' decisions to come out and live openly as LGBTQ.

The heterosexual assumption pervades interactions in everyday lives in both the public and private spheres. Alongside assumptions about the primacy of heterosexuality are those constructing the flawed, dangerous, threatening nature of those who are not heterosexual. We also argue, however, that gender must be understood as an intricately embedded aspect of the heterosexual assumption. Thus ways in which people live their intimate and familial lives are understood to be shaped not only by their sexuality but also by the simultaneous expectations of conformity to gendered expectations about how they might interact as children, friends, employees and employers, service users and providers, intimate partners and as parents. These gendered expectations themselves are constructed and mutually shaped through the diverse nuances resulting from ethnicity and 'race' both from within minority communities but also from the stereotyped and prejudiced perceptions and expectations of the majority communities. We argue that these gendered expectations develop in parallel to expectations attached to heterosexuality and that discourses and ideologies about heterosexuality are central to constructing and shaping ideas and expectations about masculinities and femininities. Thus hegemonic masculinity is fundamentally heterosexual: gay masculinity can only be a subordinated masculinity (Connell, 2000). Likewise, emphasised femininity can only be understood if it is understood as heterosexual femininity. Thus, both gay men and lesbians are still typically understood to stand outside not only the norms of heterosexuality but also outside the norms of gender. Furthermore, these experiences of subordinated masculinities and femininities are, at the same time, interpreted through individuals 'raced' and ethnic positioning, their social class positioning, their age and whether or not they are disabled.

Such assumptions about gender and sexuality are nowhere more important than in the doing and living of intimate lives. The heterosexual assumption not only shapes ideas about what is possible in an intimate life for those who live in heterosexual relationships but also, as we will demonstrate, has an impact on those entering same sex relationships. At the same time, service providers also have expectations about how intimate lives might be lived in same sex relationships that are 'read off' from the heterosexual assumption, and includes the way gender might be enacted in those relationships, with added assumptions made about how gender might be performed by different cultures, at different ages, in different social classes and if an individual is disabled or not. Thus responses from service providers from a range of agencies responding to the criminal justice system, relationship breakdown, housing and DVA to those in same sex relationships will be influenced by the heterosexual assumption. Because historically, responses from providers of services have been shaped more by perceptions of the differences and dangerousness of LGBTQ people, the heterosexual assumption can also help explain the help-seeking decisions made by LGBTQ people. The latter includes making a judgement about their safety in coming out and the negative consequences of making the wrong decision: they could experience homophobia from those from whom they seek help, their confidentiality might not be respected, they may feel they have to come out in other spheres of their life when they do not feel ready, and/or they may fear how their decision might elicit homophobic responses to their partner, children, and others to whom they are close (see also Irwin, 2006). Similar arguments have also been made in relation to how the responses of service providers have been shaped by assumptions about 'race', ethnicity and social class (for example, Sokoloff and Dupont, 2005).

To begin the discussion about these issues, in this chapter we specifically focus on the extent to which heterosexual intimacy is similar or different to same sex intimacy; what impact a heterosexist and homophobic society has on experiences of DVA in same sex relationships; and whether and how coming out has any impact on the experiences of DVA in same sex relationships. First of all however we build on the outline in Chapter One, looking at how social and legislative change has provided a challenge to the heterosexual assumption and opens up spaces for more inclusive ways of living and loving for those in same sex relationships.

The changing legal and social landscape for those in same sex relationships

In the UK and most liberal democracies, those living in same sex relationships are now able either to marry or otherwise enact a civil partnership or union conferring all or most of the same rights and responsibilities of marriage on the adults. In most countries, parental rights and responsibilities in same sex relationships have also been secured (France and Ireland are significant examples of exceptions where adoption and fostering is excluded from the partner registration models). In the UK lesbian couples becoming parents using licenced fertility clinics and donated gametes are also allowed to register both the biological and non-biological mother as the legal parents on the child(ren)'s birth certificate (2008 Human Fertilisation and Embryology). In addition, since April 2010, gay male couples are allowed to apply for a parental order which if granted will allow the birth to be registered and show both men as the parents in the Parental Order Register. Same sex couples are now able to adopt and foster as couples (2004 Children Adoption Act) and LGBTQ people are protected from discrimination by the 2010 Equality Act and the 2008 Employment Act in the provision of goods and services and in employment respectively. There is, however, still provision made for providers of single-sex services (such as refuges) under the law to refuse access to a trans person if the provider can show that to do so is reasonable. Clearly this has implications for trans women's access to refuge if they experience DVA.

For trans people the 2004 Gender Reassignment Act now enables individuals who have had medical treatment (not necessarily surgery) for severe gender variance to be given a Gender Recognition Certificate (GRC) which they can use to change their birth certificate and be legally identified in their chosen gender. While this is an important change in legal recognition for trans people there were important caveats such as a married trans person having to divorce their partner in order to be given a GRC. This was because, until April 2014, same sex marriage was not legal. In addition, those who do not wish to have medical treatment may not qualify for a GRC and therefore will not be able to change their birth certificate with all the ramifications this has for citizenship such as getting a passport and gaining services as a survivor of DVA.

Nevertheless there has been a sea change across public sector services in the design of equal opportunities policies and development of best practice to provide an inclusive service to all service users regardless of sexuality, gender and gender identity. The 2010 Equality Act requires those agencies providing public services (including in the voluntary and private sectors) to provide evidence about the extent to which they are being successful in achieving the goal of inclusion across a range of what are called protected characteristics: age, disability, gender, gender reassignment, pregnancy and maternity, 'race', religion or belief and sexual orientation (see Richardson and Monro, 2012 for a detailed analysis of these changes). Yet, we would argue that the extent to which activism and scholarship have been successful in achieving these legislative changes must be measured not only by the ways in which individual rights and obligations have been recognised and protected but also by their impact on the everyday expression of those rights through their intimate, familial and parental relationships.

It is true that the legislative landscape is unrecognisable now, as we enter the second decade of the twenty-first century, to that which it was only 25 years ago. Not only did the Conservative government then pass the notorious Section 28 (see Chapter One), but the age of consent for gay men was five years higher than that for heterosexuals, being found out as gay or lesbian in the military could result in a dishonourable discharge and lesbian mothers could lose custody of their children because of their sexuality (Weeks et al, 2001). Yet, notwithstanding the gains outlined briefly above there is also evidence that there is a sizeable minority of the population who have not been persuaded by the arguments for inclusion. This ongoing unease with minority sexualities and trans people is most clearly articulated in debates about what could be understood as the heart of human existence: adult intimacy and the creation of families. Here we explore briefly the impact of this unease in two areas: sex and relationship guidance in schools and same sex marriage.

Sex and relationship guidance

Led by organised religions, dissenters from the equality arguments are a vocal minority who claim to speak for a silent majority. They argue that sex between two women or two men is not only unnatural but immoral and that children should not be exposed to such an environment if they are to reach adulthood as mentally healthy, normatively gendered, heterosexual women and men. These more overt objections to inclusive legislation based on equal rights have not been the only signs that there is a struggle going on in society to accept equality arguments, however. There have been several pieces of policy and guidance that express the ambiguity that exists about full acceptance of different ways of living and loving. Of relevance here is the UK government Department for Education and Employment's *Sex and relationship education guidance* (2000, hereafter the *Guidance*) for England and Wales which provides advice for schools on how to achieve their obligation to adopt a sex and relationship education policy. Given the evidence from this study and others that young people, regardless of sexuality and gender, are at higher risk of experiencing DVA than older people (Mullender et al, 2002; Hester et al, 2007; Donovan and Hester, 2008; Barter et al, 2009), prevention, begun in schools, would suggest itself as an obvious strategy. The *Guidance*, however, contains at least two potential barriers to the development of sex and relationship education that could be inclusive of young people who are lesbian, gay, bisexual, and/or trans and/or questioning their sexuality. The first springs from the ambivalence articulated around what kinds of relationships children and young people should be encouraged to enter. On the one hand the document recognises that children are brought up in different kinds of families and that there are 'strong and mutually supportive relationships outside marriage'. Thus, out of respect for difference and the recognition that these relationships can provide well for their children, pupils should learn the 'significance of marriage *and stable relationships* as building blocks of community and society' (DfEE, 2000, 4, our emphasis). On the other hand, and on the same page in the guidance, the responsibility of schools to teach 'the nature and importance of marriage for family life and bringing up children' is given priority.

The second barrier is what can be seen as a legacy of Section 28. The *Guidance* has a specific section on 'Sexual identity and sexual orientation' and advises that schools are expected to meet the needs of all their pupils 'whatever their developing sexuality' ensuring that sex and relationship education should be 'relevant to them and sensitive to their needs' (DfEE, 2000, 12). Homophobic bullying is specifically mentioned as behaviour that should be dealt with, although a caveat is added in the advice that arguably undermines what has gone before. The advice continues to encourage teachers to: 'deal honestly and sensitively with sexual orientation, answer appropriate questions and offer support. *There should be no promotion of sexual orientation*' (DfEE, 2000, 13 our emphasis).

In the same document in relation to the role of youth work in the provision of sex and relationship education the same message is given: '[i]t is inappropriate for youth workers, as with any professional, to promote sexual orientation' (DfEE, 2000, 28). Before Section 28 was repealed it was never tested through the courts. Its power was in its symbolic status and censoring role. Not only did it encourage self-censorship by those who might otherwise have engaged in activities the Section intended to prevent, for example, in schools (Moran, 2001) but it also provided those who agreed with the Section a rationale for discriminatory policies. For example, some local authorities were challenged with the use of Section 28 to stop their proposed spending on lesbian and gay events (Moran, 2001). It was, however, always misunderstood in terms of its jurisdiction over sex and relationship education because local authorities were not responsible for sex and relationship education policies in schools since that responsibility had been handed to school governors by the same government. When the New Labour government came into power in 1997 and attempted to repeal Section 28 they nonetheless faced strong opposition because of the perceived role the Section had in relation to sex and relationship education (Moran, 2001). As Weeks et al (2001) argue, a society's response to lesbians and gay men in relation to children is the litmus test of how far tolerance, let alone acceptance, has been achieved. The *Guidance* (2000) (and the Scottish equivalent) reflects this discomfort and relies on its interpretation by school governors to ensure that individual schools provide sex and relationship education that is inclusive both of young lesbians, gay men, bisexual women and men and those questioning their sexuality and of the prevention of DVA for all children and young people. More recently in 2013 the legacy of Section 28 was evidenced by the finding in a survey conducted by the British Humanist Society that 44 schools 'stress in their sex-education guidelines that governors will not allow teachers to "promote" homosexuality, or are ambiguous on the issue' (Morris, 2013). Thus, though there is material evidence of positive change in society based on an equal rights argument, there are still significant pockets of resistance to this argument and the campaigns to change minds, policies, as well as laws continues. This is nowhere clearer than in the campaigns in the UK and elsewhere for same sex marriage.

Campaigns for same sex marriage

Without engaging with the campaign for same sex marriage in too much detail it can be characterised as a 'last stand' for many who oppose it. The Pope has suggested that in acceding to same sex marriage there lies a threat to the future of humanity:

> [P]ride of place goes to the family, based on the marriage of a man and a woman…This is not a simple social convention, but rather the fundamental cell of every society. Consequently, policies which undermine the family threaten human dignity and the future of humanity itself. (Pullella, 2012)

Other faiths have spoken out very strongly as well and some, typically right of centre political parties, have been anxious to follow suit. In the UK the personal commitment in favour of same sex marriage of the Conservative Prime Minister has been criticised by some senior members of his party, and a large part of its traditional constituency in the country as signalling a move too far away from their traditional roots that have championed traditional heterosexual marriage and the nuclear family (Pierce, 2012). In the first reading of the bill 137 Conservative members of parliament (MP) voted against it and a further 40 either did not vote or abstained (Urquhart, 2013). However, the Marriage (Same Sex Couples) Bill received Royal Assent on 13 July 2013 and became law. The first same sex marriages will be able to take place on Saturday 29 March 2014.

The core issue in the debates has been whether or not the definition and purpose of marriage can be changed or understood to include those in same sex relationships. The argument underpinning those who say it cannot rests on the belief that marriage *is* heterosexuality as expressed in male/female penetrative sex from which will result children who require parenting from their biological parents; and that these relationships, are at the centre of society around which the economy, its legislative frameworks, its welfare, its distribution of power and money has been organised for centuries (see Osterlund, 2009 for a discussion of these arguments in the Canadian context; and Grossi, 2012, in the Australian context). The argument of those who say it can, rests on the belief that marriage *is* the love, connection and commitment for life between two people which are the same regardless of sexuality or gender; and which can include agreement to parent together children who may or may not be biologically connected to one or both parents (as currently happens in many heterosexual marriages). The act of procreative heterosex is deemed unimportant next to the other aspects of love that are considered to be universally felt, desired and lived, including parenting.

The campaigns for same sex marriage are, however, not universally supported from within LGBTQ communities and neither are the arguments that underline those campaigns. These differences within LGBTQ communities also have a bearing on how and whether adult intimacy is understood and perceived as different or similar across sexuality and gender and it is to these differences that we now turn.

Assimilation or separation

There have been fierce debates within LGBTQ communities and the academy about the basis of the successful arguments presented by LGBTQ activists and their allies for equal rights. An alliance between an expedient and/or genuinely believed essentialism, what Plummer (1995) calls essential truths (see also Richardson, 2005), has argued successfully that sexuality is a fixed part of human nature. While this argument has been more politically necessary in the United States context where changes to the constitution to protect minorities must define them on the grounds of genetic differences (Gamson, 1994), elsewhere too in Western societies, the argument has been persuasive. Successful campaigns across many western neo-liberal democracies have used slogans that focus on the apparent universality of human feelings (love), human organisation (family) and human need (for example, a job, housing, security) to shift public opinion. In his re-inauguration speech, President Obama of the United States of America captures this argument when he said about same sex marriage: 'Our journey is not complete until our gay brothers and sisters are treated like anyone else under the law...If we are truly created equal, then surely the love we commit to each other is equal as well' (Obama, 2013).

It has, therefore, become increasingly acceptable that society should be organised in such a way that accepts different sexualities neutrally, and non-hierarchically, so that nobody's status as a human with universally recognised and declared needs should be undermined. Increasingly, major political parties of every persuasion have become more willing to author inclusive legislation on the basis of this argument.

Yet, there have been some (perhaps unintended) consequences of the championing of this fundamental shift in the perception of minority sexualities. Richardson (2004, 2005) and others have pointed to the ways in which these assimilationist (Gamson, 1994) arguments have constructed new norms within LGBTQ communities and society at large about 'good gays' and 'bad gays'. As Richardson argues, the normalisation of lesbians and gay men in citizenship debates may have created new 'others' – those who do not want to have children or to have long-term monogamous relationships – with the potential for an emerging new 'sexual and gender fundamentalism' (Richardson, 2004, 403). The unprecedented gains in sexual and gender tolerance within society may have inadvertently created new concerns about old fears of making public the less positive aspects of the lives of sexual minorities, for example the high levels of alcohol and drug use, serial monogamy, casual and recreational sex and DVA. Historically, silences about these issues have been promoted in order not to give credence to those who have constructed sexual minorities as pathological, deviant, dangerous, even diseased and contagious. There has been a desire not to wash dirty laundry in public (for example, McLaughlin and Rozee, 2001; Ristock, 2002b; Duke and Davidson, 2009). In addition, many lesbian feminist groups have been reluctant to acknowledge that the utopian goal of love without men might actually be business as usual for some women living with abusive partners (for example, Hart, 1986; Ristock, 1997).

Another problem with the assimilationist or, as Seidman et al (1999) call it, the normalisation agenda is that its full implications have been avoided, that is, the question of 'equal rights with whom?' White, middle-class, able-bodied, heterosexual intimate and familial relationships represented in the nuclear family have become the gold standard providing the benchmark against which alternative ways of living and loving have been compared. This has left intact and unchallenged not just the assumption that heterosexuality in this mode represents all that it is to be human including their desires/needs/goals but that this mode of heterosexuality has become synonymous with normality. Minority sexualities (and genders) are then left either agreeing that this is the benchmark to which they aspire or accepting that they are thus placed outside normality. There are consequences with both positions. In the former there are the pressures LGBTQ people are then subjected to in showing how like heterosexuals they are, which can mean suppressing any accounts of difficult issues such as DVA. In the latter, living outside the norm can lead to being targeted for abuse, discrimination and hate crime with subsequent fears about revealing any need for help from mainstream services as well as possibly remaining in and/or returning to abusive relationships for fear of living alone in a hostile world.

A further consequence of assimilationist approaches has been that the status of being human has been elided with questions of access to the social structures for shaping, organising and regulating human existence. These structures, whether they are the nuclear family with its breadwinner/nurturer gender roles, the marriage contract, or a gender segregated labour market have all been simultaneously and unproblematically taken as given and (unintentionally) reified within arguments for equality. Thus arguments in favour of same sex marriage propose that love, regardless of sexuality or gender, is felt equally and should therefore be awarded the same legal and social recognition in marriage. The institution of marriage itself is rarely critiqued. A notable exception in the UK campaign in favour of same sex marriage is a group called Equal Love whose agenda is to make civil partnerships open to heterosexual couples and marriage open to same sex relationships so that those who wish to opt out of the latter contract because of its patriarchal connotations can opt into the more egalitarian civil partnership. They use evidence from the Netherlands in support of this by pointing to the fact that two thirds of those entering civil partnerships are heterosexual couples (http://equallove.org.uk/). Increasingly the language of assimilation based on ideas about the sameness of human desires and needs to argue for access to existing social, legal and political structures is normalised within LGBTQ communities. This has not always been the case.

Assimilation or separation: then and now

Critiques of marriage from within feminist or LGBTQ communities including academics or activists have been rare in the build up to campaigns for same sex marriage (for exceptions, see Saalsfield, 1993; Donovan, 2004) but this signals a sea change in the attitudes and agenda of LGBTQ communities in the UK from only 15 years ago. In their exploration of families of choice in the mid-1990s, Weeks et al (2001) found that there was a desire among those who took part to use the language of family to describe the people who were the closest to them in their lives. That this meant their families were chosen and included friends, specific members of a family of origin, ex-lovers, children and so on did not, for them, undermine the relationships and practices they believed constituted family. The language of family was adopted to evidence the validity of their lives and core relationships. Choice was important not just because it meant that families were created but also because it signalled a reshaping of values traditionally associated with the heterosexual family: for example, duty and obligation were re-configured as commitment, responsibility and positive choices to look after and care for family members (reflecting the findings of Finch and Mason, 1993). As Weston (1991) argues, these families can be fragile because those chosen as belonging to a family may not reciprocate, and/or they can change over time in a way that blood ties are assumed to be life-long. There was also, however, a consciousness that being able to choose family members and relationships signified opportunities to create something new rather than being restrained by the heterosexual assumption about intimate and familial relationships. An egalitarian ethic was espoused by many who talked about expecting there to be power differences between partners in a relationship or between parents and children but who also believed that these could be negotiated to temper any negative abuses of that power. Negotiation and reflexivity (Giddens, 1992) were central to many of the accounts given and there was awareness by many, particularly of the non-heterosexual women, that these were more possible in comparison with heterosexuality and their own previous heterosexual relationships, where gendered expectations and power inequalities had been difficult to resist. Most participants believed that new ways of being, 'experiments in living', were possible as a result of living outside the heterosexual assumption especially in relation to assumptions about gender (a similar argument was made by Dunne in relation to lesbian parenting (1999)). Of course these experiments in living were tempered by the positionalities of those who took part and the intersectional identities they inhabited. As has always been the case, having access to resources is crucial in being able to realise opportunities to live in new ways and social class, 'race' and ethnicity and age were crucial mediating realities in respondents' attempts to live in ways they felt reflected their desires. Nonetheless most felt that living outside the heteronorm provided spaces in which to try new ways of living that they could feel were worthwhile and a challenge to the heterosexual assumption.

The potential for, and celebration of, being different and more egalitarian in living outside the heterosexual assumption resulted in most participants in the research by Weeks and colleagues rejecting same sex marriage. Though most could see the inequity of a legal framework that unfairly discriminated against lesbian, gay and bisexual intimate, family and parenting relationships, most did not want to get married. Instead they wanted another kind of legal framework that conveyed equal rights on their personal and intimate and family lives (Donovan et al, 1999). In that study, the differences between intimate and familial lives that were the result of their sexuality were understood to be worth protecting in order to avoid the unequal power dynamics that resulted from unconscious patterns of behaving and relating associated with heterosexual relationships. Living outside the heterosexual assumption was understood to have benefits as well as penalties for intimate lives because of the opportunities for living and loving differently.

By contrast, in our study, comparing love and violence in heterosexual and same sex relationships, survey respondents were asked whether they thought that DVA was the same or different in same sex and heterosexual relationships. Responses here, just a decade later, reflect much more an assimilationist approach of sameness across sexuality. The majority of those who answered the question (69 per cent, 482/701) said that there are no differences and the same proportion of those who said that they had experienced DVA agreed. This reflects the wider social trend to argue that 'we are all the same'. Some respondents seemed surprised that we would ask about differences and similarities, with one respondent writing that it was a 'stupid question'. Others emphasised the idea that 'violence is violence' or that 'all domestic violence is equal and wrong'. The underlying message is clear: we are all the same and experience the same social problems as our heterosexual counterparts. As one respondent put it: 'heterosexuals and homosexuals have the same human rights.'

Of those who said that there are no differences between domestic abuse in same sex and heterosexual relationships two types of response were given: the majority who gave a categorical 'no' or those who said 'no but'. There was overlap between the explanations given by this latter group and the minority who said that there are differences between DVA in same sex and heterosexual relationships (25 per cent), and these are considered together. The most common explanations for responses given were related to sexuality (n=80), the lack of recognition and support available to those in same sex relationships (n=74), the more hidden nature of DVA in same sex relationships (n=57) and gender (n=34). Thus the majority of responses reflect the consequences of the heterosexual assumption, that is, whether or not SSDVA is visible as a problem and whether or not appropriate support is available (often both referred to together) rather than whether the DVA experiences in themselves are different. For the majority differences arise from the (assumed) perception and (potential) response from outside the same sex relationship. For example:

> No [there is no difference], but outside perception might
> be different. Not taken as seriously or believed.

There were some who referred to gender in making the same point,
that is, an assumption is made that where there are two women or two
men in the relationship DVA is assumed to be less serious:

> Yes, to some degree, as both partners have the same physical
> strength and emotional background.

> Yes, because if someone of the same sex hits you it isn't seen
> as bad as say a man hitting a woman.

This last response makes reference to how physical violence might be
perceived rather than how it might be experienced and reflects fears
that those outside a same sex relationship might not take the DVA as
seriously as they might when it conforms to the public story. Other
references to gender similarly reflected the impact of the public story
of DVA: that men cannot be victims/survivors and women cannot
be perpetrators and the impact this has on receiving an appropriate
response and/or keeping DVA in same sex relationships invisible.
    References to the potentially unhelpful responses of others were
both general (as above) and specific about the source of help:

> No difference other than perhaps the help you may get
> from the police?

The hidden nature of DVA in same sex relationships can be seen
to follow on from the fact that same sex relationships in general are
not visible: as one respondent said, "same sex relationships are not
recognised." How DVA remains hidden is also dealt with in some
responses. A gap of trust (Donovan and Hester, 2010, and see Chapter
Seven) is identified between LGBTQ communities and helping
agencies that act to keep the issue hidden:

> Broadly similar. Stigma of sexuality may prevent individuals
> seeking help.

Throughout these responses, there is no reference to the nature or
impact of the DVA. The focus is on the response to it – from the
survivor, their informal friendship/family or community networks
or from the more formal mainstream or DVA or LGBTQ specialist

agencies. The heterosexual assumption is referred to implicitly or explicitly to explain why DVA in same sex relationships remains in what West (1998) refers to as a second closet:

'It's more secret and no where [*sic*] for help.'

'No, its [*sic*] an abuse of power and trust either way, although I think it is viewed differently by the health community.'

Both covertly and overtly these responses make clear that the impact of DVA in same sex and heterosexual relationship is not necessarily different, but that the social/cultural frameworks that regulate or provide recourses to support act as if they are. Society, they are saying, does not respond to people in same sex relationships as if they are the same as heterosexuals but problematises them as different, hence relationship problems such as DVA are more hidden and/or invisible and existing support agencies seem unable to respond appropriately.

Those who referred to gender and/or sexuality as leading to differences gave a variety of explanations about how these might have an impact on the experience of DVA in same sex relationships. Some talked about how sexuality might have an impact on the kind of DVA experienced and referred to threats to out a partner. A handful talked about there being more DVA in same sex relationships than in heterosexual relationships and another handful said that there is less DVA in same sex relationships. The impact was referred to by some as being worse, especially for women who might have expected other women not to be violent, while others said it was worse in heterosexual relationships. Some talked about same sex relationships, particularly lesbian relationships, being more intense. Others said that, particularly gay male, relationships might be more competitive though none of these explained why these factors might result in DVA. There was also a small group who referred to the different power and/or relationship dynamic that they believed occurs in same sex relationships that they inferred might have a different outcome in terms of domestic abuse:

Yes, because the power dynamics between two women/two men and one man and one woman are different.

Different because of different power balance and absence of traditional roles.

Again, there was no further explanation of how these differences might have an impact on DVA in same sex relationships. Thus sexuality and gender were believed by many respondents to have a variety of impacts on the experiences of DVA in same sex and heterosexual relationships.

The trend to reflect more assimilationist views was also found in the response to the question asking what kind of help could be made available to those experiencing DVA in same sex relationships. Most of those who responded to this question (47 per cent, 114/243) referred to the need for generic support without specifying whether this should be provided by mainstream or LGBTQ specific agencies. In fact only 9 per cent (21/243) referred to LGBTQ specific services while just over 26 per cent (40/243) referred to making mainstream services (for example, the police, refuges, or GPs) either better able to respond to LGBTQ people or making it clear that they do provide services to LGBTQ people. The fact that so few felt that specific LGBTQ services were needed is further evidence of a belief that 'we are the same' and 'we need the same'. Forty-three respondents (18 per cent, 43/243) also referred specifically to the need for counselling to be available for those experiencing DVA. We will return to the apparent preference for privatised solutions to same sex DVA in Chapter Six. While the majority believed that DVA in same sex relationships is the same as DVA in heterosexual relationships, there is also recognition that living in a heterosexist and homophobic society might make a difference to how DVA in same sex relationships might be perceived. However, there has been a growing debate within North America about the extent to which living outside the heteronorm might have further consequences that have an impact on why and how DVA is experienced and it is to this that we now turn.

Consequences of living under the heterosexual assumption: 'minority stress'

A small group of our survey respondents explained that living outside heterosexuality can result in differences that might have an impact on experiences of DVA:

> Yes, because of externalised and internalised homophobia, which exacerbates issues in relationships.

Other commentators have referred to these factors as minority stress, a way of recognising the ways in which living in a context which is heterosexist and homophobic might create stresses that have consequences for intimate relationships, including DVA (Balsam, 2001). Minority stress is used in the North American context in relation to any group with minority status, that is, whose position in society results in the experience of specific inequalities related to access to resources (material, financial, educational, formal sources of support and so on), or of assumptions made about competence, character and potential. This would include black and minority ethnic groups, working-class people, disabled people, older and younger age groups, trans groups and so on (Balsam, 2001). The notion of minority stress is a more individualised and psychologised approach than the social positionality and intersectionality framework that we favour in this book (see Chapter One). In relation to those who are LGBTQ, minority stress specifically relates to the stresses believed to result from living 'in the closet' and/or experiencing direct or indirect discrimination because of sexuality, and/or living with the fear of and/or actual experience of hate crime. The consequences of living with these stresses, it is argued, could precipitate DVA. Stresses can be experienced from both internal (to the individual LGBTQ person, called internalised homophobia) and external sources (from hate crime, rejection from family of origin, homophobia at work, and so on), sometimes referred to as internal and external stressors (see Balsam, 2001).

There is now substantial evidence of the consequences of living outside the heterosexual assumption for the mental and physical health of LGBTQ people who count among those at the highest risk for key indicators of mental health problems such as suicide, substance use, depression, anxieties and so on (for example, Hunt and Fish, 2008; King and McKeown, 2003; Whittle et al, 2007; Kelly et al, 2011; Lewis et al, 2012). The impact of homophobic bullying in schools and workplaces as well as the impact of hate crime in public spaces on the health and wellbeing of LGBTQ people as well as their educational and life chances is also well documented (for example, Warwick et al, 2004; Russell et al, 2011). It is of no surprise therefore that some commentators have suggested that another consequence of living in a hostile environment might be DVA in same sex relationships (for example, Mendoza, 2011; see also Balsam and Szymanski, 2005). Tigert (2001) argues that DVA is a response to internalised homophobia, cultural oppression and 'religious and psychological shame'; and Mistinguette et al argue that lesbian abuse is a form of 'oppression sickness' (in Tigert, 2001, 75). These authors argue that the experience of violence over a lifetime as a result of minority stress results in lesbian, gay men and bisexual people normalising interpersonal violence and therefore either being more willing to use violence or more accepting of violence in adult intimate relationships (see for example, Balsam, 2001).

Our research suggests that the concept of minority stress is currently limited in its definition and measurement and relies too much on assumptions about individualistic and/or psychological responses to pressures that arise from intersecting, oppressive social, cultural, economic and faith contexts that fall unequally on members of different social groups. At worst it is understood as the result of remaining in the closet which is conceptualised as an individual's 'maladjustive behaviours...[in] concealing one's sexual identity' (Mendoza, 2011, 170), although others have recognised that not coming out might also be a more rational and safer strategy than coming out (for example, Balsam and Szymanski, 2005). Nevertheless, coming out is presumed to be an individual, cognitive decision rather than a social and relational process wherein being out or being closeted can be enacted in different ways in different spaces and within different relationships. For example, while one might be out to all of one's friends and work colleagues one might not (yet) be out to one's family of origin. Alternatively, while one might be out in every social network one belongs to, in public spaces – on the way home from a night club for example – one might never give any sign (holding hands with a partner, wearing a visible badge or t-shirt with a pro-LGBTQ slogan) that one is out. Seidman et al (1999, 14) also argue that the closet is not 'a metaphor only of containment and denial' but also a temporal, physical, geographical, relational space where a self and a life can be tested, experimented with and tried on; otherwise they argue how can 'a dominated self manage resistance and liberation'. In other words not coming out can be experienced in identity affirming ways.

Yet for those who argue that staying closeted leads to minority stress that can then be implicated in DVA, social behaviours and socially constructed beliefs and perceptions are re-categorised as problematic individual cognitions that might influence individualised (de-contextualised) behaviours. Consequently, variations occur across the literature in what factors are identified as representing minority stress, and how they are measured, typically using quantitative methods. This also leads to an inconsistency in findings that are typically associated or correlated with DVA rather than causally related. For example in the study by Mendoza (2011) stigma, homophobia and discrimination are used as measures of minority stress while Balsam and Szymanski (2005) focus on internalised homophobia, experience of heterosexism and levels of outness; Lewis et al (2012) focused on substance use as an indicator of minority stress; and Miller et al (2001) explore what they believe are the consequences of minority stress, that is, fusion, lower self-esteem and levels of independence.

At the same time the way in which violence/abuse is defined and measured is also variable which has the same consequences for moving the debates forward. Sometimes adaptations of the Conflict Tactics Scale (see Chapter Two) are used in studies of minority stress which means that context, meanings and impacts of the violent/abusive behaviours being used are not taken account of (for example, Mendoza, 2011). As we have already argued, understanding the context in which violent behaviours take place is crucial in order to understand why violence has occurred and identify whether it is DVA as coercive control, self-defence, mutual couple violence, violent resistance or mutual abuse (Johnson, 1995; Johnson and Ferraro, 2000) so that responses can be appropriate. In their study, Carvalho et al (2011) also make this point and conclude that more research is needed to explore the extent to which indicators of minority stress are associated with different types of violence.

Taken as a whole most of the studies conducted on the relationship between indicators of minority stress and DVA are inconclusive. While correlations have been found the direction of the relationship is not clear. For example, as Carvalho et al (2011) suggest, the correlation they found between what they called interpersonal violence and stigma consciousness, might have been the outcome of the experience of interpersonal violence rather than the cause of it. Finally there is also some evidence that such individual orientations vis-à-vis internalised homophobia, experiences of discrimination, substance misuse and so on might be positively mediated by the existence of social networks and community support (for example, Lewis et al, 2012). Thus it would seem that the social and cultural contexts in which individuals live their intimate and familial lives which might also be a valuable focus for making sense of how DVA might occur.

Another limitation of the focus on minority stress and its relationship to DVA, echoes discussions in heterosexual DVA about its relationship with social stresses brought about by, for example, financial and/ or material insecurities, redundancy and/or unemployment. Similar concerns can be raised about this approach. First, there is an apprehension that lesbians, gay men and bisexual people are, like working-class men in the heterosexual debate, demonised and constructed as inherently unstable and violent. Second, while there will be places (geographical) and spaces (occupations, workplaces, families, neighbourhoods) in which there will be those who are more or less willing to use violence and/or discriminate against lesbians, gay men and bisexual people it is also the case that most people coming out as LGB (and this would also apply to those identifying as trans who come out about their gender identity) might experience fear, anxiety and stress but will not engage in DVA. In relation to this it is entirely possible that both partners are living with similar kinds of stresses so the question remains about what would lead one partner to be an abusive person and the other less likely to do so? Of course it is entirely possible that they are both as likely to take their stresses out on each other but again the question needs to be asked whether this constitutes DVA or whether this is Johnson's common couple violence or mutual abuse that, therefore, needs a very different response. Some studies have studied the psychological profile of partners to lesbian relationships in relation to dependency and fusion in a way that partially addresses this latter point but again the findings remain correlative or associated rather than causal (see Miller et al, 2001; Poorman and Seelau, 2001).

Nevertheless, sexuality is implicated in the experiences of DVA in same sex relationships as it can be used as a way of exerting control by one partner over the other. Typically this is possible for two reasons. First if one or both of the partners in the abusive relationship are not out or not out to key people in their lives (for example, employers, members of family of origin). When the survivor is not out the abusive partner can use this knowledge to control their partner's behaviours with the threat that they will out them. Second, if the abusive partner is not out, this can be used to control the victim/survivor's behaviours with the rationale that the abusive partner's identity needs to be kept in the closet. These controlling behaviours would hold no power if it were not for the socio-cultural context that reinforces the heterosexual assumption and results in material consequences for many lesbians, gay men and bisexual people in their everyday lives. These are issues we explore further in Chapter Four.

First same sex relationships: impacts of the heterosexual assumption on experiences of DVA

As the respondents to our survey explained above, being out or not might have an impact on the ability to help-seek and/or get recognition and support for experiences of DVA not just from mainstream agencies but from informal sources of help such as family or friends. While help-seeking is taken up in more detail in Chapter Five, it is worth considering here how the different experiences of coming out, especially into first same sex relationships might make an experience of DVA different because of its hidden nature.

While there are still those LGBTQ people who live their intimate relationships and families of choice over much of their lifetime in isolation from their families of origin, it is with the experiences of those entering their first same sex relationships that it is possible to explore the extent to which intersecting identities and socio-cultural positioning might have an impact on the experiences of DVA. These accounts suggest that there might be a period of time when a first same sex relationship is embarked upon during which many opportunities for vulnerability can arise because individuals feel that they cannot be out either to erstwhile family of origin and (heterosexual) friendship networks of support or potential new sources of support; and an individual does not feel confident about what they should expect to happen in a same sex relationship. Yet this might not necessarily have a negative impact, especially if there are other potential sources of help or community knowledges available. Community knowledges (Weeks et al, 2001) include LGBTQ specific knowledge and/or resources that can be local or national and enable LGBTQ individuals to feel connected to or part of larger LGBTQ communities or networks. Unfortunately, for too many of those we interviewed there was little evidence of the existence of community knowledges and it seems that there are still very few places and spaces that might equip those entering same sex relationships for the first time about how same sex relationships might happen, about what to expect, about what to do if something does not feel right in the relationship (Donovan and Hester, 2008). This is true both for young and older people coming out and/or questioning their sexuality. As we will argue in Chapter Four, the intersection of sexuality and age can result in older aged LGBQ people (and this might also be relevant for those identifying as trans) being positioned as 'young' and therefore subordinate in terms of their experience and knowledge about living in a same sex relationship.

Emma's account illustrates how a lack of knowledge about being in a same sex relationship led to her remaining in an abusive first same sex relationship when she and her abusive partner were 17 years old:

> EMMA: 'I don't really think I thought that much about it. I just thought this is how relationships are, this is how it is and you have to give up this for the relationship, you know...'
>
> INTERVIEWER: 'What did you feel that you were giving up?'
>
> EMMA: 'My personal freedom. My, you know, my desires to do things, the things that I wanted to do. I kind of gave all that up and I had to, I had to be with [her partner] all

the time.' (Emma, a white queer woman who was aged 30–34 at interview, and 17 when she began her first same sex relationship which was abusive)

Emma's family of origin did not figure in the start or development of this relationship. Her only reference to her parents was to say that she was out to them, but that her abusive partner was not out to her own parents and that this acted as a further way her abusive partner was able to control the terms of the relationship because Emma 'didn't exist'.

As Emma's account suggests, other vulnerabilities can arise because the abusive partner is willing to use issues relating to sexuality to control their partner's behaviours and relationships with other people. Jeb, a white, gay man similarly talks about having his 'wings clipped' by his abusive partner, who used his own fear of being outed as a way to try to control where Jeb went, who his friends were and whom he brought to the house:

> 'And when he was away I wanted to go out and make friends, and he didn't think that was necessarily the best idea because you know we had a house together and he didn't want me to be bringing people back to the house, or people where we lived to be realising that we were gay. Because he wanted to keep all that very, very hush-hush because of his work, and his parents…were very strict Irish Catholics. So he was constantly trying to hem me in, box me in when all I wanted to do was, you know, grow and continue to grow. I had no issues with my sexuality. I'd come out to my parents when I was 15. And all of a sudden to be put back in this box, and being told to sit there and shut up, that was quite challenging.' (Jeb, 25–29 years old at interview, and 15 years old when he began his first same sex relationship which was abusive)

Edward, another white gay man also explained that it was because it had been his first same sex relationship he had not been able to recognise what was happening to him as DVA. Rather, he explained that his abusive partner's behaviours and reasons given for those behaviours led him to believe that this was what love was and to be expected in a same sex relationship:

> 'I don't know whether he loved me or just clung to me because he, er, because he wanted help in some kind of way,

'I'm not sure. But at the time I didn't know any differently either. Obviously it was my first relationship and I wasn't, I wasn't to know what to expect at all.' (Edward, a white gay man aged 35–39 at interview, 16 when he began his first same sex relationship which was abusive)

Worryingly, accounts like Edward's and Emma's suggest that they believed or expected that having a same sex relationship might include experiences that made them unhappy. Sarah, who had experienced previous heterosexual relationships before her first girlfriend also reflected on this:

'[S]he did a lot of drugs and she was quite abusive. But I think because she was my first girlfriend I didn't know any different. Even though I recognised…that's not [what] a relationship should be, you know, none of my relationships with my brother's friends had ever been like that…But yeah, I did love her.' (Sarah, a white lesbian, 30–34 years old at interview, and 25/26 when she began her first same sex relationship which was abusive)

In many of the accounts we were given about first same sex relationships expectations were low about how they might be experienced. It is not difficult to argue that one of the consequences of the heterosexual assumption is being played out in these relationships when victims/ survivors assumed that same sex relationships are to be negatively experienced. Similarly, William, a police officer, explained that it was only because of the way that society has changed about DVA that he came to realise that he experienced DVA in his first same sex relationship:

'I think at the time I thought that was just the way a same sex male relationship was…Obviously since then I've sort of grown up, become more mature, more worldly wise. I've seen that, you know, violence issues does [*sic*] affect an awful lot of people in a lot of different ways. So, at the time that's how I just thought it was. And again, there wasn't the emphasis on it that there is in today's society. And it was a lot more covered up.' (William, a white gay man aged 40–44 at interview, and 22/23 when he began his first same sex relationship which was abusive)

Of course heterosexual young women and men might also experience feelings of being nervous and wary of their first relationships as they, too, do not know what to 'do' or expect. For young heterosexuals, however, there exist plenty of relationship role models in cultural imagery or their own families and neighbourhoods to which they can refer. For example, Theresa, a white heterosexual woman talked about how she would make comparisons between her relationship and the heterosexual relationships she saw represented on the television or on the streets:

> 'Aha, cos I used to think, like, if you see things on the telly and stuff, and how everything's always happily ever after, I used to think "Well, it's not like what I'm living like," and then…[because] I wasn't seeing me friends you couldn't really talk with them about what was going on in their relationships but, like, if you were out and about, like shopping or whatever, you would see people and think, "Well, they're smiling and they're holding hands and like." D'y'know wharra mean? Where, I didn't ever feel like that when I was walking along with him.' (Theresa, aged 40–44 at interview, and 16 when she met her abusive husband)

For young people contemplating their sexual identity and first same sex relationship there is still a paucity of role models to consider or spaces in which those relationships can be discussed and explored.

Another consequence of coming out into a first same sex relationship without having community knowledges to draw on about what to expect is the scope for the creation of sub-cultures where abusive behaviours become normalised. Kay's experience reflects this concern:

> 'I was very naïve about women and, now that I've been through that experience about, sort of, manipulation and control, it's made me realise that a lot of people are like that. And through the discussions I've had with other gay women, it seems to be sort of pretty common, and it's made me a bit jaded I suppose. It just seems to go with the territory, you know, this sort of co-dependency, jealousy, splitting up, getting back together again, splitting up, getting back together again…It's just made me think that people that are secure with themselves and are willing to let their partners live their lives without that control, are very, very few and far between.' (Kay, a white lesbian, aged 35–39 at interview,

and 32/33 when she began her first same sex relationship which was abusive)

The lack of security that Kay refers to as being a common experience in her circles of 'gay women' may also reflect the impact of the heterosexual assumption that constructs same sex relationships as pathological, dangerous and diseased and lesbians as needy and dependent, yet predatory. Her first same sex partner had more experience of being out, had had previous same sex relationships and tried to control how Kay did her own coming out:

> '[S]he'd had quite a few relationships with women. She'd been out since she was 18 and she went around with a lot of gay women. It was just this big crew of gay women, so you know. You know what that's like. She'd just had that for all her life whereas with me, it was completely different... when I met her, I was just beginning to have gay female friends in this area, just beginning to be out at university and confident about that, you know, it was all opening up for me, whereas she'd again, been there, seen it, done it, really. And her attitude was, "Oh you don't want to be going out on the scene. You know, it's awful," and all the rest of it, whereas yeah, I know that now, but to say that to somebody that's just beginning to dip their toe. You can't put restrictions on people like that.' (Kay)

Heterosexual women also describe the ways in which their abusive partners isolate them from their friends and prevent them from going out without the abusive partner, often using jealousy as a rationale. In the accounts of those in same sex relationships, however, it becomes clear how powerful this isolation can be when they may already be disconnected from their family of origin because of their sexuality and are then expected either to stop seeing their LGBTQ friends or to stop developing connections with local LGBTQ social scenes and friendships, especially because there are very few other community knowledges available to draw on in the way there are for heterosexual women (in women's magazines, television, literature, film and so on). That many of those experiencing SSDVA did so in their first same sex relationship suggests that a search for confirmation of identity can have consequences in terms of being vulnerable for experiencing DVA. The sense of excitement or even euphoria with coming out that is reinforced by a first sexual relationship can then get mixed up and articulated as love for the partner. As Kay explained:

> 'Because it was my first relationship with a woman and it felt absolutely fantastic. It was just all of that, you know, completely right, "Hallelujah, here I am. I've done it at last." This is great. I think I was just in love with the feeling rather than the person, cos that's about acceptance isn't it? I love you because you know, you've accepted me and I'm not the freak anymore.' (Kay)

Any growing sense of unease with the ways a partner in a first same sex relationship is behaving can be countered by a self that is still feeling the strength of feeling often attached to the experience of a first love as well as the sense of loyalty attached to a relationship that has played such a role in an individual's journey to coming out. Anthony, a white gay man, also explains how his first same sex relationship, entered into when he was 20 years old was abusive, but an important relationship because, at the time, he did not have other gay friends:

> 'I didn't really have that many gay friends then either…it was, sort of, like, really hard to, sort of, meet people. And I was still, I'd only just come out to my parents, and so that was all kind of up in the air and it was just nice to have someone who sort of understood.' (Anthony, aged 20–24 at interview, and 20 when he started his abusive relationship)

A first same sex relationship can be extremely important in confirming an individual's sexual identity as well as providing support through the initial coming out process including coming to terms with their sexuality. Yet, the survivor often lacks community knowledges which add to their vulnerability and isolation. Edward was asked how his first same sex relationship became a relationship and his response encapsulates all of these strands; of being out of one's depth with an older partner, about feeling inexperienced about what to expect in a same sex relationship and about feeling unable to speak about this to anybody. The pauses and repetition of 'I don't know' in his explanation underlie the difficulties he had in making sense of what had happened:

> 'I don't know. I really don't know. I think [exhales] oh! I don't know. It should never have happened, to be honest, but I [pause] wasn't forced into it. I sort of fell into it, somehow.

> [pause] Oh, I don't know. Cos I was young, and I was [coughs] not frightened but I was [pause] I didn't like any conflicts, I didn't like arguments and, and he said something. He sort of, he said something and assumed that we were now in a relationship, and I didn't, I didn't feel as though I could say "No, we're not in a relationship." And because of that, that's how it suddenly got labelled a relationship.' (Edward, a white gay man aged 35–39 at interview and 16 when he began his first same sex relationship which was abusive)

Edward's abusive partner was his boss and six years older than him when they met when Edward was 16. He expected Edward to join him going out for meals and to pubs and clubs after work and to pay his way even though he knew that the money Edward earned would not cover the costs. Edward's lack of knowledge about what to expect in a same sex relationship was compounded by the isolation of not being out to his family of origin who, in other circumstances, might have been thought of as a possible source of counsel about his intimate life. Edward could not seek help from his family with his abusive relationship because he was not out to his father and because he had run up a credit card bill on his father's credit card in order to meet his abusive partner's expectations about his financial independence.

Being alone when entering a first same sex relationship that is imbued with the import of confirming a sexual identity can provide the context for DVA (see also Ristock, 2002a). It is not difficult to understand why DVA in same sex relationships might not be recognised or sought advice about when LGBTQ lives and relationships are still difficult to find represented in the media as an ordinary part of society. Formal and informal sex and relationship education rarely include LGBTQ identities and/or relationships or those who are questioning their sexuality (for example, Formby, 2011). Both covert and overt hostility still has to be expected and/or prepared for from families of origin, friendship networks, neighbours, work colleagues and employers, and so on. The heterosexual assumption perpetuates simultaneously both that authentic relationships are heterosexual relationships and that those of LGBTQ people are 'other'.

Not knowing how to talk about DVA and not knowing who to talk to are very common features of the accounts of heterosexual women when they talk about their help-seeking but this occurs only when they have initially recognised that something is happening for which they need help. For those entering their first same sex relationships, however, identifying that help is needed might well be delayed because of their lack of knowledge about how a same sex relationship might be experienced; because their feelings for a partner in first same sex relationship might be confused with the excitement associated with coming out and confirming a self–identity; because they may not yet be part of any local community or friendship networks of LGBTQ people; and as a result of the public story that DVA is a heterosexual problem. Tess's account reflects how she juggled some of these factors, feeling her way in a first same sex relationship but also feeling her way with other lesbian and gay friends and wary of mainstream agencies:

> 'I think there was something in, you know, being in my first, kind of, significant same sex relationship and not knowing really what was ok to talk to other people about? So, you know, didn't have so many friends in the gay community. Um – but definitely wouldn't have gone to them and gone, "Oh god, you know, I'm having this, this is happening in my relationship and I really don't know how to handle it,"… You know, wouldn't have known about, kind of sources of support at that point. Definitely wouldn't have gone to my doctor.' (Tess, a white lesbian aged 40–44 at interview, and 24 when she began her first same sex relationship which was abusive)

The broader context within which LGBTQ people come out and come to terms with their sexuality, make friends, negotiate relationships with their families of origin, proceed through their education, enter employment, meet prospective partners, initiate relationships, live their relationships and create families of their own with or without children must be taken into account when understanding the experiences of LGBTQ people in abusive relationships. While there will be individual responses to these structural, social and cultural factors, the question of whether this constitutes minority stress and therefore an explanation for DVA is moot. The impact of the public story about DVA along with a lack of community knowledges, which can result in a belief that same sex relationships might be expected to be difficult and a lack confidence about what to expect from a same sex relationship, can contribute to an inability to recognise and name experiences as DVA. These factors are the result of the heterosexual assumption and the positioning of LGBQ and/or T people outside the heteronorm. Sexuality intersecting with age and/or coming out can position individuals in even more vulnerable positions in terms of recognising and/or naming their experiences as DVA. The isolation experienced by same sex victims/survivors may also be exacerbated by the isolation that results from fears about discrimination, homophobic bullying and/or hate crime. These factors may be further exacerbated by the experiences of other intersecting identities and social inequalities such as those resulting from 'race', faith, age, disability and social class and result in survivors remaining loyal to a partner rather than speaking out about their behaviour to service providers. Informal sources of support for relationship troubles (as it was often considered at the time by our respondents) such as family of origin and/or friends might also be considered and dismissed if these sources are expected to be ignorant of same sex relationships, unsupportive and either/both reinforce their sense of rejection or/and increase their sense of protection and/or loyalty to an abusive partner.

Summary

• While the legislative landscape across many western neo-liberal democracies have changed in favour of equal rights across sexuality and gender, the heterosexual assumption results in many individual LGBTQ people still living in fear of coming out and/or experiencing discrimination and/or hate crime as a result of their sexuality and/or gender identity. The evidence also suggests that being LGBTQ can have implications for people's health and well-being as well as their life chances.

• The arguments for equality based on the idea that everybody, regardless of sexuality, is 'the same' and wants the same things increasingly characterises the self-perception of LGBTQ people. An example of this trend in our survey was that the majority of respondents said that they would expect the experience and impact of DVA to be the same across sexuality.

• North American writers have suggested that minority stress, the pressures of living in a heterosexist and homophobic society and of living in the closet, create stresses/tensions within same sex relationships that might lead to DVA. We argue that minority stress is a problematic concept for three reasons:
  – its focus is too individualistic and, in most accounts, focuses on the psychological adjustment of LGB people to what we argue are social structural implications of heterosexism and homophobia;

- methodological problems make this an unstable concept, particularly in terms of making distinctions between different kinds of, and motivations for, violent and abusive behaviours;
- while all of those who are LGBTQ and in same sex relationships could be 'at risk' of minority stress it is self-evident that not all same sex relationships are abusive.

• We found evidence that the heterosexual assumption does have an impact on:
  - the kinds of abuses that are enacted: controlling where, when and to whom survivors are out; threatening to out them; using fears of being outed to isolate survivors from potential sources of friendship or family; undermining survivors by calling into question their status as an authentic lesbian, gay man, bisexual and so on;
  - whether or not DVA is recognised by survivors and named as such;
  - those in first same sex relationships, regardless of age, lacking community knowledges about what it is to have or 'do' a same sex relationship. This means, especially if their first relationship is with somebody already out and who has experience of having same sex relationships, or somebody older, that an unequal power dynamic can be constructed in which the survivor is controlled, isolated and abused by their partner.

• It is the positioning of LGBTQ people as outside the heteronorm and the intersections of multiple identities that LGBTQ people inhabit that create unequal knowledge and skills about and experiences of intimacy and inhibit the recognition of DVA in same sex relationships.

FOUR

Identifying and experiencing domestic violence and abuse

Introduction

In this chapter we begin to explore the nature and impact of DVA experiences for individuals in same sex relationships, drawing on some of the main findings from our national COHSAR (COmparing Heterosexual and Same sex Abuse in Relationships) survey and combined with material from our interviews. In carrying out the survey we were asking individuals to say whether they had experienced, or possibly perpetrated, one or more of a long list of emotional, physical and sexual behaviours that might be construed as abusive (see Chapter Two). Most studies tend to use the term 'abuse' when describing such behaviours. In this book we are not making that assumption, as doing so can make it more difficult to understand the nature of the behaviours involved, the context, and whether they have an abusive, harmful, impact, as opposed to being merely 'negative' behaviours without harmful effect. As described in Chapters One and Two, our approach is unique in asking not only about behaviours but also about a range of potential impacts, and additionally, whether individuals self-identify as experiencing DVA. As will be explored further in this chapter, this approach allows us to ask important questions about the impact of those experiences, and about whether the behaviour identified by respondents had an impact on their lives, constituted abuse of themselves, abuse of another and/or defensive/protective/ retaliatory behaviour. These are very important questions as they help us to understand more about the complexities of DVA, allowing us to ask if something is the type of DVA involving fear and control (the coercive control and or intimate terrorism discussed by Stark (2007) and Johnson (2006) respectively), or behaviours without the range of impacts associated with such DVA. Our approach also allows us to move the analysis beyond the static binaries of victim/perpetrator.

Identifying and recognising DVA

Liz Kelly (1996), talking about heterosexual DVA, has outlined that an important feminist principle has been:

> not to create hierarchies of oppression/abuse; to insist that experiences which the law and institutions define as 'minor' may have major consequences for women and children; and to recognise that many women and children are able to marshal internal courage and strength and find external support in surviving brutal attacks without permanent or inevitable damage. (Kelly, 1996, 44)

Although she is referring to heterosexual DVA, these are also issues of relevance to the analysis of our same sex relationship data. In many other studies based on surveys, a hierarchy of DVA is often imposed, where physical violence is accorded the greatest 'weight' and emotional abuse the least. This is the case in survey approaches based on the Conflict Tactics Scale and the ratings used there. Similarly in criminal law, physical harm is the main marker for criminal offences linked to DVA (within crimes under the English and Welsh *Violence Against the Person* legislation). While coercive control is now part of the English and Welsh Home Office definition of DVA, there is no legal basis for an offence based on this (see Chapter One). Individuals, however, may not experience different forms of DVA behaviours in this hierarchy or order of magnitude. What is especially important is the impact of particular (often sets of) behaviours, and such impact is more likely to be linked to the positioning and contextual meaning for the individual concerned.

This brings up another problem, which is that some individuals may construe as abusive behaviours that others do not construe in this way. Kelly (1996), for instance, expresses concern that definitions of lesbian DVA may be wider and include more emotional factors than other DVA definitions, especially experiences such as manipulation, conflict and disrespect. She has highlighted problems with some of the quantitative research on lesbian DVA, arguing that DVA is defined in much broader ways in these surveys than in comparable studies with heterosexual women. She suggests that lesbian respondents, being sensitive to issues of power and violence, may be more willing to define their partners' behaviour as violent, thus resulting in higher figures for lesbian DVA than might otherwise be ascertained. Ristock also takes up this critique about studies based on surveys, arguing that 'we have to be careful in how we understand the gender differences of lesbians using more violence than gay men as reported by Waldner-Haugrud and others' (Ristock, 2002a, 12). Lesbians as well as heterosexual women may report higher levels of DVA than men, because they perceive such behaviour where it is carried out by women as especially violent, 'and this is the case whether they are reporting themselves to be victims or perpetrators' (Ristock, 2002a, 12), and/or because lesbians are more likely to have learnt to recognise and name abuse 'because many lesbians have been politically active in the antiviolence movement' (Ristock, 2002a, 12). Hassouneh and Glass (2008), however, based on a small interview study, suggests that lesbians may also underreport DVA because they are reluctant to see women as violent. Yet gay men may be even more likely to apply the more restrictive and gendered 'domestic violence as physical violence paradigm' that Hearn and others have described (Hester et al, 2007). As Cruz outlines: 'when we remember that males are typically socialized to express anger and aggression via physical means; some gay men might view domestic violence as proscribed and gender-typical behaviors' (Cruz, 2003, 310).

These difficult issues regarding defining and recognising experiences of DVA are also reflected in various ways by our interviewees, for whom a range of key factors appeared to influence their perception and definitions of their own relationship experiences. These included the public story of DVA with its focus on physical abuse. Childhood or heterosexual adult experience of DVA also fed into the public story and played a part in the interpretation of their experiences. And those who were working directly or indirectly with victims/survivors of DVA, tended to have deeper awareness and understanding of the issues. Interviewees particularly influenced by the public story found it more difficult to define their experiences as DVA if physical abuse was not the main feature. This included a small number of the survey respondents who reported on the questionnaire that they had not experienced domestic abuse, but subsequently, in the interview, re-defined their experiences as domestic abuse. This was more likely to be the case for the gay men. For example, Edward, a white gay man, answered 'no' in the questionnaire to ever being in a domestically abusive relationship, but his experiences and discussion of these in the interview indicate that he did experience DVA abuse, involving physical and control elements. Edward did not define his experience as DVA at the time it was occurring, but knew that he did not like what was happening to him:

'Well, the only thing that I knew at the time was that I didn't like it. And I didn't put a label to it, I just knew I didn't like it, and, I had to somehow get rid of it [the relationship].' (Edward, a white gay man aged 35–39 at interview and 16 when he began his first same sex relationship which was abusive)

In the interview he began to link his relationship experiences of ongoing control and physical restraint as DVA. He also describes using violence against his partner in retaliation:

'I think in some way that I was abused. [pause] Maybe teetering on physical abuse actually, because sometimes when we used to have arguments he used to literally restrain me, you know, stop me, and I used to pull away so much that [laughs] my clothes would rip. Um. You know, it was horrible. He never, you know, attacked me or anything like that, but…just…I dunno. Certain things – certain things that he would do just purely to [pause] not allow me to do the things that I wanted to do. I wanted to get away from him, he would not allow me to do that. [pause] You know, and we got into so many arguments. Oh my god. So many arguments. I mean, I hit him, at one point, because he was rattling me up so much. Oh, it was horrible. [pause] So. It was difficult [laughs].' (Edward)

Audrey, a lesbian when we interviewed her, was previously in a heterosexual relationship. She left that male partner because she recognised his very physically and emotionally abusive behaviours as what she termed the 'classic signs' of heterosexual DVA. By contrast, she found it difficult to identify the abuse in her subsequent lesbian relationship as DVA because of her lack of knowledge of such relationships (it was her first), and due to prior expectations about both sexuality (with ideas of a lesbian utopia) and about gender (lesbians are not violent, men are):

'I didn't know what being a lesbian meant and there was a lot of, I think where I found the relationship abusive, um, emotionally was that, um, I was kind of, there was some markers and I didn't necessarily know what these markers were.' (Audrey, a white lesbian, aged 55–59 at interview, and

53 when she began her first same sex relationship which
was abusive)

The lesbians and gay men we interviewed who had lived with
childhood DVA, where fathers were abusing mothers, also tended to
have a perception of DVA as physical, ongoing heterosexual DVA. For
instance, Valerie, a white lesbian, grew up in a household where her
dad was abusive to both her mother and her. When she experienced
emotional abuse from her female partner she did not initially recognise
it as DVA because it did not include the physical abuse her father had
used. As she says:

> '[Dad] was a perpetrator so it's surprising that I didn't pick
> up on it [in own relationship] to be honest...I think if she'd
> ever raised her hand to me it would have been different
> because that is what I equate with my dad...I'd made a
> conscious decision when my dad left, when I was 14, that
> no one was ever going to hit me again so I think if she'd
> done something that directly it would have been over.'
> (Valerie, aged 30–34 at interview, and 24 when SSDVA
> relationship began)

Amy, a white lesbian, also lived with DVA as a child, and in this
instance it did help her identify what was happening in her first lesbian
relationship when she was beaten by her partner, and to leave:

> INTERVIEWER: 'When you were in that relationship,
>   experiencing domestic abuse, did you recognise it at
>   the time as that?'
> AMY: 'Yeah. And that's why I thought I can't stay...Because
>   I was really quite badly beaten, and this – out of nowhere,
>   well what felt like completely out of nowhere...I was
>   completely shocked and that somebody who I was so in
>   love with and who I did really love, we had a fantastic
>   relationship...And that, 10–15 minute encounter just
>   completely, completely trashed the relationship...But
>   yeah, I did recognise it because as I say I experienced
>   domestic violence as a child.' (Amy, aged 30–34 at
>   interview, and 16 when she began her first same sex
>   relationship which was abusive)

Another lesbian interviewee, Barbara, had lived with DVA from her father to her mother as a child. As a consequence, she differentiated between the negative behaviours that she experienced from time to time in her lesbian relationship, and what she saw as the ongoing, everyday, controlling DVA that her mother had experienced:

> INTERVIEWER: 'So would you say that your relationship was domestic violence?'
>
> BARBARA: 'No, but I think, um…things that she did would verge on it. If that became a regular thing, like every day, then I would say it would be a domestic violence relationship, but I wouldn't say it was because…I dunno. There wasn't the…through the experience of me mam, the way she was controlled and the way it was an everyday thing, I wouldn't say it was…I dunno.' (Barbara, a white lesbian, aged 19 years at interview, and 18 when SSDVA relationship began)

Kay, a white lesbian, had not experienced DVA as a child, but eventually worked with victims/survivors in her job. This was what made her decide, with hindsight, that behaviours in a previous relationship had bordered on DVA, and if she had stayed in the relationship it would have led to more serious abuse in the longer term. In this instance the abusive partner appeared to present as the victim and used this as part of her abusive behaviour, thereby creating the manipulative, 'skewed/warped' context of coercive control. Kay thought the abusive behaviour was related to her partner's insecurities about the relationship and consequent need to control: "When she was away from me and she wasn't confident about what I was doing, or started feeling insecure about what I was feeling about her." When she finished the relationship her ex-partner continued to harass her, which in the end was what had the greatest negative impact on Kay:

> 'I do think it was quite a controlling relationship, yeah. And, you know, when I was filling out the questionnaire…I did think, "Well actually, is this really going to count, or are they really going to want to interview me?" because in comparison to what some of my friends have been through, you know, it's probably not on the greatest scale of long term, abusive, violent behaviour…You know, it was pretty short term. Uhm, but it does fall into it, I think…if I was dealing with somebody, uhm, as a worker, and they were a

client, I'd be saying, "Yes, it does and that isn't acceptable," and everything else, whereas because it's me, you think, "Oh no, I don't actually fall into that. It's OK, I'm in control, I can handle it," and it was just one of them. But em, now I look back on it I think, yeah actually, it was pretty controlling, more control and bordering on abuse I think, but then, I think that longer term, it would have been more abusive. It was just really bizarre stuff.' (Kay, aged 35–39 at interview, and 32 when she began her first same sex relationship which was abusive)

The gay men we interviewed generally had greater difficulty identifying their experiences as DVA, and appeared, as Cruz (2003) indicates, more steeped in the public story of DVA. Like the lesbians above, however, men who had other experiences of DVA, for example because they had become involved in work in this area, were more likely to have redefined their own experiences as DVA. For instance, Kenneth now worked in a social support role where he came across DVA. He felt that he had denied his earlier DVA experiences partly because he did not understand or recognise what was going on at the time:

> INTERVIEWER: 'And you've talked about your experiences in your worst relationship. Would you define that as domestic violence, domestic abuse?'
>
> KENNETH: 'I would now. At the time I didn't. Um, and part of that was about denial of where I was and part of that was about not knowing, cos I hadn't, I think, because…in the field I work in now I'm much more aware of those sort of issues anyway…Cos I still wanted that relationship, so I would have found it very difficult to label it as, emotional abuse, or physical, domestic violence, anything.' (Kenneth, a white gay man aged 50–54 at interview, and 39 when SSDVA relationship began)

Ted was a member of the local domestic violence forum when we interviewed him, and that had informed his understanding of his own experiences in his first same sex relationship, which he had not previously identified as DVA because his male partner did not use physical violence:

> 'I didn't realise that I did suffer domestic violence because it wasn't physical…And I didn't realise it was about the power

control thing, basically, and I did not realise till I joined the domestic violence forum and started talking to people and I realised I was a sufferer for 15 years.' (Ted, a white gay man aged 55–59 at interview, and 28 when he started his first same sex relationship which was abusive)

Alistair was also working in a job where he came across DVA. He was now taking a wider view of what might be included as 'abusive' behaviour and as a consequence was also redefining his own experience of 'mind games' from a previous male partner as involving elements of abuse, if not entirely as a DVA relationship:

INTERVIEW: 'Do you think you've ever experienced domestic abuse?'

ALISTAIR: 'Um, if you'd of asked me that [pause], kind of, years ago I'd've probably said no. I suppose if I think back to my first relationship, I think because my first partner had [pause] a lot of things that he couldn't, kind of, talk about, or, kind of, express himself or, he was very guarded sometimes, I think he, rather than be put in this, kind of, vulnerable situation, he would be [pause] what's the best word to use, um – I suppose, kind of, he would mebbes play mind games a little bit. And I would never've said that it was, it was abuse, but I know, kind of, with the job that I do now abuse can mean all sorts of different things, and I suppose there were some, not very often at all, but there were some times that, um, I felt [pause]… there was… something around, kind of, being made to feel guilty, or being made to feel that it was my fault, or something like that, you know…' (Alistair, a white gay man, aged 35–39 at interview, and 21 when relationship began)

The accounts from our interviewees thus indicate the difficulties in identifying negative relationship behaviours as DVA, and how previous experience feeds into such identification. What is also interesting is that identification of DVA appears to have 'moved on' since the concerns raised by Kelly and others in the 1990s, with greater awareness of the issues by our respondents, both women and men, who have worked in DVA related fields. The notion of a lesbian utopia also appears to have diminished, perhaps suggesting greater acceptance that such relationships do not necessarily promise a 'rose garden' (Hester, 1992, 105).

Nature of DVA: Experiences of survey respondents

We now turn to some of the main findings from the COHSAR survey and the prevalence of potentially abusive behaviours experienced by respondents, or used against their partners, and the impact on them. Clearly, the complexities involved in identifying and defining one's experiences as DVA, and also potential differences between behaviour that is harmful and merely 'negative' behaviours, create difficulties in interpreting survey data. It is therefore important to bear in mind the earlier discussion about identification of DVA in relation to the survey findings, and we also describe the data in a variety of ways in order to accommodate some of these complexities. Moreover, we attempt throughout to discuss how understanding of positionality and intersectionality with regard to individuals' location and identities also helps us to unravel the experiences and impacts of potentially abusive relationship behaviours.

More than a third of our COHSAR survey respondents (38 per cent) had at some time experienced what they themselves defined as domestic abuse in a same sex relationship. An even greater number of respondents indicated that they had experienced at least one form of negative or potentially abusive behaviour from their same sex partners. More than half (54 per cent) reported that they had at some time experienced potentially abusive emotional behaviour from a same sex partner, and between a third and a half that they had experienced such physical (41 per cent) or sexual (41 per cent) behaviours. These figures are considerably larger than the findings from the more general UK health surveys with lesbians, bisexuals and gay men (Henderson, 2003; Hunt and Fish, 2008; Guasp, 2012), and larger than those reported in the Crime Survey for England and Wales (CSEW) (Smith et al, 2010), suggesting that the focus of the COHSAR survey on 'problems in relationships' may have increased the proportion of respondents reporting experiences of DVA. Yet, as we shall see later, when we take into account severity, less than one in five of the COHSAR respondents appeared to have experienced the DVA that is defined as intimate terrorism or coercive control, and only one in ten experienced severe DVA in the last 12 months.

Echoing other studies involving same sex or heterosexual relationships (for example, Ristock, 2003; Walby and Allen, 2004) emotional abuse appeared to be more widespread among the

COHSAR survey respondents than physical and sexual abuse. As in the interviews, however, survey respondents were more likely to identify physically and sexually abusive behaviours as 'domestic abuse', and self-definition was most closely identified where individuals had experienced multiple forms of abuse.

Table 4.1 shows the overall incidence of potentially abusive behaviours experienced by the respondents to the COHSAR survey during the past 12 months or ever. Incidents reported in the past 12 months is usually deemed the most accurate measure, as memory

Table 4.1: Emotional, physical and sexual behaviours from same sex partners (%, N=746)

	Individual behaviour items	Ever	Last 12 months
Emotional behaviour	Being isolated from your friends	53.1	34.5
	Regularly insulted/put down	45.1	25.4
	Told what to do/whom to see	39.9	22.5
	Frightened by things your partner says/does	41.0	21.8
	Isolated from relatives	34.6	21.6
	Made to do most housework	27.6	18.5
	Your spending controlled	26.7	18.1
	Your age used against you	22.7	14.0
	Your education used against you	20.4	11.5
	Your class used against you	18.2	9.9
	Your sexuality used against you	16.1	8.7
	Accused of not being a real gay man/lesbian	17.4	8.7
	Blamed for partner's misuse of alcohol/drugs	15.3	7.8
	Malicious/pestering phone calls	20.5	7.7
	Your religion used against you	8.6	6.3
	Blamed for partner's self-harm	13.5	6.1
	Property damaged/burnt	15.3	5.3
	Children actually hurt	7.3	4.7
	Your disability used against you	6.3	4.3
	Threats to stop contact with your children	7.5	3.9
	Threats to harm someone close to you	8.3	3.4
	Threats to 'out' you to lose your children	7.3	3.1
	Threats to hurt your children	7.5	3.0
	Threatened with being 'outed'	8.6	2.8
	Your race used against you	3.4	1.5
	Your pet abused	4.1	1.5
	Your medicines withheld	1.4	0.7

(continued)

Table 4.1: Emotional, physical and sexual behaviours from same sex partners (%, N=746) (continued)

	Individual behaviour items	Ever	Last 12 months
Physical behaviour	Slapped/pushed/shoved	32.3	14.3
	Physically threatened	20.8	8.9
	Kicked/punched	17.5	7.0
	Restrained/held down/tied up	14.8	6.2
	Threatened with an object/weapon	4.4	4.0
	Stalked/followed by partner	13.7	3.7
	Bitten	7.3	2.9
	Choked/strangled/suffocated	7.7	2.8
	Hit with an object/weapon	7.5	2.8
	Beaten up	9.2	2.6
	Locked out of house/room by partner	7.8	2.6
	Prevented from getting help for injuries	4.4	1.7
	Burned	1.6	0.6
Sexual behaviour	Had sex for sake of peace	32.3	18.4
	Touched in way that caused fear/alarm/distress	14.6	5.3
	Hurt during sex	14.1	5.3
	Forced into sexual activity	14.4	4.1
	'Safe' words/boundaries disrespected	9.3	3.8
	Refused your request for safer sex	7.8	2.7
	Sexually assaulted/abused	8.6	2.1
	Threatened with sexual assault/abuse	5.7	1.2
	Raped	5.3	0.8

may be better over a shorter period. Incidents reported in relation to a lifetime of intimate partner relationships (as in our use of 'ever') inevitably involve greater frequencies as experience accumulates, although may also be subject to underreporting due to memory lapse. As outlined in Chapter Two, the questionnaire asked respondents to consider a wide range of potentially abusive emotional, physical and sexual behaviours from their partners within these two separate timeframes.

What stands out from the data in Table 4.1 are the large numbers of individuals experiencing potentially abusive behaviour from their same sex partners. More than a third said that in the past year their same sex partner had isolated them from friends or family, and more than one in five regularly experienced being insulted and/or put down, being told what to do and whom to see, and/or was frightened by what their partner said or did. There is also a sizeable group of respondents (about one in ten in the past 12 months) who said that their age, education, class or sexuality were used against them by their partners, or were accused of not being a real gay man or lesbian. More than one in ten said that they had been slapped, pushed or shoved by a same sex partner in the past 12 months, and nearly one in five had had sex for the sake of keeping the peace and having a quiet life. These patterns of emotional, physical and sexual behaviours from partners remained the same across time, although, as expected, were magnified. Thus more than half of the respondents said that they had at some time ('ever') experienced being isolated from friends, more than 40 per cent had at some time been regularly insulted or put down or had felt frightened by what their partner said or did, and a third had at some time been slapped, pushed, shoved or had sex for the sake of peace.

While Ristock (2003) emphasises the heterogeneity of DVA experiences in lesbian relationships, our survey data also indicated many similarities between lesbians, gay men, bisexuals and queer people in their experiences of a range of abusive behaviours and the impacts of such behaviour in same sex relationships (the number of trans individuals were too small to make accurate assessment). This contrasts with surveys such as the Crime Survey England and Wales, Statistics Canada and the National Intimate Partner and Sexual Violence survey in the United States, where bisexuals were found to experience considerably more abusive behaviours than lesbians or gay men, although that appears to be because bisexuals were experiencing such DVA from opposite sex partners rather than same sex partners (Smith et al, 2010; Ristock, 2011; Walters et al, 2013; and see Chapter One).

Slightly more women than men in our survey self-identified as experiencing domestic abuse at some time, although the differences were not significant (40 per cent women, 35 per cent men). There were, however, some interesting differences in relation to experiences of particular behaviours that appear to reflect wider processes of gendering and gendered norms. Men in same sex relationships were significantly more likely than women in same sex relationships to experience physically and sexually abusive behaviours (at Chi Square $p<0.05$). Sexual abuse was where the greatest gender differences occurred, both in relation to the previous 12 months and ever. Male respondents were significantly more likely than women to be forced into sexual activity, be hurt during sex, have 'safe' words or boundaries disrespected, have requests for safer sex refused, and to be threatened with sexual assault (at Chi Square between $p<0.001$ and $p<0.05$). In contrast, women were significantly more likely to be made to do most of the housework, have their sexuality used against them or be accused of not being a real lesbian, and women were more vulnerable to abuse if they had children (at Chi Square $p<0.05$). Our interviews also indicated that abusive behaviours can in some respects be understood to be gendered: the heterosexual women and gay men more typically reported experiencing physical violence and physically violent sexual coercion from male perpetrators; lesbians and heterosexual men more typically reported experiences of emotional abuse from female perpetrators; gay men typically experienced more financial abuse; and lesbians typically experienced more emotionally abusive sexual coercion.

Gender did not, however, provide the main difference between survey respondents, and in most cases was not significant at the 0.05 level (based upon Pearson's Chi Square with continuity correction). Other risk factors for potential abuse included age (being under 35 years), lower income levels and lower educational attainment, and these were much more marked than differences related to gender. While differences by gender are more obvious in the general, largely heterosexual, population data on domestic abuse, our findings that younger age and low income may be associated with DVA echo the general population findings regarding heterosexual women in the UK and elsewhere (Smith et al, 2010; Watson and Parsons, 2005). From the list of potentially abusive behaviours, respondents to our survey who were under the age of 35 or had low income reported experiencing significantly more emotionally, physically and sexually abusive behaviours (at Chi Square $p<0.05$), while those with low educational attainment reported significantly more emotionally and physically abusive behaviours. The behaviours that were especially prevalent among these three sub-groups were as follows:

1. *Younger respondents (under 35)* were significantly (at Chi Square $p<0.05$) more likely to report that they been isolated from friends; accused of not being a real gay/lesbian; threatened with 'outing'; had their spending controlled; their age used against them; and/or their sexuality used against them. They were significantly more likely to be slapped/pushed; kicked/punched; bitten; held down; strangled; hit with an object; stalked. They were significantly more likely to be hurt during sex; refused safer sex; safe words disrespected; and sexually assaulted.
2. *Low income respondents* were significantly (at Chi Square $p<0.05$) more likely to be isolated from friends; put down/insulted; threatened with 'outing'; had their religion used against them;

their disability used against them; blamed for self-harm; had medicines withheld; and/or been frightened by their partner. They were significantly more likely to be bitten; held down; prevented from getting help; stalked. They were significantly more likely to be touched inappropriately; hurt during sex; have safe words disrespected; sexually assaulted; experience threats of abuse; and be raped.

3. *Low educational attainers* were significantly (at Chi Square $p<0.05$) more likely to report being isolated from relatives; not seen as a real gay/lesbian; had their spending controlled; told what to do; their property damaged; received threats to harm someone close; had malicious phone calls; and/or were frightened by their partner. They were also significantly more likely to be slapped/pushed; kicked/punched; held down; physically threatened; stalked; or locked out.

Where age is concerned, our interviews indicated a strong link between experience of DVA and first same sex relationship for both gay men and lesbians, which tended to be associated with younger age groups (Donovan and Hester, 2008). Risk linked to income and educational levels are more difficult to explain, although our survey data indicated that gay men were significantly more likely than women to have their spending controlled (beyond the previous 12 months, Chi Square significance at $p<0.05$), and low income was especially prevalent for those who said that they had a disability, of whom two-thirds earned less than £20,000. Association between individual behaviour items and specific groups can, however, be difficult to interpret and the direction of association is not clear. For instance, while low income level has been identified as a risk factor for DVA in the CSEW (Walby and Allen, 2004), the question remains whether low income/poverty provides the actual risk for DVA or whether women become poorer *following* a DVA relationship (and see Worcester, 2002). Moreover, a number of factors may intersect to provide the overall picture of apparent association.

This brings us back to the ideas of positionality and intersectionality, the social context of same sex relationships (Chapter Three), as well as the greater detail provided by our interviewees. For instance, one of our queer interviewees, Lynn, indicated that it was the intersection between age, sexuality and low income that were important in providing the possibility for her partner to sexually abuse her. Lynn was in her late 20s and five years younger than her partner (young age) and this was her first same sex relationship (sexually 'young'). Her partner had a lot more money (low income) and was 'quite a vibrant character on the scene' (sexuality and 'community knowledge'). The combination of these factors meant that Lynn 'often did feel stupid' and 'belittled', although she did not think her partner necessarily intended to abuse her. It also meant that the sexual aspect of the relationship was particularly difficult and unpleasant for Lynn:

> '[Partner] was big on instigating sex and I remember trying to instigate sex but being very scared of it at the time, erm, partially because it was my first relationship, but partially because she did seem to lead things, I suppose, in the relationship…if I tried it the other way, it never seemed to work…because a couple of times it didn't work, so I got scared and so I didn't do it again…And I wasn't aware at the time, I could actually say "no" to her. I mean it wasn't like I was raped or anything but it was [pause] I wasn't aware enough to be able to say, "I'm not entirely comfortable."'
> (Lynn, a white queer woman, aged 25–30 at interview, and 20 when she started her first same sex relationship which was abusive)

In this instance notions of sexuality give meaning to notions of age, and vice versa, such that the first same sex relationship in itself becomes equated with and situates Lynn as someone of a 'young age', whatever her actual biological age. The lack of community knowledges often associated with first same sex relationships (see Chapter Three) provides an important part of how sexuality and age are mutually shaped in this way. In this instance, income provides a further context for power differential and oppression. As Eriksson argues: 'Different power relations construct and are constructed in relation to each other. Systems of meaning that can be separated analytically are intertwined empirically' (Eriksson, 2008, 99).

Marcus, a white gay man, was in a relationship with a man whom he described as 'a tight bastard', and who would use his higher level of education to control Marcus around money and spending (intersection of class, low educational attainment and control of spending). Marcus talks about having a 'chip on my shoulder' because he was a 'working-class lad' with a comprehensive education. In contrast his partner was '[elite university]-educated, private, very middle class'. Money was important to Marcus, because 'it represents stuff', but his partner would only 'buy pound shop presents for Christmas' while he expected Marcus to give him expensive presents in return. He describes how his partner made him feel especially exploited and put down by charging him to travel in his car and used his superior education to manipulate Marcus to do this:

> 'So he'd like count up, you know...you'd fill up the, the petrol tank, erm, when we got there and then – well he did some clever subtraction – [university]-educated and very clever...did these things and I would have to pay him petrol, you know, for the miles that we did, basically. So he got round the fucking mileage bills in that way and I always felt very uncomfortable about that and felt exploited on another level, materially...' (Marcus, aged 35–39 at interview, and 35 when the abusive relationship began)

Ted, a middle to low income earner in his 50s (income), had been in a relationship with his male partner for 15 years. In the interview he talked about how his partner increasingly controlled the bank accounts and spending (spending controlled), which was also an indication of the wider control his partner wielded over him. His abusive partner's ability to set the terms and make key decisions, particularly about spending money and how leisure time was spent, had enabled the partner to have many affairs with other men. As discussed earlier in this chapter, Ted eventually recognised the 'power and control thing' that he had experienced for a long time.

> 'At the time it wasn't equal. In the beginning I suppose it was, then it sort of slowly changed, if you like, then you realised he was in total control, of, sort of, the bank accounts and stuff like that, cos we had, sort of, joint accounts and everything was, sort of, you know, could do what he wanted, but I couldn't.' (Ted, a white gay man aged 55–59 at interview, and 28 when he started his first same sex relationship which was abusive)

In the example of Valerie we see how the apparent risk factor identified in the survey data, in this instance low income, may not be the actual basis for abuse, but may instead be a marker for other factors that provide the abusive context. With regard to the abuse experienced by Valerie there was complex intersection between low income (linked to motherhood) and illness (easier to manipulate). Valerie had always wanted a baby and she and her partner became co-mothers, although the child was 'probably the only thing in that whole relationship which has happened which [partner] didn't want'. Prior to the birth of her daughter, the partner was already increasing her control of Valerie. Valerie describes that her partner:

> 'kind of just, slowly but surely over time, kind of, sucked me in and broke down any sort of sense of individuality and, kind of…I lost touch with a lot of my friends. We went where she wanted to go, we did what she wanted to do, so if we went out it was because she wanted to.' (Valerie, aged 30–34 at interview, and 24 when SSDVA relationship began)

After the birth, Valerie went back to work full time but became depressed as she wanted to spend more time with her daughter. She therefore reduced her working hours and her income decreased. The low income (highlighted as a risk factor by the survey data) was thus linked to motherhood as the actual context of her partner's abusive behaviour. Valerie's depressive illness created further possibilities for her partner to manipulate and abuse her. As she became well again, Valerie started to notice the abuse and eventually left the relationship. However, although the partner had resisted being an active parent in the care of their daughter while they were together, she pursued child contact post-separation as a means of continuing her control of Valerie (see also Radford and Hester, 2006):

> 'We are going through a court case over contact with Lauren now. So as I say she's still pressuring me.' (Valerie)

Impact of emotional, physical and sexual behaviours

Valerie talks about her ex-partner 'pressuring' her. The emotional, physical and sexual behaviours discussed in the previous section can of course lead to a wide range of impacts – from no impact at all, to increasingly detrimental and harmful impacts. Moreover, when potentially abusive behaviours and the impact of those behaviours are considered together it is clear that individuals experiencing a combination of emotional, physical and sexual abuse, rather than merely one of these forms of behaviour, experience much greater impact (Hester et al, 2010).

It was possible to explore the association in the COHSAR data between the various social demographic variables and the scales related to any one form of abuse (separate abuse scale for last 12 months) or combined abuse (combined abuse scale for last 12 months) using one-way ANOVA and Cramer's V (see Chapter Two for detail of abuse scales). The results from such association suggest that both low educational attainment and relative youth were both significantly though weakly associated with an elevated risk of DVA, either in terms of relatively more extreme forms of abuse (combined emotional, physical and/or sexual behaviour) or at a lower threshold of abuse (only one of emotional, physical or sexual abuse behaviour). Neither gender nor sexuality were significant predictors of elevated risk of DVA in the bi-variate association, although a limited number of individual items of potential DVA behaviours were significantly associated with gender (Table 4.2, and discussed later). Results which were significant in the analysis at the 0.1 confidence level are as follows, and show significant impacts for younger respondents and low educational attainers, both for separate types of abuse behaviour (that is, separate scales for physical, emotional and sexual abuse) and for the more severe combined abuse (that is, where physical, emotional and sexual abuse items are combined in one scale) (see Chapter Two for the scales and their validity):

- *Separate emotional, physical or sexual abuse:*
  - younger respondents (under 35) ($V=0.077, p<0.0$)
  - low educational attainers ($V=0.072, p<0.0$)
- *Combined abuse:*
  - younger respondents (under 35) ($V=0.062, p<0.0$)
  - low educational attainers ($V=0.069, p<0.0$)

Key: 0=no association and 1=perfect association

It is perhaps unsurprising (given its higher incidence within the COHSAR survey sample) that, with regard to individual items of impact, emotional behaviours were most frequently cited by the survey respondents as having an impact (see Table 4.2). At least one in five respondents reported that more than half of the emotional behaviour items had an impact on them. Similar numbers also reported that five of the 27 items applicable to physical behaviour had a detrimental impact on them, and one in five reported that sexual abuse 'had affected the sexual side of [their] relationship'. Particularly concerning are the small proportion of respondents who said that they feared for their lives due to their partner's emotional (6 per cent), physical (7 per cent,) or sexual (4 per cent) abuse.

The survey respondents mostly 'felt sadness' following potentially emotional abuse (42 per cent). Yet, more than a third of respondents felt that they had to watch what they said and did as a result of their

Table 4.2: The impact of emotional, physical and sexual behaviours from same sex partners – ever (%, N=731)

	Emotional	Physical	Sexual
Made you feel loved/wanted	6.6	2.6	2.2
Lost respect for partner	33.9	22.3	15.2
Made you want to leave partner	35.2	21.0	13.6
Emotional/sleeping problems/depression	34.7	18.6	14.4
Stopped trusting people	13.7	10.4	6.2
Stopped trusting partner	32.0	21.8	14.0
Felt unable to cope	20.2	14.3	10.0
Felt worthless/lost confidence	34.7	18.4	13.8
Felt sadness	42.3	21.0	16.0
Felt anxious/panic/lost concentration	28.5	17.8	13.6
Felt embarrassed/stupid	30.4	17.0	14.8
Felt isolated/stopped going out	24.2	13.8	7.3
Felt angry/shocked	33.8	24.5	12.6
Self-harmed/felt suicidal	13.1	9.2	6.7
Worried partner might leave you	20.1	8.8	6.0
Defended yourself/children/property/pets	8.2	8.2	2.9
Feared for your own life	6.2	7.4	3.8
Retaliated by shouting at your partner	30.2	14.9	4.8
Retaliated by hitting your partner	6.8	9.3	2.1
Physical injuries, eg bruising/scratches	na	14.7	5.5
Injuries that needed medical help	na	5.1	1.9
Affected sexual side of your relationship	37.1	18.9	20.0
Worked harder to make partner happy	21.6	8.8	6.4
Worked harder to stop making mistakes	18.1	8.1	5.2
Felt had to watch what you say/do	35.3	16.6	8.9
Lost contact with your children	0.4	0.3	0.1
Negatively affected relationship with children	3.7	1.6	0.7

partner's emotional behaviour, said that they felt worthless or lost confidence, and/or experienced emotional or sleeping problems or depression. What might perhaps be construed as a more 'active' response was exhibited by the third of respondents who felt angry or shocked by their partner's emotional behaviour, and more than a third wanted to leave the relationship as a result. One in five respondents, however, was concerned that their partner might leave them.

Of respondents subject to physical behaviour from same sex partners the largest group felt angry or shocked as a result (25 per cent), or lost respect for their partners (22 per cent). One in five also stopped trusting their partner, felt sadness, and/or wanted to leave the relationship as a result. More than one in ten sustained bruising or scratches (15 per cent), and one in twenty (5 per cent) had had physical injuries that required medical attention. Respondents who experienced potentially abusive sexual behaviours from their same sex partners also mainly felt sadness (16 per cent), lost respect for their partner, and/or had emotional or sleeping problems or depression as a result, although others reported that they felt embarrassed or stupid.

The effects of the individual items of impact were in many respects similar across the respondent sample, and more prominent than the differences. There were no significant differences by sexuality. Some significant differences were apparent with regard to gender, low income and educational attainment of the respondents, although emotional impact was a significant feature for some *older* rather than younger respondents.

Gender differences regarding individual items of impact were most prominent in relation to emotional abuse, and women in same sex relationships were significantly more likely to report some impacts of emotional abuse on their lives than male respondents. In response to Kelly's (1996) concern that lesbians over-report emotional abuse, our findings suggest that women in same sex relationships are indeed reporting greater experience of emotional behaviour, although this is also experienced as having a negative impact. Women were much more likely to report that the abuse made them work harder so as 'to make their partner happy' or in order 'to stop making mistakes', and/or that it had an impact on their children or their relationship with their children (at Chi Square $p<0.1$, $p<0.01$ and $p<0.001$ respectively). The impact on men was to make them 'feel loved/wanted' (at Chi Square $p<0.05$). There were fewer significant differences with regard to the impact of physical behaviour. The impact on women was especially to stop them 'trusting in people', to make them work harder so as 'to make their partner happy', and/or that it had an impact on their children or their relationship with their children (at Chi Square $p<0.1$, $p<0.05$ and $p<0.05$ respectively).

Some of these impacts were also reflected by our interviewees. For instance, Amy, a lesbian who said she was 'really quite badly beaten' by her first female partner and saw it as DVA talked about wanting to make her partner feel better:

> 'You know, and after the, after the event, I remember her just breaking down and there was me picking her up and trying to make her feel better, and I thought, "What on earth am I doing? What on earth am I doing?"' (Amy, aged

30–34 at interview, and 16 when she began her first same
sex relationship which was abusive)

Sarah's first same sex relationship was abusive, including physical
violence, yet she stayed because she loved her partner and wanted to
try and help her to change:

> 'She didn't make me feel good about myself. [laughing] She
> used to beat me up. Um, [pause], I don't know. I think part
> of me wanted to help her, um, and I thought loving her
> would fix everything.' (Sarah, a white lesbian aged 35–39
> at interview, and 25/26 when she began her first same sex
> relationship which was abusive)

The one significant difference regarding impact of sexual abuse
behaviours and gender was that women were more likely to fear for
their lives as a consequence of sexual abuse from their female partners
(at Chi Square $p<0.05$). When experience of potentially abusive
behaviours and impact were taken into account together, however,
sexual abuse stood out even more clearly as a risk factor for gay men.
This was also reflected in the interviews.

For both Kenneth and Anthony, whom we interviewed, instances of
sexual violence from male partners were what they described as their
worst relationship experiences. Kenneth found it difficult to describe
as 'rape' the forced sex he had experienced and had minimised it at the
time. For Anthony, however, it had meant the end of the relationship.

> 'There was a whole interesting potential around the use of
> the sexual dynamic. Cos there was…I mean one, one time,
> fairly early on in our relationship, he [breathes out] and I
> still find I can't actually say that he raped me, cos it wasn't
> quite as simple as that, but he certainly forced, and forced
> very violent sex on me…Against my will…So it's effectively
> rape.' (Kenneth, a white gay man aged 50–54 at interview,
> and 39 when SSDVA relationship began)

> 'The worst thing about it was when – he was the first
> person I ever had like full penetrative sex with, and we
> tried once, and you know, it sort of worked but not very
> well, and then he tried again, and then he sort of pinned
> me down, and I said "Stop," and he didn't, and that was the
> pivotal point, and that was it, it was *no more*.' (Anthony, aged

20–24 at interview, and 20 when he started his first same
sex relationship which was abusive)

Heinz and Melendez (2006) looked at the risk of HIV or other sexually
transmitted diseases as part of intimate partner DVA in a convenience
(DVA service based) sample of 58 LGBT individuals, mainly men in
same sex relationships. They found that individuals who had been
forced to have sex with their partner were at least ten times more likely
not to use protection in sexual activity as they feared their partner's
response to safer sex. Our survey data suggest that there is a group
of younger men, especially, at risk of similar DVA experiences: being
forced into sexual activity, hurt during sex, having requests for safer sex
refused, and being threatened with sexual assault. While some of our
interviewees talked about experiences of sexual assault and rape, only
one, however, talked specifically about fears around safe sex and how
requests around safe sex were also used as part of a pattern of coercive
sexual activity by abusers.

   As already mentioned, in our survey low income and educational
attainment were associated with heightened impact of emotional,
physical and in some cases sexual abuse, although this typically related
to a limited number of indicators. In relation to the individual items
of impact listed in Table 4.2 the impact of emotional abuse was
significantly (at Chi Square $p<0.05$) more prevalent among older
respondents (35 and over) and negatively affected their relationship
with children. This feature may perhaps be explained by an intersection
with gender, as the female respondents were almost three times more
likely to be parents than the men (see Chapter Two).

   Respondents who were low educational attainers were significantly
(at Chi Square $p<0.05$) affected by emotional, physical and sexual abuse
behaviours from same sex partners. The impacts for some were quite
extreme, with both emotional and physical abuse leading some to fear
for their own lives. Both emotional and physical abuse led to feelings
of sadness. Some responded to emotional abuse by retaliating and
shouting at their partner. Other emotional impacts included: emotional
problems or depression; stopped trusting people; felt worthless; felt
panic/loss of concentration; felt angry/shocked; self-harmed/felt
suicidal. Physical abuse also led to concerns that the partner might
leave, and made the respondent watch what s/he said or did. Sexual
abuse led to injuries that needed medical help, and to loss of respect
for partners.

   Respondents in the low income group were significantly (at Chi
Square $p<0.05$) more likely to stop trusting people, and to self-harm

or feel suicidal as a result of emotional abuse. Physical abuse led to feelings of being loved or wanted.

Although the survey data identifies significant risk groups who may experience detrimental and harmful impacts from emotional, physical and sexual behaviours by partners, the experiences of interviewees remind us that these 'risk factors' are signifiers of positionality that situate individuals experiencing DVA as having less power and abusers as having control and power over their partner. For instance, Bruce, a white gay man, had lower income than his abusive male partner, and at the time of the relationship was in the 'low income' group. His partner 'had quite a bit of money' and 'was independently quite well off', which provided a key inequality between them. The money provided the partner with:

> 'quite a lot of power in terms of being able to just [clicks his fingers] do what he wanted and go when he wanted, be, do whatever he wanted to do. Buy things and so on and so forth.' (Bruce, aged 30–34 at interview, and 19 when he began his first same sex relationship which was abusive)

Bruce talks about his partner's power and that this meant '[partner] was prepared to do things that I wasn't prepared to do', which included using violence. Bruce experienced physical violence and wider abuse from his male partner, part of what he saw as a domestically abusive relationship which had a controlling impact on him:

> 'Well, there was a lot of physical violence…He was very physically violent, he was emotionally very controlling and he was very, erm, he, invaded various aspects of my life. Like he would turn up at work. He would turn up at my parents' house. I was still kind of living at my parents' house all the time. He would cause great scenes in public, erm, particular if there was an event about me…Yeah, but certainly the physical, the physical violence was the worst aspect of it.' (Bruce)

It was the combination of physical violence with other abuse, which created the impact of fear that his partner also used to control Bruce, exert power over him and keep Bruce in the relationship:

> 'Erm, there was, but…he controlled me through *fear*, you see, so the fear just didn't come from nowhere. Fear came

from the fact that he hurt me physically and hurt my relationships or hurt my, damaged my property. So...he didn't actually have to do very much to, you know, at some points all he had to do, I could detect him bristling and building and building and you could see it and you knew what potentially was gonna come next, so therefore without the kind of physical violence and the history of his [violence] and the actual reality of it, his controlling behaviour wouldn't necessarily have had such an impact because I actually think I would have said "Well, bugger off, I'm not having this." It was that which gave him his power if you will.' (Bruce)

Severity of potential DVA behaviours and impact

In the previous section the significance for particular groups (based on gender, age, income and/or educational attainment) of the separate items of emotional, physical or sexual behaviour and items of impact were outlined. As explained in Chapter Two, however, a particular strength of the COHSAR research is the possibility for exploring the intersection of potential abuse behaviours and impact that the approach provides. Thus it is possible to begin to statistically differentiate between experiences that constitute DVA on the one hand (intimate terrorism and coercive control), and those negative experiences without the harmful impact that DVA involves, on the other. Where individuals experience higher levels of abuse from a partner, this may be assumed to be associated with a greater impact upon respondents. By combining statistically both behaviours and impact this association was indeed found to be the case, reflected in the relationship between the frequency of incidents of potentially abusive behaviour and their impact on respondents' lives (Hester et al, 2010). Establishing the optimal threshold for any set of impacts and abuse items was achieved by maximising the statistical 'fit' between these scales using one-way analysis of variance (ANOVA). The relationship between abuse and its impacts can be represented graphically, as illustrated by Figure 4.1 and ANOVA methods can then be applied to estimate an optimal threshold.

The graph in Figure 4.1 plots values for the impact and abuse scales relating to emotional abuse at any unspecified point in the respondents' lives. These data show a clear relationship between abuse and impact, but also a smaller number of cases where respondents were experiencing either a high number of potentially abusive behaviours and low impact or vice versa. Through analysis of variance we identified the optimal fit

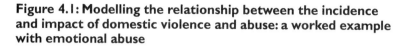

**Figure 4.1: Modelling the relationship between the incidence
and impact of domestic violence and abuse: a worked example
with emotional abuse**

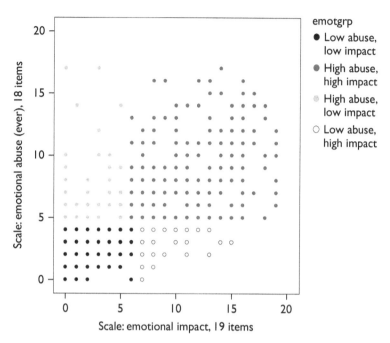

between these two variables – in this case at about seven on the x-axis
(impacts) and four on the y-axis (abuse). Pursuing this approach gave
rise to four distinct groups: high abuse and high impact, high abuse
and low impact, low abuse and high impact, low abuse and low impact.
Respondents were consequently deemed to have experienced DVA in
the sense of intimate terrorism and coercive control if they reported
both high levels of abusive behaviour experience *and* reported that this
had a significant impact upon their lives. We used this approach with
the two separate scales mentioned earlier (see Chapter Two) – a scale
for separate types of potential abuse behaviour (any one of emotional,
physical or sexual), and a scale for combined abuse.

The separate abuse scale estimated the incidence of abuse for each
of the emotional, physical and sexual abuse behaviours based on
multidimensional measurement, with prevalence rates varying between
7 per cent (sexual) to 14 per cent (emotional). The summary indicator
used here defines a respondent as 'abused' if their scores on *any* of the
separate incidence/impact scales was above the threshold. This includes
19 per cent of the valid sample. The individual thresholds are defined
as follows:

- *Emotional*: Respondents were classified as 'emotionally abused' if they scored 5+ on this scale and 7+ on the emotional impacts scale – identifying 105 respondents (14 per cent of the valid sample).
- *Physical*: Respondents were classified as 'physically abused' if they scored 1+ on this scale *and* 4+ on the physical impacts scale – identifying 72 respondents (10 per cent of the valid sample).
- *Sexual*: Respondents were classified as 'sexually abused' if they scored 1+ on this scale *and* 4+ on the sexual impacts scale – identifying 50 respondents (7 per cent of the valid sample).

The combined abuse scale estimates the frequency of respondent abuse, and of the impacts of abuse, based on a unified measurement scale. It is assumed here that emotional, physical and sexual abuse are one-dimensional, in other words that all items are tapping into the same (that is, singular) underlying phenomenon. The summary indicator used here defines a respondent as 'abused' if their scores on the *combined* incidence/impact scale is above the threshold that is 8 per cent of the valid sample.

With regard to the combined incidence and impact of emotional, physical and sexual abuse, overall, 122 respondents (16 per cent of 746) experienced at least one form of abuse in the last year. Of these, the largest groups were those reporting only emotional abuse (30 per cent) and emotional and physical abuse (20 per cent). Respondents experiencing multidimensional abuse constituted just over half (56.4 per cent) of all those reporting abuse. Our combined abuse scale is also assumed to be multi-dimensional, and theoretically involves the same sample of respondents, and this was found to be the case. Of those 56 respondents identified as 'abused' based upon the combined abuse scale, 52 (93 per cent) were separately identified as abused on at least two of the three separate dimensions (that is, emotional, physical, sexual: see Table 4.3). All of those identified as 'abused' using the separate individual abuse scales were also classified as 'abused' on the combined abuse scale.

In Table 4.3 respondents self-defining as abused are classified by the separate emotional, physical and sexual abuse scales as the unit of classification. The data in Table 4.3 suggests that, in the view of respondents, DVA is most closely associated with experiences of physical abuse and, to a lesser extent, with sexual abuse, rather than with emotional abuse per se. As discussed earlier, this was also echoed in the follow-up interviews. Of those survey respondents classified as experiencing significant abuse relating to one dimension only in relation to the separate abuse scale, only 27 per cent of those experiencing 'emotional abuse only' (Group 1) also self-defined as

Table 4.3: Domestic abuse group memberships and proportions within groups self reporting DVA and 'combined abused' (last 12 months)

	Abuse scale		~AND self-defined		~AND combined	
	N	**%**	**N**	**%**	**N**	**%**
1. Emotional only	42	29.6	11	27	2	5
2. Physical only	22	15.5	16	73	2	9
3. Sexual only	11	7.7	5	45	0	0
4. Emotional and physical	28	19.7	20	71	23	82
5. Emotional and sexual	17	12.0	7	41	12	71
6. Physical and sexual	4	2.8	3	75	0	0
7. Emotional, physical and sexual	18	12.7	18	100	17	94
Total	142	100	80	56	56	39

abused. In contrast, nearly three-quarters (73 per cent) of those defined as experiencing 'physical abuse only' (Group 2) also self-defined as abused, and nearly half (45 per cent) of those experiencing 'sexual abuse only' (Group 3) also self-defined as abused. Self-defined DVA was most closely identified with multiple forms of abuse (Groups 4 to 7), and especially with abuse in all three dimensions where *all* 18 respondents classified in this way also self-defined as 'abused'. Combined emotional and physical abuse also scored highly (71 per cent) in relation to self-definition.

Perhaps unsurprisingly, therefore, the fit between these summary measures and self-defined abuse is also much closer for the combined scale than for the separate abuse scale measure. In total, 77 per cent of those identified as 'combined abused' also defined themselves as having experienced domestic abuse, compared with 56 per cent of respondents classified as 'abused' on the basis of their group membership within any of the separate scales relating to emotional, physical and sexual abuse.

In other words, the most severe instances of DVA involved combinations of emotional, physical and sexual abuse and these experiences were also most likely to be associated by the survey respondents with having been in a domestically abusive relationship.

Perpetration of potentially abusive behaviour against partners

The COHSAR respondents were also asked about potentially abusive behaviours they had perpetrated against their partners, using similar items of emotional, physical and sexual behaviours as those they might themselves have experienced. Respondents generally reported fewer instances of potentially abusive behaviour against their partners than they reported from partners to themselves (Table 4.4). This is not surprising, echoes previous studies, and may reflect the social undesirability associated with domestic abuse as well as unmeasured differences in sampling probabilities. What is particularly interesting is that a similar hierarchy of behaviours were used against partners as had been experienced by respondents. Thus behaviours such as insulting and putting down one's partner, telling them what to do and say, causing fear, isolating them from friends and using age, class and education against them featured strongly in the list of emotional behaviours, as did kicking, shoving or pushing in relation to physical behaviour. The respondents seemed even more reluctant to express what sexual behaviours they had used against partners, although causing fear, hurting their partner during sex or forcing them, were most prevalent (but stated by very few respondents).

In order to differentiate between actions that might be motivated by self-defence and retaliation against the partner, rather than by a desire to control their partners, respondents were asked why they had used the behaviours. There were 21 possible reasons given as options for respondents and of these, five can be broadly defined as 'defensive' strategies:

- they hit you first (positive response by 7 per cent)
- to protect yourself from them (positive response by 8 per cent)
- to retaliate against them (positive response by 9 per cent)
- to protect children/relatives/friends (positive response by 1 per cent)
- to protect property/pets (positive response by 2 per cent).

In total, 108 respondents answered at least one of these five questions and 64 respondents answered two or more of these questions positively. This suggests that a significant proportion of respondents living in relationships where both partners are using potentially abusive behaviour may simply be seeking to defend themselves or others from further abuse. In other words, what some describe as symmetrical or 'mutual abuse', may actually involve a primary aggressor. Of those respondents reporting four or more instances of potentially abusive behaviours of their partner (from the separate abuse scale mentioned earlier), more than half (51 per cent) cited one or more reasons related to protecting themselves or others, or retaliation against their partner's violence, and well over a quarter (29 per cent) cited two or more reasons of this nature. Of those respondents reporting two or more

Table 4.4: Emotional, physical and sexual behaviours used by respondent to partner (%)

		Ever	Last 12 months
Emotional behaviour	Insulted/put them down	17.2	13.8
	Told them what to do/whom to see	13.5	11.0
	Frightened them with things you said/did	13.3	10.1
	Controlled their spending	11.8	9.5
	Isolated partner from friends	9.2	7.3
	Age/class/education used against them	7.4	5.5
	Made them do most of the housework	6.3	5.4
	Isolated partner from relatives	5.1	4.1
	Blamed them for your misuse of alcohol/drugs	6.6	3.8
	Blamed them for your self harm	6.0	3.4
	Religion/disability/race against them	2.5	2.5
	Made malicious/pestering phone calls	3.3	2.0
	Threatened to 'out' them	3.4	1.7
	Damaged/burned their property	2.6	1.1
	Abused their pet	0.7	0.8
	Threatened to harm someone close	0.7	0.6
	Withheld their medicines	0.4	0.2
Physical behaviour	Slapped/pushed/shoved	21.9	9.2
	Restrained/held down/tied up	7.0	4.1
	Physically threatened	7.1	3.4
	Kicked/punched	6.8	3.2
	Bitten	3.0	1.9
	Hit with an object/weapon	2.2	1.2
	Threatened with an object weapon	2.7	1.2
	Choked/strangled/suffocated	1.6	0.9
	Locked a partner in a house/room	1.9	0.9
	Stalked/followed a partner	3.7	0.6
	Beaten up	1.2	0.3
	Burned	0.5	0.3
	Prevented from getting help for injuries	0.4	0.2
Sexual behaviour	Touched in a way that caused fear/distress	2.2	1.8
	Hurt during sex	2.7	1.7
	Forced into sexual activity	2.2	1.5
	Disrespected their 'safe' words/boundaries	1.4	0.9
	Refused their request for safer sex	1.0	0.8
	Raped them	0.1	0.2
	Sexually assaulted/abused them in any way	0.4	0.0
	Threatened them with sexual assault/abuse	0.0	0.0

instances of potentially abusive behaviours of their partner (from the separate abuse scale mentioned earlier), nearly a third (32 per cent) cited one or more reasons related to protecting themselves or others, or retaliation against their partner's violence, and over one–fifth (21 per cent) cited two or more reasons of this nature.

Clearly, it would be inappropriate to characterise a relationship as symmetrical or 'mutually abusive' where the motivations for the respondent's actions are strongly associated with a desire to protect themselves or others, or constitute retaliation against their partner's violence. In cases where respondents responded positively to *two or more* items of this type these cases were thus classified as asymmetrical and 'abuse against respondent' rather than as involving symmetrically abusive relationships (Table 4.5).

Table 4.5: Relationship type by abuse scale (last 12 months)

| | Separate abuse scale | | Combined abuse scale | |
Relationship type	**N**	**%**	**N**	**%**
Symmetrical	51	7.5	9	1.3
Respondent is abused	89	13.1	47	6.9
Partner is abused	60	8.8	26	3.8
Non-abusive	481	70.6	599	88.0
Total	681	100	681	100

Summary

- Our approach is unique in asking not only about behaviours but also about a wide range of potential impacts, and additionally, whether individuals self-identify as experiencing DVA.

- The accounts from our interviewees indicate the difficulties in identifying negative relationship behaviours as DVA, and how individuals' previous experience feeds into such identification. A range of key factors in particular appeared to influence interviewees' perception and definitions of their own relationship experiences, including the public story of DVA, their own childhood or heterosexual adult experience of DVA, and working directly or indirectly with victims/survivors of DVA.

- More than a third of our survey respondents had at some time experienced what they themselves defined as domestic abuse in a same sex relationship. In the last 12 months less than one in five respondents appeared to have experienced DVA that is defined as intimate terrorism or coercive control, and one in ten experienced the most severe DVA in the last 12 months. An even greater number of respondents indicated that they had experienced at least one form of negative behaviour from their same sex partners.

- Our survey data indicated many similarities across the LGBTQ sample, including the range of abusive behaviours experienced by respondents and the impacts of such behaviour.

- There were some gender differences in relation to experiences of particular behaviours that appear to reflect wider processes of gendering and gendered norms. Men in same sex relationships were significantly more likely than women in same sex relationships to experience physically and sexually abusive behaviours, and sexual abuse was where the greatest gender differences occurred.

- Risk factors for potential abuse and heightened impact included age (being under 35 years), lower income levels and lower educational attainment, and these were much more marked than differences related to gender. At the same time, association between behaviour items and specific groups can be difficult to interpret and the direction of association is not clear. Intersectional factors also appeared to be important in creating contexts of risk of DVA with differences and inequalities between partners in terms of age, income, community knowledge, class and education being especially apparent. These features intersected and mutually shaped in a variety of ways that fed into the power and control exerted by abusers.

- The most severe instances of DVA involved combinations of emotional, physical and sexual abuse and these experiences were also most likely to be associated by the survey respondents with having been in a domestically abusive relationship.

- Most of those indicating that they had used abusive behaviours against a same sex partner did so for reasons related to defending themselves or others from violence and abuse initiated by an abusive partner. Thus our findings suggest that violence and abuse in same sex relationships is not characterised by mutual abuse or common couple violence but is asymmetrical violence and abuse with a primary aggressor.

FIVE

What's love got to do with it?

The research on which this book is based started from two premises. First, that not enough was known, certainly in the UK context, about DVA in same sex relationships to warrant a wholesale rejection of feminist approaches to understanding it. Second, relationships that become violent and/or abusive, regardless of gender or sexuality, mainly start out consensually and motivated by love or, as with the case of arranged marriages, motivated by positive feelings and hopes for love between partners. In this chapter we explore the ways that love, as expressed and interpreted by abusive partners and victims/survivors, can maintain abusive relationships. Love, experienced and constituted through verbal and nonverbal expressions, feelings and behaviours is usually understood positively and this is the case even in abusive relationships (Fraser, 2008). Here, love can act to confuse victims/survivors about how to make sense of and name their experiences as DVA. What we call practices of love, then, underpin and reinforce relationship rules in abusive relationships: that the relationship is for the abusive partner and on their terms and that the victim/survivor is responsible for the care of the abusive partner and the maintenance of the relationship, including parenting children where they exist, and the household if they cohabit. Relationship rules are established and enacted through relationship practices that establish the abusive partner as the key decision-maker who is able to set the terms for the relationship; and through their expressions of need and neediness. The victim/survivor is positioned as responsible for caring and emotion work for the abusive partner, their abusive behaviours and the relationship. We propose that relationship rules can be understood to reflect gendered understandings of roles in dominant constructions of adult (heterosexual) love, for example those of decision-making (masculinity) and carer (femininity). Yet the fact that they are enacted by partners in same sex relationships as well suggests that it is not the gender of the partner to a relationship per se that necessarily defines which role they will inhabit. Rather, we suggest that it is the dominant scripts about how (heterosexual) relationships might be lived that influences and shapes the relationship dynamic. Within this, however, other relationship practices challenge what have become these gendered assumptions about how roles in relationships might be divided between partners which, in abusive relationships can further confuse victims/survivors about what they are experiencing. For example, abusive partners' propensity to disclose 'fragile' selves (which is more associated with femininity) can act to position victims/survivors as emotionally stronger (more associated with masculinity) than their abusive partners. In addition, aspects of love that are expected in adult intimacy such as jealousy and dependence can be read, understood and experienced (by both partners) not necessarily as controlling but as evidence of love and commitment. Thus we conclude that an important way of understanding DVA relationships can be a focus on how practices of love act to embed the relationship rules in abusive relationships. Before we begin to explore these ideas in more detail we first continue the discussion we began in Chapter One about how love can be understood across gender and sexuality.

Love matters

When considering what is known about DVA in same sex and heterosexual relationships, what is striking are the similarities in victims/survivors' accounts. This is apparent from our research (see Chapter Four) as well as others' (Renzetti, 1992; Ristock, 2002a; Carvalho et al, 2011; Tellez Santaya and Walters, 2011). Victims/survivors in both same sex and heterosexual relationships experience a range of physical, emotional, financial and sexual abuses, are systematically undermined and experience isolation from friends and/or family or other potential sources of help. The differences that occur are mainly found in experiences of identity abuse, that is, using sexuality and/or gender identity as a way of further controlling and/or undermining and isolating a victim/survivor (identity abuse has also been evidenced in the accounts of DVA from trans people (see Bornstein et al, 2006; Roch et al, 2010)). Furthermore, gendered norms of behaviour can explain the more typical use of particular types of abuse by women and men in either same sex or heterosexual contexts and the different impacts on them. For example, as discussed in Chapter Four, we found that female abusive partners were typically more likely to use emotional violence and abuse and emotionally coercive sexual violence and abuse while male abusive partners were typically more likely to use physical violence and abuse and physically coercive sexual violence and abuse. In addition, as we will explain in Chapter Six, help-seeking can be differentially affected across gender and sexuality by the public story of DVA. Nonetheless, the similarities in experiences and impact of DVA across sexuality and gender are remarkable. Consequently, other researchers (for example, Rohrbaugh, 2006; Tellez Santaya and Walter, 2011), have questioned the extent to which feminist approaches explaining how and why DVA occurs are relevant for same sex relationships (as well as the experiences of heterosexual male victims/ survivors). The evidence from the experience of those in same sex relationships, which we began to outline in Chapter Four, suggests that this analysis of coercive control can also be applied in same sex relationships.

Feminist approaches, however, have also problematised dominant constructions of masculinity, femininity and heterosexuality. They argue that these create unequal, gendered power relationships between women and men in their adult intimate and familial relationships that are enacted, reinforced and mirrored in both public and private spheres and produce not only the conditions for abuse in individual relationships but collusion with and protection of abusive men by patriarchal social, economic and cultural structures. These structures are argued to create conditions of structured dependency for women in heterosexual intimate relationships, particularly when they become mothers, which not only reinforce unequal power relationships between women and men but also make it financially, materially, culturally and emotionally difficult to leave. More recent contributions to understanding DVA in the feminist literature have included an analysis of so-called 'honour'-based violence and forced marriage that have also implicated the role of family members in enacting and/or colluding in DVA (for example, Gangoli et al, 2011; Chantler and Gangoli, 2012), although the role of families and communities in colluding with abusive men had been recognised prior to these more recent discussions (for example, Hanmer, 2000).

These unequal relationships through and in which heterosexual intimacy and family life are constituted are, in western societies, increasingly underpinned by the importance of love. In Chapter One we pointed out how love, as a catalyst for adult intimacy has been both problematised in western societies (for example, Evans, 2003; Bauman, 2003) and applauded for freeing up personal lives from traditional strictures that have oppressed, particularly heterosexual, women (Giddens, 1992; Beck and Beck-Gernsheim, 1995). Early feminists critiqued romantic love for the ways in which it inculcated in heterosexual women a desire for marriage, depicted as the ultimate patriarchal trap wherein women and their desires were subjugated to those of their husband and children (for example, de Beauvoir, 1972). More recently, Evans (2003), Bauman (2003) and others (see Jackson, 1993) have cautioned that a focus on love can too often engender a selfish focus on individual wish fulfilment that leaves family, parental and personal lives unstable. It has also been argued that being encouraged to prioritise the achievement of love and happiness in our personal lives acts to deflect concerns away from endeavours to promote progressive social change (see Jackson, 1993). Giddens (1992) would argue, on the contrary, that love is becoming democratised, breaking down patriarchal authority and, instead, focusing on egalitarian relationships that are, as Giddens would put it, contingent.

Western cultures are saturated with narratives about love being a fundamental purpose of life: to feel and to know love is said to be 'all you need'. In Chapter Three we explored how the belief in the universality of love as a human need, feeling and right has persuaded many that marriage should be opened up to same sex couples (see Osterlund, 2009, for a discussion of this). As a universal feeling, love is understood, in the main, to be a feeling over which humans have no control (Jackson, 1993). This essentialist construction has it that love is somehow magical, inexplicable or, on a more prosaic note, an impenetrable chemical reaction, the solution to which lies outside human understanding. Love is understood to 'just happen', often without anybody expecting it, and with such force as to shake the foundations of an individual's world. That such an emotion could be shaped or influenced or constructed through historical, cultural and social forces is seen by some to degrade it (see Jackson, 1993). Yet though we each construct a sense of what love means to us we do not do this in a social vacuum. Rather, as Jackson argues:

> We do this by participating in sets of meanings constructed, interpreted, propagated and deployed throughout our culture, through learning scripts, positioning ourselves within discourses, constructing narratives of self. We make sense of feelings and relationships in terms of love because a set of discourses around love pre-exists us as individuals and through these we have learned what love means. (1993, 212)

Furthermore, we have argued that these narratives of love are also constituted through and of adult heterosexuality which is itself comprised through particular gendered norms. These gendered norms infused with beliefs and understandings arising from racial and ethnic identities, faith, social class and age or generation, typically position woman and men differently with regards to tasks such as responsibility for care and emotion work, housework, the provision of, and decision-making attached to the provision of, material and financial resources and so on. These gendered activities become important in discussions about love because their enactment or not can be read as signs that relationships are working. In addition, however, expressions of love including through sharing experiences, histories and problems, desires and personal goals, what Jamieson (1998) calls disclosing intimacy, as well as through sex and care, are also understood to be part and parcel of what can be expected when two people are in love and become intimate. Yet often, these, too, can be enacted in ways that reflect gendered understandings of what (heterosexual) women and men are like.

In fact, Duncombe and Marsden (1995, 150) argue that 'asymmetry in intimacy and emotion work may be the last and most obstinate manifestation and frontier of gender inequality'. As a result, they suggest, heterosexual women often feel disappointed at the disconnect between their expectations of a shared emotional life with men and the reality. The men, for their part, can often be mystified and/or irritated by what they perceive as unreasonable, if not irrelevant, requests to emote. Instead, many men believe that initiating sex represents their emotional connection with their female partners (Duncombe and Marsden, 1993; 1995). These authors also argue that inequalities in heterosexual relationships result in large part because of the construction of dominant masculinities in which emotion work is neglected, which leaves heterosexual women with difficult choices about how they make sense of and maintain their relationships. The evidence suggests that heterosexual women convince themselves that their relationships are sustaining and equal even in the face of evidence to the contrary (Duncombe and Marsden, 1993; 1995; Wilcox, 2006).

Using a Foucauldian approach to power, Lloyd and Emery (2000) argue that the unequal gendered power relationship implicit in abusive heterosexual relationships can be hidden by the myth of equality between the sexes. Differences between heterosexual women and men can be recast as inherent and complementary but often are rendered invisible by the enactment of routinised gendered behaviours understood to be 'normal' and therefore not worthy of note. Acts of physical or sexual aggression can then be dismissed or explained away as heterosexual men assuming their (complementary) role as initiator in courtship and authority figure who is in charge in the relationship. The construction of women as dependent on the relationship may elicit feelings in them that any relationship is better than no relationship resulting in women remaining in the abusive relationship. Hester (1992) has also argued that the inequalities embedded in the differences between constructions of male and female sexuality have been eroticised which can also act to position women as being to blame for their victimisation since they can be argued to have been attracted to abusive men.

Lloyd and Emery (2000) argue that a second discourse, of romance, can provide a language or metaphor and salve that facilitates forgiveness, isolation of aggressive behaviours as atypical and a belief in the strength of the love the couple has for each other to endure any obstacles to their happiness (Lloyd and Emery, 2000). Cultural artefacts such as fairy tales, Valentine's Day, romantic literature and films can act to seduce heterosexual women into a commitment to a relationship which includes tolerance of abusive behaviour (see also Wood, 2001). Another consequence of the romantic discourse, they argue, positions heterosexual women as the carer, both of the abusive partner and the relationship: 'if she tries hard enough, love will conquer all' (Lloyd and Emery, 2000, 27). While women are engendered to the maintenance tasks in the relationship, men are positioned as having 'autonomous motives'. In other words men are expected to face outwards from the relationship and serve their own interests with the support of their female partner. Lloyd and Emery (2000) also argue that the romance discourse creates fears about ending relationships in relation to losses, of the self as part of a relationship, of the partner, and/or of the relationship. We would also argue that the fear of the loss of self is exacerbated by a culture that promotes the central importance of being attached to another person in a committed relationship together with the belief that still has currency, that there is only one possibility of 'true love' for each of us.

Thus, the enactment of heterosexuality can be understood through a set of binaries that shape how women and men 'fit' together in sexual and intimate relationships. These binaries are seen to embody complementary characteristics, feelings, values, behaviours and expectations. Their existence as powerful ideas that are also rendered real by their enactment in everyday life as well as in cultural artefacts are important to understand the ways in which those who are not heterosexual come to understand who they are in relation to heterosexuals, not only in terms of how they are perceived but in how they live intimate lives. Making a commitment for life, wanting to protect a partner from the opprobrium of friends and family, making investments in a relationship that makes leaving difficult to contemplate much less enact, and/or feeling a responsibility to care for a partner are not inherently or exclusively the behaviour of heterosexual women. Likewise, wanting to control a partner, to be looked after and cared for exclusively and to be willing to cajole, wheedle, threaten and/or actually use force to ensure these are not inherently heterosexual male characteristics. The psychodynamics of couples and/or the pathology of perpetrators are one set of explanatory tools on which we may draw to make sense of DVA, but the socio-cultural context in which adult intimacy is understood and conducted must also be included as another. For example, dependency and jealousy have been formulated as indicative pathological factors in abusive partners' psychological profile, but they could equally be understood as very ordinary aspects of being in love and accepted as evidence of love and of neediness by both partners in an abusive relationship. Developing Lloyd and Emery's (2000) discourse of romance provides the basis for explicating how beliefs and expectations about love might provide scripts that accommodate abusive behaviours regardless of gender and sexuality (for example, see also Tellez Sahtaya and Walters (2011)).

To move the discussion on we unhook relationship practices and practices of love from heterosexual gender norms and restate them in terms of dominant expectations of love relationships held by anybody regardless of gender and/or sexuality. The accounts of abusive relationships we were given by our research participants made clear that certain behaviours, expressions and feelings were accepted as signifying love across gender and sexuality. These accounts will be discussed further in this chapter, and at the heart of the relationships being talked about is a paradox: what victims/survivors believed constituted a love relationship was not what they experienced in their abusive relationship yet most of them maintained a belief that their abusive partner loved them. The accounts of victims/survivors were peppered with expressions of love towards their abusive partner: care, affection, a sense of responsibility, loyalty, protectiveness. Yet the accounts they gave of how their abusive partners behaved describe selfishness, cruelty, a willingness to hurt and punish – sometimes severely – possessiveness, jealousy and expectations of care, loyalty, support, protection and forgiveness. The latter expectations were often elicited after declarations of love, promises to change and sometimes threats to commit suicide. Such expressions of love, need and neediness often provoked guilt and self-blame in victims/survivors but also obligations of care that became increasingly difficult to resist the more they had invested in the relationship (by moving in together, having children, getting married and so on). While the practices of love enacted by abusive partners persuaded victims/survivors to remain in abusive relationships for longer than they might have done with hindsight, their more general beliefs about love and adult intimacy also acted to confirm their decision to stay. Thus practices of love were in effect a part of the perpetrator's 'toolkit' of abusive practices, providing context and avenue for the coercive control of their partners. Beliefs included that marriage is for life, if you love somebody you should stay with them through good times and bad, that a commitment to a relationship should not easily be broken, that to break up a relationship would be a source of shame, embarrassment or sense of failure (particularly for heterosexual women in the eyes of their parents), a desire to prove that love could overcome the abuse being experienced and lead to change in the abusive partner for the better. All of these beliefs were both personal and reflective of the scripts and narratives available to them in society, regardless of gender and sexuality. In addition, many of the respondents explained that they felt love for their abusive partner, that they had felt their abusive partner loved them and that they had experienced happy and loving times as well as abusive times (see also Fraser, 2008).

All except one of those interviewed who had experienced DVA had done so in prior relationships. While, as we have explained in Chapter Two, the time lag between the interview and the abusive relationship will have had an impact on their memories, it is also the case that making sense of how they had come to remain in an abusive relationship had an impact on how they responded to our questions about love. Echoing many of the participants, Hazel, a white lesbian, explained that 'real' love would only be found with one person, so any relationships that had not worked could not have been 'real' love even if it was thought to be so at the time:

> 'Em, I think in general my, my perception is the same as it always has been, you only ever fall in love once but you can have varying degrees of love before you find that one person that you want to spend the rest of your life with. Um, and prior to that I was very much, "No, you just, you only ever fall in love once and anything else, you know, there's no point being in relationships unless you know that one person is for you." Em, but now I can see that there are very much, there's a very, sort of, sliding scale with that.' (Hazel, a white lesbian aged 20–24 at interview, and 15 when she began first relationship with a man which was abusive, and 20 when she began her first same sex relationship which was abusive)

Only one interviewee, Fran, a white, heterosexual woman, maintained that she had never loved her abusive ex-husband, with whom she had a daughter, and that she had 'no idea' whether he had loved her. Her marriage, at 18 years of age was described as a route out of an abusive family.

Other respondents described how careful they had been entering a relationship that they had felt an inner warning about. Audrey, a white lesbian, who had an abusive relationship with a man prior to her abusive relationship with her first lesbian partner, conveys this sense of caution:

> 'Yeah, we met on holiday…I knew [laughing] bad news right from the beginning. I just knew and I could see this was quite a controlling man and, um, I did that thing that women do, thought I could change him. Thought I could save him from his self.' (Audrey aged 55–60 at interview, and 35/36 when she met her abusive male partner)

Later in her interview Audrey described how, in retrospect, she realised that this abusive partner had groomed her. She described a feeling of being very attracted to a man she 'knew' was no good for her, of always being cautious of him, but of responding to his seduction of her in ways that positioned her as being responsible to care for and 'save' him.

For the rest of the interviewees love had either been explicitly present on both sides of the couple as they began their relationship or had been expected or hoped for by the victim/survivor and expressed by the abusive partner. However, as indicated earlier, because the relationships they talked about were over, some interviewees retrospectively questioned whether they had 'really' been in love. Edward, a white gay man illustrates the way in which this questioning took place:

> 'Well, I would say that I've felt as though I've been in love, for all of the relationships at the time that I was going out with them, but it's only when I started going out with the next person that I actually realise that "No, I wasn't in love with that person."' (Edward, aged 35–39 at interview, and 16 when he started his first same sex relationship which was abusive)

Like Hazel, above, Edward and others believed that 'real love' was a one-off event that, depending on their experiences, they pursued through different relationships. For those who had hoped for love as they entered what became an abusive relationship, their motivation to give the relationship a go had been the love expressed to them by their partner. As the account by Amy, a white lesbian, shows, she, too, invokes the benefit of hindsight in her answer:

> AMY: 'No, I don't think I did call it love. I think I, well, I know at the time I just said to her I wasn't sure how I felt really, but the only thing that I did know was that I wanted to be with her and I couldn't say how long that would last for…'
>
> INTERVIEWER: 'And…did she love you?'
>
> AMY: 'I think so. It certainly felt so…it's by the little things that she'd do; or her body language or – you know, from – silly things as well…how can I explain it? When somebody perfectly identifies what you'd like, and they can do it, they've got a gift of doing it, on a regular basis, and again the element of surprise…She was very, very caring, actually, she really did look after my feelings and was very interested and we'd talk a lot. And in quite a few ways [pause] I quite admired the person whom she made herself out to be.' (Amy, a white lesbian aged 30–34 at interview, and 21–23 when she began her second same sex abusive relationship)

Amy's account mirrors Audrey's account of her abusive heterosexual relationship where she also felt 'taken in' by her abusive partner even though Audrey had, as Amy had not, seen warning signs that this partner was 'controlling'. Taken together, love, expressed by the abusive partner or hoped for by the victim/survivor was central in most accounts of those we interviewed who had experienced DVA. This included relationships that had not lasted for very long. In general the gay men we interviewed who had experienced DVA had shorter relationships and did not live with their abusive partner. The lesbians, queer women and heterosexual women who had experienced DVA were more likely to have lived with an abusive partner and to have been with them for longer. There were some respondents, both women and men, who had experienced DVA in what might be called dating relationships. These were typically not longer than about eight months in length yet respondents still talked about having had positive feelings that could have been love and that their partners also expressed love for them. Consequently while we might question the extent to which a dating relationship can be included in a discussion about love, for most of our respondents love or hopes for love were central motivators for the relationship they discussed. In the next section we consider the ways in which practices of love, which might include behaviours enacted in courting relationships (or 'grooming' as Audrey would have it) are able to establish an abusive dynamic in a relationship regardless of sexuality or gender.

Relationship practices of love: establishing relationship rules

Morgan (1999) provides us with the concept of relationship practices to free up academic discussion to talk about 'doing family' rather than the structure of 'the family'. This not only allows us to explore what family means to its members, and to capture the changing nature of what constitutes family, it also allows us to move beyond discussions that assume the heterosexual nuclear family to be the gold standard against which other families are compared. The concept of relationship practices is similarly used in this book to explore how adult intimacy is lived and understood. Yet while this is helpful the concept in itself does not lend itself to discussions of power. Rather it conjures up a more neutral way of speaking about and describing how adult and familial intimacy is enacted and understood as such.

Another way of conceptualising familial and intimate relationships is through Finch's (2007) concept of display. This adds another dimension to the discussion about how members of families and, we would add, relationships, situate themselves as such and represent those relationships more publically. She focuses on the more visible diversity of behaviours that (mutually) create/reinforce family relationships from photographs of grandchildren on television sets to expectations that personal phone calls in professional settings can be taken in emergencies because they are family related. Display is used both as an activity of family relationships and a concept for analysis of these activities. While this concept focuses on the multiple ways that family relationships are known and represented both to each other and to those outside the family there is an assumption that display is necessarily reinforcing of family relationships. There is less focus on the ways in which display might not take place when, for example, family members are rejected because of their sexuality or, in the case of DVA, when signs of abuse may be covered up in order to present an edited display of intimate and familial relationships. Again power, though implicit in discussions about display, is not explicit in the use of this concept.

In order, therefore, to facilitate a more explicit discussion of how power operates in intimate relationships we suggest the concept of relationship rules. There are three advantages to this concept. First relationship rules suggest that they can be imposed by one partner on the other. Admittedly they may become norms of the relationship so that DVA is minimised with reactions such as 'he's always like that when...' or 'I should have known she'd react that way because...'. Using the notion of rules, however, reminds us that they are not mutually constituted but more deliberately enforced. Of course there are examples we can think of that might be thought of as unspoken relationship rules, such as trust and fidelity which can be broken and lead to relationship breakdown. Yet, we suggest that these can be conceptualised as everyday expectations of adult relationships assumed and constituted through dominant socially and culturally produced scripts about adult intimacy rather than specific rules of engagement to be learned in a DVA relationship. Second, using the concept of rules implies that breaking them might constitute grounds for punishment. Punishment in DVA relationships is meted out by the abusive partner to remind the survivor that they are expected to conform to and obey the rules. Third, the knowledge that consequences will follow for breaking relationship rules acts in and of itself to prevent them being broken. This means that while often DVA relationships are experienced as a mixture of good and bad times, there is almost always the understanding on the part of victims/survivors that they should be vigilant to ensure that relationship rules are not broken. There now follows a discussion of the relationship rules we identified from the interview responses.

Relationship rule one: the relationship is for the abusive partner and on their terms

We found evidence of two sets of relationship practices used to establish and enforce the first relationship rule, setting the terms of the relationship in favour of meeting the needs (and whims) of the abusive partner: key decision-making and, as an aspect of disclosing intimacy, what we call expressions of need or neediness.

Decision-making that sets the terms of the relationship

In any adult relationship, regardless of whether partners cohabit, relationship practices involve the everyday decisions that have to be made about how households run, how the household tasks are distributed between the partners (and children if they exist), how children are parented, how money and leisure time are spent, holidays taken, and so on. Heteronormatively, gender has shaped expectations about how these decisions are taken and by whom. In our interviews, however, we found that the abusive partner, regardless of gender or sexuality made the key decisions that set the terms for the relationship. Key decisions might not be the same across relationships nor indeed remain the same within the same relationship; and in addition they might not follow traditional gendered expectations. For example, several women who recounted abusive relationships with men talked about their abusive partner being able to set the terms by not doing paid work and expecting the victim/survivor to provide financially and materially for the relationship. In these relationships, the abusive heterosexual men might also expect to be able to control how the money that their partner brought into the relationship was spent.

The experience of Tanya, a white heterosexual woman, illustrates this as her husband refused to take responsibility for anything in their marriage. His ability to avoid almost any relationship practices embedded his entitlement to establish the terms for the relationship. In practice this meant that Tanya had to take all the responsibility for their home and the parenting of their son which freed up her husband to live the life he wanted to. This included taking paid work which took him away from home for most of the time:

> 'He was gone all the time. So I was left, I had to arrange all the childcare, you know, for [their son]. And it was, again it was like, Denis always said, "Well, you wanted the baby, so you can organise it." He didn't do it nastily, he did it in a, well he just [physically] went, you know. He just did all his own stuff first, and then I just had to arrange it.' (Tanya, aged 45–49 at interview, and 19 when she met her abusive husband)

On one level the key decision-making in this relationship is not obvious since Tanya made decisions about every aspect of their home life. On another level the key decision-making had been her husband's in abnegating any responsibility for their relationship. Tanya explained that over time she withdrew from organising the family's finances because she wanted to force her husband into taking some responsibility, but this meant that they faced many financial problems because he took out loans and remortgaged the house without telling her; and then resented her for leaving the finances to him. He did assume other decision-making, such as where they went on holidays but how this occurred mirrors the accounts of others in that Tanya took what she called the easy route of submission:

'I just, I think I was so easy going. I just used to, for a quiet life. Because he, although he wasn't, he wouldn't shout and scream, he was moody, he was very moody, and he would be sulky, and he would withdraw into himself and I would say, "Oh, what's the matter?" and he'd say, "Nothing's the matter, I'm just being quiet." But I knew that there was something he was either worried about or cross about, or unhappy about.' (Tanya)

Similarly in same sex relationships the abusive partner was able to establish the key decision-making and did so by employing relationship practices that eventually acted to prevent any resistance. For example, Ted, a white gay man, explained that, without any physical violence being used, his partner gradually eroded his will so that eventually he 'gave up' trying to resist his partner's demands:

> TED: 'I mean, I earned a lot more than he did but he always had control if you like: "We'll do this, we'll do that." Like, "We'll decorate, but we'll have it this way." It was never what I wanted, it was always what he wanted…it was easier just – "Well, do it." It just saved the arguments and you know and it was, "Oh, you've got no taste." And like, if we were out with people, it was, "Oh, you shut up, you don't know what you're talking about," and you were always, sort of, put down.'
>
> INTERVIEWER: 'So he was sort of making most of the big decisions?'
>
> TED: 'Yeah. Oh all of them, all of them. I mean where we went – he would come in – "I've booked a holiday we're going to such and such." There was never any discussion, "We're going here," and that was it.' (Ted, aged 55–59 at interview, and 28 when his first same sex relationship began which was abusive)

We have explained, in Chapter Four how, by keeping control over these aspects of the relationship Ted's abusive partner had been able to have many affairs with other men. That these relationship practices occurred gradually is of interest in explicating how patterns of abuse can emerge in relationships. Like Tanya above, Ted suggests that it became easier to 'give in', though not because of the moods of his abusive partner as Tanya had to face, but because of the arguments that ensued if he did try to resist his partner's behaviour. In relation to his partner's insistence on making most of the financial decisions he says:

> 'I just thought he was, sort of – cos I had quite a high pressure job and I just thought he was doing it to save me the hassle. Oh, you know, it was "Oh, isn't he good, he's doing this, he's doing that, you know, he's saving me," you know. I'm sitting doing paperwork from work and I thought, "Oh, he's taken everything out of my hands," but that was the way it was manipulated, if you like, and I didn't realise until afterwards, I must admit.' (Ted)

In Ted's explanation he drew on practices of love as the rationale behind his abusive partner's behaviours: that his abusive partner took over their finances because he cared for Ted. He also referred above to those explicitly abusive practices that his abusive partner used to convince Ted that Ted was too incompetent to make decisions including financial ones. This was how the relationship proceeded over 15 years, with only one episode of physical violence when they were about to break up. Yet Ted believed until after the relationship was over that his partner's actions were motivated by love and care for him.

Emma, who identified as white and queer, also talked about her partner making the key decisions and thus being able to set the terms for their relationship. She, too, referred to the ways in which it became easier to go along with her partner than to challenge anything:

> INTERVIEWER: 'And so, in terms of decision-making, did, was it, did she make all the decisions?'
> EMMA: 'Absolutely. All of them…I think at the time I thought, "Well, I can't make a decision. I, you know, I don't know what I should be doing, or I don't know what we should be doing," [s]o it's better to, you know, say, "Ok, you, you decide." It's easier that way, which is, that's what it felt like. It's easier that way and I, I wouldn't know so obviously that's the best thing to do.' (Emma, aged 30–34 at interview, and 17 when she began her first same sex relationship which was abusive)

Like Ted, in Emma's account there was evidence that her abusive partner's behaviour had eroded Emma's self-esteem and confidence which led her to believe that her abusive partner was better able to make decisions than she was.

Tanya, Ted and Emma, as did others, felt unable to resist the ways in which their partners were able to exert power in the relationship and were often convinced that their partner's behaviour was motivated by love of and/or care for them. They also talked about the ways in which they had come to realise that resistance was futile, however, either because their partner became argumentative, as in Ted's case, or moody and withdrew their affection, as in Emma's and Tanya's cases. Such relationship practices that elicited guilt, care and attempts to avoid conflict in the survivor are subtle abuses that control the emotions of victims/survivors and lead them to give in to their abusive partner's demands in order to attest to their own love for their abusive partner.

Findings from our survey showed that women were significantly more likely to 'try harder' as a result of experiencing abuse (Chapter Four) and while this came across in the interviews as well, several gay men also talked about their attempts to appease their abusive partner in similar ways. The ways in which relationship practices and practices of love were experienced, both negatively and positively, as they exerted control over the survivor, contributed to the difficulties Tanya, Ted and Emma had in recognising their relationships as abusive. Incrementally, Tanya, Emma and Ted's abusive partners were able to establish the first relationship rule. They did so from very early on by using different kinds of tactics that eventually wore down any attempts to resist them. Other interviewees were also able to describe the ways that they were worn down by abusive partners insisting on their own way. Tactics included: being ground down to give in or not object through wheedling, persistence, shouting and screaming; keeping the victim/survivor up late into the night to 'talk' or argue; sulking, moods and silences; returning to the issue continually over days, weeks or months. The success of these behaviours is evidenced in victims/survivors' explanation that they eventually attempted to pre-empt their use by 'giving in', saying things such as Ted describes: 'It was easier just not arguing, just saying "fine."' Valerie, a white lesbian, explained that she had never challenged anything her abusive partner had demanded within the relationship because, as she explained:

VALERIE: ''Cause it was less stress.'
INTERVIEWER: 'Yes. What could happen if you didn't?'
VALERIE: 'If I didn't – I've never, until actually after we'd split up, ever not caved in…in the whole relationship. Whenever she put pressure on me to change my mind, I'd change my mind…I don't know, it was easier to say "yes" than it was to say "no" and I'm not particularly

> confrontational…I don't like arguing. I like to have quite
> a chilled, laid-back life.' (Valerie, aged 30–34 at interview,
> and 25 when she began her abusive relationship)

Valerie blamed herself for not standing up to her abusive partner and
her account suggests that she had no evidence of what might have
happened if she *had* refused to acquiesce because she had never done
so. Her account illustrates the way in which many victims/survivors
are able to read their abusive partners in non-verbal ways and be able
to tell without being told what is allowable or acceptable (see also
Wilcox, 2006). Again, in this excerpt, Valerie explained how the terms
of the relationship were set by her abusive partner conveying the first
relationship rule.

Decision-making in an adult relationship can be seen as an indicator
of how power operates within it. It does not necessarily follow that
an abusive partner in a relationship makes all the decisions, that the
survivor is always subordinated to or by particular relationship practices
or that the same kinds of decisions are made by abusive partners across
different relationships. Typically, however, abusive partners make
the key decisions as defined in each abusive relationship, including
their decision to do nothing to contribute to the relationship. These
decisions supported the first relationship rule: that they set the terms
for the relationship. While dominant constructions of masculinity have
been associated with decision-making, it emerged from our study
that decision-making was co-opted by abusive partners regardless
of sexuality or gender. Thus, abusive partners come to inhabit the
relationship practices of what have come to be associated with
embodied heterosexual men, although they were neither necessarily
men nor did they necessarily represent a masculinised role in their
relationship.

Other accounts, most often given by heterosexual women, provided
examples about how the abusive partner was able to set the terms of
the relationship very early on by their use of physical and/or sexual
violence. Such aggression might be experienced routinely within
weeks of the relationship starting, as was the case with Theresa (a
white heterosexual woman, aged 40–44 at interview, who was 16 years
old when she met her abusive husband), where it began 'within, like,
weeks'. Alternatively, and with sexual violence, this might happen out
of the blue. A couple of women were unable to speak about the sexual
violence they experienced in relationships with men; as a result, these
relationship practices were pivotal. For example, Donna, who identified
as a white lesbian when we interviewed her, had been divorced from

a previous heterosexual marriage which she identified as her worst relationship experience. When her husband, as she put it 'sexually abused' her, the relationship was changed, "Literally, it was overnight," and threw everything that had happened before into strong relief:

> DONNA: 'I, I just couldn't believe it, but that's when the fear kicked in as well, I think, and because, because I felt so powerless anyway. I'd not noticed that I didn't have any power in the relationship up until that point, I think, when it was completely taken away from me. Em, and then, then it was a case of being so scared and needing to kinda keep things going because I didn't know what the next thing would be, you know, I didn't know whether he WAS GONNA COME IN DRUNK AND WELL YOU KNOW, I JUST DIDN'T KNOW…'
>
> INTERVIEWER: 'Right, ok. So up until that point it wasn't, you didn't think this is great but you still thought this is ok…'
>
> DONNA: 'No, I thought this is quite nice, you know, it wasn't that it was just ok, it was "Oh, this is nice," you know, it's, maybe a bit different to what I expected but that's all right, you know, I can get on with it and you know, "Let's enjoy what we've got," and you know we had quite a good life.' (Donna, aged 35–39 at interview, and 26 when she began her abusive relationship with her husband)

While this incident of sexual violence fundamentally changed Donna's perception of her abusive husband and made her fearful of what he was capable of, up until that point she had accepted him establishing the terms of the relationship as part of settling down into married life with somebody with whom she was very happy. The practices of love her husband had engaged in to that point had not provided her with any signs that this was an abusive relationship.

Expressions of need and/or neediness

As we discussed in Chapter One, femininity has been constructed around the belief that disclosing intimacy, listening and sharing and emotionally connecting are embedded within what it is to be an adult woman. Yet what became clear in accounts of abusive relationships is that abusive partners, whether they are women or men in heterosexual or same sex relationships, can be extremely eloquent in providing rationales for their behaviour that elicit feelings of sympathy and emotion work in the abused partner. These feelings led victims/ survivors, particularly women, to not only want to fix their abusive partner, but also to protect them from outside criticism, stay loyal to them and the relationship and to either remain in or return to the relationship. What became apparent is that many respondents came to feel responsible for their abusive partner who they saw as dependent on their care. Ava, a white lesbian's account, exemplifies this in her response to the question asking what the worst things were about her abusive relationship:

> '[pause, breaths out, long pause] Uh, probably the fact that I could, I knew exactly what her problems were. And the worst thing was that she knew that I knew but didn't, was so pigheaded and stubborn, um, and just didn't, didn't acknowledge it. The violence. Um, the nastiness, verbal. Er, the arrogance, just, just everything…I should never have, hmm, never have gone back. But, I did. Er, the worst thing? [pause] Flogging a dead horse; um. Staying up all night, listening, going over the same ground over and over and over again. Um. Just everything. Um. It was a bad time.' (Ava, aged 45–49, and 33 when she began her first same sex relationship which was abusive)

Ava explained that understanding her abusive partner's violent behaviour and attributing it to alcoholism was, with hindsight, a mistake because it convinced her to return to the relationship with the hope that things would change and that her partner would stop drinking. Staying up late to talk to and listen to her abusive partner's expressions of need and neediness was finally understood to be of little use and the second part of their relationship was finished by Ava. Yet her abusive partner had, during the course of their on–off relationship, clearly been able to talk about and show how damaged she was because of the alcohol misuse in ways that elicited care from Ava.

Amy's second abusive partner also revealed to Amy her alcohol problems which she attributed to childhood experiences of sexual abuse. The revelations had such an impact on Amy that she decided to speak to a counsellor to enable her to support her abusive partner and so that she would not have to break the confidence of her partner by seeking support from her own friends. In addition, Amy decided that she would not leave her partner because she wanted to support her through her difficulties and show her commitment and support for the changes her partner said she wanted to make:

'Yeah...I thought...the nice side of her outweighed the ugly side of her, for want of a better word. Um. Yeah, and I felt like it wouldn't be fair for me to say, "Oh, right, I've seen this behaviour, it's really ugly, I'm going, bye," after a couple of years or something. It wasn't fair at all. So I did feel responsible to try and help her out and try and look after her and try and support her...But also I think I felt a greater responsibility because it was the first time in all of that time that she'd ever disclosed the alcohol use and the events which led to the alcohol use. You know, and a lot of that stuff was around abuse. So it was very difficult.' (Amy, white lesbian aged 30-34 at interview and 21-23 years old when she began a second SSDVA relationship)

Such an obligation of care towards abusive partners who expressed need and/or neediness was not uncommon across gender and sexuality in our interviews. Gay male victims/survivors also gave accounts of abusive partners who had expressed their need or neediness in explanation for the abuses they perpetrated. Kenneth, a white gay man, had an abusive relationship with a man 17 years younger than he was and who was, like Kenneth, HIV+. In the following excerpt, Kenneth explains what his partner had disclosed to him:

'I wouldn't forgive it, but...he'd grown up in an abusive family...abusive father, but yeah, he got violent towards me. Never seriously hurt me. But, on more than one occasion – p'raps three or four occasions, kicked and hit. And that was absolutely awful...He died at age 26...so he died like two and a half years after we split up. Um, and he was...as healthy as I am at the moment when we split up...I'm not saying that I kept him alive but...he would constantly say to me...how he really admired the way I coped with HIV. Um, looked up to the way I handled taking the drugs and that. He really didn't like it...I mean, bit odd for someone who would push anything down his throat, um, but in terms of taking medication he was terrible, and really didn't like it at all. And he did and he admired me for that, and he did say that I kept him alive, that I gave him a reason to wanna keep going.' (Kenneth, aged 50–54 at interview, and 39 when he began his abusive relationship)

His abusive partner's experiences of childhood abuse provided Kenneth with an explanation that made sense of the abuse Kenneth experienced. In addition, his abusive partner intimated that he needed Kenneth in coming to terms with being HIV+ which enabled Kenneth to feel wanted and responsible to look after his abusive partner for over two years. Underlying many of these accounts is the relationship of dependency abusive partners are able to contrive with victims/survivors. The latter, in their turn, see the vulnerabilities of their abusive partners not as signs to leave but to remain in a caring role because this comes to be understood as the evidence of what their love for each other means. Scripts about dependency and care, staying loyal and committing to support a partner dealing with their problems are not individually created, however, but result from their resonance with scripts that exist in wider society.

Explanations given for partners' abusive behaviours ranged from abusive families of origin to being an outsider or not 'fitting into' society. Often heterosexual men were in the latter category and described as being 'different' in some way. Tanya, talked about how her husband was not like other men because he did not want to possess anything, including her or their children and that he had a 'terror' of responsibility. Others talked about their abusive partner being creative, radical, being different or an outsider in some way and that this meant that they were not to be judged or treated the same as others. Consequently, abusive partners were able to set the terms for their relationships which typically meant they were able to live as they wanted to, but with the emotion work of their partners to support and protect them from outside opprobrium. In addition, the explanations given for their abusive behaviours were such that victims/survivors could empathise and remain caring and loyal to them. Audrey's account of how she tried to support her abusive male partner illustrates this; and towards the end echoes the account of Emma we gave earlier in this chapter:

> 'Yeah, what that meant was being understanding and yeah [pause] being able to see it from his point of view, whatever it was. Giving him space to talk, agreeing with him that his boss was a bastard or his mother was a cow or whatever you know, cos it seemed like nobody was on his side. Of course I [laughing] quickly realised why…cos, you know, you don't behave in a relationship in isolation, you're like that everywhere at some level and – not violent, you know he wasn't violent other places, but his attitudes were violent

and you know I just saw him as this little misunderstood boy and, I guess, like mummy, I would understand him. I'd make – I'd make our relationship and our home and our life a safe place.' (Audrey aged 55–60 at interview, and 35/36 when she met her abusive male partner)

Both Emma and Audrey articulated experiences of abusive relationships that resulted in them believing that loving and/or caring about somebody inevitably must result in giving up one's own desires. This depiction of love reflects exactly what is expected by the first relationship rule.

Victims/survivors also expressed need or neediness in their relationships but the effect of this could be profound (Donovan and Hester, 2011). Tanya's revelation to her husband that she deeply regretted her abortion, which she had in the fourth year of their relationship, and desperately wanted to have a child was understood by her as the act that effectively ended her husband's love for her even though they remained married for another 21 years. Revealing strongly felt desires, insecurities, ambitions and so on, can, inadvertently provide abusive partners with knowledge which they could exploit and use to further control them. Theresa had told her husband about her ambitions to become educated and get on in life and to learn to drive, but these became activities that she was specifically kept from achieving. Marie 'confessed' to her abusive partner that, on the only occasion in the previous seven years of their abusive relationship, that she had gone home for a week to her family who lived abroad, she had begun an affair. This elicited behaviour from her partner that resulted in feelings of such guilt and shame in Marie that she remained in the abusive relationship for a further five years, continually attempting to make up for her failings. Marcus's abusive partner was aware that Marcus had invested an enormous amount in trusting that their relationship would be monogamous, as a result of which he either threatened to, or did, engage in sexual encounters with other men which thoroughly undermined Marcus's self-esteem. Thus revelations from victims/survivors could provide new ways for abusive partners to control them or rationales for punishing them.

Like jealousy, threatening to commit suicide is widely recognised as an extreme form of controlling behaviour that can put (heterosexual) victims/survivors at increased risk of harm from abusive partners (for example, see CAADA, 2012b). The end of an abusive relationship is also recognised as a time when heterosexual women face increased risk of severe harm or homicide (CAADA, 2012b). In our study accounts were given by several heterosexual women and gay men in which abusive partners had threatened to kill themselves; however, what also became apparent was that when these threats were given they were often understood either or both as an expression of neediness or love on the part of the abusive partner. Theresa, white a heterosexual woman explains:

> 'Because like if I ever used to get upset and want to end it all, he used to be like, "Oh, but I'll kill meself and I love you," and which I know is like getting an emotional bloody thing that he used to play but *then* I didn't used to appreciate that so I used to be "Oh well he must really love us."' (Theresa, a white heterosexual woman, aged 40–44 at interview, who was 16 years old when she met her abusive husband)

Thus was Theresa, like other victims/survivors we interviewed, persuaded that she was both loved and needed by her abusive partner: two powerful reasons to stay in a relationship that are lauded in wider society. Other respondents who had ended their abusive relationships found this did not necessarily put an end to the abuse they experienced from their partner. Post-separation abuse included various ways of trying to persuade the survivor to re-engage with abusive partners. Anthony, a white gay man, ended his three-month abusive relationship when he was raped by his partner. Very soon after this relationship ended, however, Anthony received a phone call at three o'clock in the morning from his ex-partner to say that the partner was contemplating suicide. Anthony had an exam at nine o'clock in the morning but, as he says, "Your mind, sort of, like, races," and he tracked down a friend of his abusive partner's to go with him and check that he was alright. Anthony failed his exam. A couple of weeks later, his abusive ex-partner rang again, this time with a more threatening message:

> 'He'd like, he'd rung me up and then he told me that, um, his ex[boyfriend] had come round when I'd gone away home, when we were [still] going out…and raped him, and hadn't used a condom, and then he hadn't used a condom on me so I should go and get myself checked out, which you know, was just [pause] – in the end it was fine, but you know… [voice trembling] it's, it's hard really not to, like, really hate him [tears in his eyes].' (Anthony, aged 20–24 at interview, and 20 when he started his first same sex relationship which was abusive)

Not content with threatening to take his own life, Anthony's abusive ex-partner also warned Anthony that he might have contracted the HIV virus. While the ex-partner was revealing his own insecurities and vulnerabilities in order to try and keep Anthony engaged with him he was also punishing Anthony for having ended their relationship. While the first phone call was heard as a cry for help and provoked a strong sense of concern in Anthony for his ex-partner, the second phone call was perceived and experienced as punitive and cruel and confirmed Anthony's decision to cut off any contact from his abusive partner. As this account suggests, expressions of need and neediness are neither confined to women nor is it only associated with femininity.

In our research many victims/survivors were only able to evidence their abusive partners' love for them when giving accounts of when their relationship had been in crisis either because victims/survivors were threatening to leave or because they had left. It was then that abusive partners would engage in more explicit practices of love, either making declarations of love or expressing need and neediness which acted to remind victims/survivors of the relationship rules. We have explained elsewhere how declarations appear to have been used strategically by abusive partners in these situations (Donovan and Hester, 2011). Not only are declarations of love centrally important in the survivor's decision to stay, they can also be as crucial in their decisions to return if they have already left. Thus engaging in practices of love can be a way abusive partners anticipate attempts by victims/survivors to leave an abusive relationship. For example, Marie believed that her abusive partner's reluctance to let her go and subsequent statements about love were indicative of her love, which had not been evident previously:

> 'I think she did love me. I mean, she really didn't want me to leave towards the end, did everything, and when we went to Relate, you know, she was – when I was able for the first time to actually say all the things that I wanted to say, she, she'd cry and she'd be unhappy and she would say, you know, "I can't believe I've behaved like that," and stuff like that. So she'd realise and apologise and things – in front of the therapist anyway, yeah. [laughing] Well I think she, she loved me, she really didn't want me to go.' (Marie, a white lesbian who was from Europe, aged 35–39 at interview, and 21 when she began her first same sex relationship which was abusive)

Leaving abusive relationships was a catalyst to post-separation abuse in many same sex relationships in our research, as it is in heterosexual relationships. This ranged from stalking and harassment, either in person, through electronic or postal means of communication, of the victim/survivor, their family, friends and employers, or the use of the legal system to establish child contact or financial settlements. There was some evidence that the initial experiences of post-separation abuse were experienced as benign in so far as they were seen as attempts by abusive partners to persuade victims/survivors to stay in or return to the relationship. Expressions of need, declarations of love and promises to change characterised these attempts. It was when these attempts were unsuccessful that the abusive partners often changed and became more relentless and punitive, as if they believed that they were entitled to punish the victim/survivor for breaking the relationship rules.

Edward, a gay man, provides a good example of this pattern. He explained that he had wanted the relationship to end from quite early on, but felt trapped in it because his abusive partner was his manager and Edward believed that he might be sacked if he were to end the relationship. This would have caused problems for Edward because, as a result of the financial abuse he experienced in the relationship, Edward had illegally taken out an extra card on his father's credit card, without his knowledge, and run up a lot of debt. Being sacked would have put an end to his ability to pay off the debt and he would have been found out by his father. Even with these clearly abuse-related reasons for remaining in the relationship, Edward's account still reveals the emotion work he was engaged in with his abusive partner and how this also kept him either remaining or returning to the relationship twice over a two-year period:

> EDWARD: 'Ended up splitting up with him on a train [laughs]…and then he decided to use, again, emotional blackmail, cos we were on one of these old rickety trains with…it had half doors, and the top door was open. And, you know, he started to say things like, "Well, if you don't go out with me, I'm gonna throw myself off the train," and stuff like that. [laughs] So.'
>
> INTERVIEWER: 'And did you believe him?'
>
> EDWARD: 'No, I didn't believe him at all… I said, "Oh, don't be stupid." [laughs] …That was the end for about a month. And then, he would [pause] and then because obviously we would see each other when we were working – he didn't sack me…but we would see each

> other when we were working. Because I still actually
> somehow wanted to be friends, with him. I felt sorry for
> him in some way, because…I don't know why I felt sorry
> for him…but he abused that as well, so, he would offer
> me a lift home and then take me somewhere completely
> different [pause] you know, and talk…I got so fed up
> with it, at one point, that I just said, you know, "Ok,
> let's go back out again, let's see, see if it's any different."
> Of course it wasn't. And we ended up going out again
> for another, about six months, seven months. And then
> finishing again.' (Edward)

Edward finally finished the relationship when he left home to go to
university in another part of the country. Unfortunately, his father then
gave Edward's abusive partner Edward's telephone number, resulting
in Edward being harassed over 'a matter of months', with demands to
meet up and talk. His abusive partner eventually moved near to Edward
and turned up in places that Edward was visiting with friends.

Some abusive partners act as if they believe they possess their (ex)
partners. When victims/survivors threaten to, or actually leave, abusive
relationships they adopt similar kinds of relationship practices and
practices of love to which they have become habituated, but when the
relationship is threatened their behaviours are more open to alternative
interpretations. Being thwarted in having their needs and demands
met, some abusive partners are willing to adopt ever more exaggerated
relationship practices and practices of love which are often experienced
as threatening to the survivor and may involve acts of severe violence.
Their intention appears to be either to convince the survivor to re-
engage with the abused partner, presumably with the intention of
reinstating the relationship, or of punishing the survivor because they
still feel entitled to dictate the terms of the relationship after it has
ended. Sarah's abusive lesbian partner abducted her, physically assaulted
her, burned her with a cigarette, and dumped her by the side of the
road miles from her home without any money after Sarah finished
their relationship. During two years of post-separation abuse, Marie's
abusive lesbian partner told her children, whom Marie had brought
up for 12 years, lies about Marie, broke into the house of Marie's
new partner and assaulted the new partner, rang the parents of her
new partner to tell them she sexually abused children, rang Marie's
workplace to tell them lies about Marie, and constantly rang Marie:
"She was all night, all night on the phone, night after night." Eventually,
Marie and her new partner left the area because Marie believed that

the post-separation abuse would never stop: after seven years with her new partner she said, "We're still on the run." We return to the impact of post-separation abuse in the next chapter about help-seeking. We discuss it here to illustrate the degree to which some abusive partners, regardless of gender or sexuality, will go when they believe the relationship might or has ended, to re-establish the relationship rules with victims/survivors, or to punish them for breaking the rules. In the face of such abusive behaviours it can be difficult to understand why the relationships remain intact for as long as they do. In the next section we consider how the second relationship rule might provide some answers to this question.

Relationship rule two: the survivor is responsible for looking after the abusive partner and the relationship

In this section we explore two aspects of the second relationship rule to discuss how victims/survivors across sexuality and gender come to feel a responsibility to take care of their abusive partner (and relationship, children and household if they shared one); and how, for several of them, this positioned them, in their own perceptions, not as victims of their partners' abuse, but as being emotionally stronger than them. Because they did not understand themselves as victims as depicted in the public story of DVA they were often less able to understand or recognise their experience as DVA at the time of the relationship.

Expectations and obligations of care

Embedded in the accounts given above about how abusive partners expressed need and neediness is the victims/survivors' responses of care, empathy and concern. What emerged in this research was that, often, emotion work dominated the practices of love enacted by the victim/survivor across sexuality and gender. Mutual feelings of love and care are expected in adult relationships entered into consensually yet, as has been discussed above, emotion work has come to be associated with femininity in embodied women. In the accounts from lesbians, bisexual and queer women it became clear that this might be true of victims/survivors, but not of their partner who expected to be cared for but not reciprocate. Sarah's first same sex relationship was abusive, including physical violence, yet she stayed because she loved her partner and wanted to try and help her to change:

> INTERVIEWER: 'How do you know you loved her?'

SARAH: 'Um [pause] That's the hard one, cos she didn't make me feel good about myself. [laughing] She used to beat me up. Um [pause] I don't know. I think part of me wanted to help her, um, and I thought loving her would fix everything. I mean there were, there were good times, but a lot of the time we were rowing, and, as I say, she was quite abusive.' (Sarah, a white lesbian aged 30–34 years old at interview, and 25/26 when she began her first same sex relationship which was abusive)

Sarah went on to explain that her partner was extremely jealous of her and wanted to control whom she saw. Sarah realised at the time that the violence was not right, yet still felt that she had to emphasise to the interviewer that she had not done anything to elicit insecurity in her partner, as if this would have made her partner's behaviour more understandable. Her attempts to explain her innocence reflect the strength of the dominant relationship script that makes socially acceptable an angry, even a violent, response to jealousy. After an assault where her partner had thrown Sarah down the stairs and then left, Sarah explained that there was a pattern to what happened after one of her partner's violent outbursts:

SARAH: 'She'd always go for a drive somewhere, after. So she'd disappear for hours, and then she'd ring and [ask] who was I with, what was I doing, and I'd just be like, "I'm sitting in the flat, bawling me eyes out, Carly, I dunno what to do." And she'd go, "Who've you got with you?…"'
INTERVIEWER: 'And what would you do then?'
SARAH: 'I'd forgive her [laughing] because I was a fool! I don't know, I think I thought she never meant it. But, there were times when she'd, like, really hurt me. I'd think, "No, this isn't right, you know. You don't do that to someone you love." She'd sit on the floor and cry and say she loved me but, I'd just say, "You don't, because you don't do that to people you love."…[S]he would say, "Yeah, it'll never happen again. I don't know what happened, you know, I don't know what came over me." And I think the hardest bit to understand was I never did anything to make her jealous…She obviously needed, felt the need to control me, but it's not that I was out doing anything that needed controlling, you know. I was just seeing a work friend and socialising.' (Sarah)

Sarah tried her best to reassure her partner that there was nothing to be jealous about and to 'fix' her violent outbursts, but when she challenged her partner's abusive behaviours her partner drew on practices of love and told Sarah she loved her as an explanation for her abusive behaviours. Jealousy has long been recognised as an acceptable emotion in adult relationships and one that, if not completely condoned, is understood as a motive for 'crimes of passion', yet it has also been identified as a motivation for extremely controlling and violent behaviours in heterosexual women's relationships (Dobash and Dobash, 1992). Many victims/survivors in this study referred to their abusive partners' jealousy as a shorthand to explain their experiences of controlling behaviours. Yet these experiences were also often explained as evidence of their abusive partners' love for them. These accounts constitute another example of abusive partners' expressions of need and neediness in expecting victims/survivors' loyalty and conformity to the relationship rules.

Occasionally, when victims/survivors described how they had perceived the need and/or neediness of their abusive partners this would result in them excusing abusive relationship practices and isolating them as incidents that were separate from the loving relationship they believed existed (Lloyd and Emery, 2000). Hazel's first relationship at 15 years of age was with a heterosexual man who was four years older than her. She attempted to explain it:

> 'Yeah, I was 15 and he was 19. Em. Yeah, I was in Year 10 at school and I think we'd met at a gig or something...and I just was completely infatuated with him. I thought he was the best thing since sliced bread. He had a motorbike he was...cool. Em. And we were together for about five/six months... it was a very sort of young relationship, but that was just awful...he was just really violent, very manipulative. But I was so dependent on him and I was so infatuated with him, you know, "I love him, he loves me." You know, "He doesn't mean to hurt me. He's drunk, he's stoned, he's pilled up...he doesn't know what he's doing," kind of thing. Em. And it was an awful relationship because in the end, we got him sectioned because he was very mentally unstable. But I, you know, still took me five/six months to see how unstable he was.' (Hazel, a white lesbian aged 20–24 at interview, and 15 when she began her first relationship with a man which was abusive, and 20 when she began her first same sex relationship which was abusive)

Hazel isolated her abusive partner's violence by explaining it as fuelled by substance abuse. She believed that mutual feelings of love existed and that she was dependent on him. However, she also felt enormous guilt because she felt that she had not cared enough to prevent his being sectioned:

> 'I was obviously very, very upset about what was happening with him and how poorly he was and I felt guilty that I'd not noticed it earlier, that um, I'd not done anything to stop it, if I'd spoken to somebody about it before, would he have got this bad?' (Hazel)

Even at 15 years of age Hazel had carried guilt and upset because she believed she had not realised his level of need – and dependency – and rescued her abusive partner before he had to be sectioned. This level of care and emotion work was not reciprocated by her 19 year old abusive partner, yet Hazel was convinced that they loved each other. The fact that her abusive partner said he loved her and the occasional times when she enjoyed his company was enough, even in the face of more frequent evidence of his violence and controlling relationship practices. At the time of the interview, almost seven years later, Hazel explained that she continued to feel guilty about how this relationship had ended, at the same time as feeling extremely anxious and fearful when she was visiting her parents in case she bumped into her abusive ex-partner in the village.

Throughout the accounts victims/survivors gave about why their partners were abusive they talked about their sense of responsibility to stay and look after the abusive partner. Women, especially, talked about trying to 'fix' the relationship. Ella, a black lesbian, summed this feeling up:

> INTERVIEWER: 'So you were really sure, then, when I said, "Did you love her?" and you said, "No," straight away.'
> ELLA: 'Mm.'
> INTERVIEWER: 'Did you feel care or affection?'
> ELLA: 'Affection yeah. Care, yes. Obligation, yes. And that very female thing [laughs] about thinking you can fix somebody. Or rescue someone.' (Ella, aged 40–44 at interview, and 26–28 when she began her abusive relationship)

This may reflect gendered constructions of femininity which not only expects women to be more literate emotionally than men, but also builds the expectation in women that achieving emotional literacy and making emotional connections with others, (especially romantically with a man), is the route to self-fulfilment. It was also the case, however, that gay male victims/survivors provided care for their abusive partners and took responsibility for the relationship. Bruce described his three-year first same sex relationship as extremely violent from the start, yet in this excerpt from his account, the fact that he showed his abusive partner affection is identified as the reason his abusive partner wanted to be in the relationship:

> 'Malcolm would do whatever, he would do whatever he wanted to do and, erm, all I wanted to do was be with him all the time and be lovely, and he didn't…he just wanted to do what he wanted to do…I honestly don't know why he wanted me around sometimes. I can't remember, I can't imagine why…there's probably two reasons, one I was very, very bonny in those days and the second was that I was also very frank and open in my kind of affection and adoration for him. And on one level he really liked that, because I don't think he got a lot of that from other people. I think other people, particularly his family, hadn't given him a lot of that and I think that…other men who were interested, were interested for different reasons, shall we say. But I was just like oh, puts [*sic*] arms round him and could spend hours looking at him and just being with him and I think he really liked that but…it wasn't enough or it wasn't quite right, or whatever.' (Bruce, a white gay man aged 30–34, and 19 when he began his first same sex relationship which was abusive)

Again, Bruce is quite clear that his abusive partner set the terms for the relationship and did whatever he wanted to do, yet Bruce also perceived that his abusive partner was needy of the affection Bruce gave him which elicited sympathy in Bruce. Regardless of the regular violence that Bruce endured, his feelings of love for his abusive partner were enough to keep the relationship going over a three-year period.

Expressions and perceptions of need and neediness can result in victims/survivors understanding that it is their responsibility to protect and take care of domestically violent and abusive partners. Information revealed constructs abusive partners as 'victims' of circumstance, can result in victims/survivors having a sense of loyalty towards the abusive partner, a willingness to protect the perceived vulnerability of the perpetrator and a sense of themselves as the partner responsible for taking care of the abusive partner and the relationship.

Emotional strength in victims/survivors

The dependency of abusive partners has been identified elsewhere as a key aspect of DVA across sexuality (for example, Renzetti, 1992; Bornstein et al, 2006) yet how it is interpreted by victims/survivors has implications that have tended not to be considered fully because of the dominance of the psychological approach that pathologises dependency in abusive partners. In our research it became clear that for many victims/survivors we interviewed, regardless of sexuality or gender, the perceived neediness and needs of their abusive partner challenged any perception of them as the only, or always, more powerful partner in the relationship. Expressions of need or neediness from abusive partners elicited a sense of emotional strength in victims/survivors which could act as a barrier to recognising the DVA they were experiencing. The public story with its focus on physical violence and the imagery of the 'stronger' man enacting physical violence over the 'weaker' woman precludes any understanding of the abusive partner as in need of protection and care. This binary of strength/weakness in the public story also challenges their self-perception as being stronger, at least emotionally, than the abusive partner. Finally, accounts suggest that abusive partners are able to contrive a smokescreen for their controlling behaviours through their utilisation of relationship practices, expressions of need/iness and expectations of care, all of which are traditionally associated with femininity, to construct a subjugated self. On the other hand, victims/survivors, regardless of gender or sexuality often positioned themselves as the responsible partner. Their enactment of relationship practices of care and concern, also associated with femininity and therefore relative passivity, were yet re-constituted in their accounts as agential (associated with masculinity) providing many of them with an emotionally stronger sense of self than they attributed to their abusive partners.

Some victims/survivors also expected that all adult relationships would be based on one partner being the stronger one who took care of the other in ways that included emotionally, but might also include practically and financially. Because they were the ones taking care of their abusive partner, this left them with a self-perception not only of strength but with a sense of responsibility towards both the relationship and the other partner. Barbara was 19 years old and gave an account of a DVA same sex relationship that had ended in the previous month before the interview. She described her understanding of what is to be expected in an intimate relationship:

> 'I think with all relationships, somebody, one person, looks after the other person, I'd – there's always, like, one person who gets looked after and one person who does the looking after, and I think I was that person. I think I, like, totally looked after her cos she was so vulnerable and, like, unstable, I was just, I had to sort of keep her on track all the time. No matter what was going on with me I had to, sort of, be, like, the strong one for her. Keep her on track all the time.' (Barbara, a white lesbian, aged 18 years when she began her abusive relationship)

Barbara's belief that relationships are based on a dynamic organised around a binary of strength/neediness enabled her to construct herself as the stronger person in the relationship which imbued in her a sense of responsibility to take care of her abusive partner. She went on to explain:

> 'I would just look at her and like, know she would have nobody else to, sort of, guide her, if I wasn't doing it, so it was, make us feel less bad about it, cos I knew I was doing something good for her. But...that I didn't get the same put into me. Like everything was, always had to be about her.' (Barbara)

The women we interviewed were more likely to resist the idea that they had been victims of DVA when they positioned themselves as the emotionally stronger person in the relationship (see Donovan and Hester, 2010). For example, some women in heterosexual relationships referred to their abusive partner, as Audrey did, as a little boy or a child. Such a construction of their abusive partner in these terms reflects their construction of self as being more emotionally mature, stronger than their partner and this reinforced their sense of responsibility and obligation to look after the abusive partner.

Amy was one of the lesbian victims/survivors who explicitly insisted that her experience had not left her feeling like a victim because she felt that she had been stronger, emotionally, than her abusive partner. Such is the power of the practices of love that abusive partners are positioned as needy: in need of protection, of loyalty and of care. Regardless of the experiences of abuse that are experienced, because they are experienced alongside relationship practices that are, in Amy's words, 'nice' they can be accommodated as part of the relationship. Amy's story is of particular interest because she had professional knowledge and experience of DVA, as did her partner, and this, Amy felt, had skilled Amy up so that she was able to resist becoming a victim/survivor of DVA:

> AMY: 'I think the place where she'd be most vicious would be in a, in a verbal assault, really, and especially, as I say, when they'd just come completely out of the blue. Um, and she'd say such things to me as, you know, about who I was going out with, who my friends were, um, about what sort of job I should do, the amount of time I spent with family or not, um. Everything, really.'
>
> INTERVIEWER: 'And did that have an impact on you? Did it make you stop seeing people as often?'
>
> AMY: 'No, it had the reverse effect, because I thought, you know, I'm, I'm very familiar with DVA and all the issues of power and control and the wheels and the models and all that sort of thing and I thought, "No, no, no, no. Not going there. Not doing it." And equally she should've known a lot better because of the sort of work that she did.' (Amy)

Yet we have discussed earlier in this chapter that when Amy's abusive partner revealed the reasons for her abusive behaviour Amy felt responsible to stay and support her in her commitment to change.

Remaining in an abusive relationship as a result of feeling responsible for the abusive partner, provides a way of understanding how victims/ survivors enact their love in their abusive relationships. In so doing they conform to the second relationship rule and challenge the public story of DVA that constructs a particular view of victims as only and always weak, passive and subjugated. Others have also challenged this depiction with evidence of the myriad ways heterosexual women resist the controlling behaviours of their abusive partners and seek help to do so (see Chapters One and Seven). In their study of the help-seeking behaviours of heterosexual male perpetrators of DVA, Hester and colleagues recommended that service providers should be wary of what they called the 'poor me' presentation of perpetrators (Hester et al, 2006). This positioning by many abusive partners and victims/

survivors of the abusive partners as needy simultaneously positions victims/survivors as responsible for their care and support. Together these contradict the construction of the public story of DVA which hangs the perpetrator/victim binary on gendered norms of male strength and female weakness and does not reflect the lived experiences of many of the victims/survivors in this study. Another consequence of how abusive partners embed relationship rules is that victims/survivors often do not recognise and/or name their experiences as DVA. This has serious implications for help-seeking which is explored in the next chapter.

Summary

- Findings from this research suggest that domestically violent and abusive relationships across gender and sexuality operate to establish two relationship rules:
  - the relationship is for the abusive partner and on their terms;
  - the victim/survivor is responsible for the care of the abusive partner, the relationship, their children, if they have them, and the household, if they cohabit.

- These relationship rules can be seen to reflect dominant ideas about how heterosexual relationships should be enacted and have been associated with gender norms such that masculinity is associated with being entitled to set the terms for adult intimacy, and femininity is associated with being responsible for providing care and nurture for the other partner and the relationship. The degree and detail of how these broad norms of gendered behaviour might be expected or enacted will also be shaped by the social positioning of individuals and their intersecting identities of 'race' and ethnicity, social class, age and generation and of being disabled.

- The first relationship rule can be seen to be established by two key relationship practices embedded in practices of love:
  - the abusive partner, regardless of gender or sexuality makes key decisions in the relationship. This includes decisions to apparently reject making any decisions or taking any responsibility for the relationship;
  - the abusive partner, regardless of gender or sexuality, expresses needs and/or neediness by revealing reasons for their abusive behaviours that elicit an obligation of care and concern in victims/survivors.

- In enacting these abusive relationship practices, abusive partners inhabit behaviours associated with masculinity (making key decisions) and femininity (expressing need and neediness). This can result in confusion about what is being experienced and can prevent recognition of DVA.

- The second relationship rule can be seen to be established by two further relationship rules also embedded in practices of love:
  - victims/survivors are expected to provide care and emotion work;
  - the self-perception of many victims/survivors that results from the care and emotion work expected of them is that they are responsible for the abusive partner and thus emotionally stronger than them.

- In enacting these practices of love victims/survivors inhabit roles and behaviours associated with femininity (providing care and nurture) and masculinity (being responsible for the abusive partner and the relationship and feeling emotionally stronger than the abusive partner). This confuses victims/survivors about their relationship experiences, making recognition of DVA more difficult.

- These relationship practices and practices of love that sustain the relationship rules act to challenge the public story of DVA which hangs on binaries of gender as embodied in women and men and strength/weakness, and thus make recognition of DVA difficult. Expressions of need and neediness from abusive partners challenges the perception of them as 'strong' as constructed in the public story while the sense of responsibility elicited in victims/survivors challenges the public story's construction of victims of DVA as 'weak' and/or 'passive'.

- The public story needs to be challenged so that the simplistic way it depicts the gendered nature of DVA can be replaced with the more realistic way gendered behaviours are experienced in DVA relationships.

- Public stories about love also need to be challenged to problematise both jealousy and normalising tendencies about violent and abusive behaviours, that tolerate, accommodate, accept and/or isolate them as exceptional.

SIX

Barriers to help-seeking:
the gap of trust

In this chapter we discuss the barriers to help-seeking experienced by those we interviewed who were in abusive same sex relationships and explore differences and similarities that exist across sexuality and gender with regard to help-seeking. In doing so, we build on the work done in North America and Australia on the help-seeking process by victims/survivors of DVA to achieve two main aims. The first is to draw attention to the particular ways that living in a heterosexist and homophobic society (see Chapter Three) results in specific barriers to help-seeking for those in same sex relationships. These barriers act at societal, institutional, communal and individual levels and are interconnected, mutually constituting and reconstituting in a dynamic, interactive process. These barriers result in what we deem 'a gap of trust' between those experiencing DVA in same sex relationships and those from whom they seek help. The second aim of the chapter is to show how practices of love (see Chapter Five) provides additional factors that should be considered in making sense of victims/survivors' help-seeking across sexuality and gender. These include the ways in which relationship rules can impede help-seeking processes in crucial ways; how practices of love are often reinforced by those turned to as informal sources of help; and to underline the importance of socio-cultural constraints on help-seeking at institutional levels. The chapter is divided into four sections. In the first we discuss possible models of help-seeking; and the next three are arranged in line with the three-staged, interactive process involved with help-seeking outlined by Liang et al (2005): recognising the problem, deciding to seek help and selecting a source of help.

Help-seeking models and help-seeking

In their review of the literature on the help-seeking behaviours of heterosexual women, Liang et al (2005), argue that help-seeking models generally include three stages: problem recognition, making the decision to seek help and selection of help provider. While these three stages suggest a linear process through which a survivor might journey, the authors argue that the process is interactive so that the survivor might instead revisit the stages a number of times. At each stage other factors are also present that may influence whether and when help seeking is undertaken and from whom help is sought and these are characterised as individual, interpersonal and socio-cultural. The authors argue that social positioning in terms of social class, gender, 'race', ethnicity and culture, faith, language, immigrant status will all shape beliefs and ideas about privacy, loyalty, entitlement, gender norms, divorce and/or separation and influence how the behaviours are understood, problematised, or not, and whether and which kinds of help might be elicited. Thus survivors' socio-cultural positioning, their beliefs about relationships, and the ways these construct their perception of what and why DVA has occurred and whose responsibility it is as well as what sources of support exist and how they are perceived as reliable, sympathetic and safe for survivors all have an impact on whether or not a survivor might seek help.

Hardesty et al (2011; and also Hardesty et al, 2008) in their study of the help-seeking processes of lesbian mothers point to the ways that the individual, interpersonal and socio-cultural factors can also be understood in sexuality-specific ways. At the individual and interpersonal levels they discuss how the degree to which lesbian mothers are confident and open about their sexuality can be crucial in eliciting informal support and formal help, but that this may or may not include being out about the DVA they are experiencing. Thus they identify two groups of help-seekers, one which was open about their sexuality and their identity as lesbian mothers and their experiences of DVA and the other who were open about their sexuality (and thus their identity as lesbian mothers) but not the DVA. A third group they identified were neither open about their sexuality nor the DVA and were self-reliant in terms of how they dealt with the DVA. Because of their tendency not to be out about their sexuality this group were less likely to live with their abusive partner or to have any shared parenting and were thus also less financially dependent on abusive partners. The authors believe that this financial factor might have been especially beneficial and made self-reliance more of a 'viable option' (Hardesty et al, 2011, 39).

The third set of factors, the socio-cultural, were also of crucial importance for the lesbian mothers Hardesty et al (2011) interviewed. In particular, legal factors were found to be important: with regard to the local state laws on DVA and whether or not they applied to same sex relationships, and the laws on child custody for children of lesbians (see also Duffy, 2011 for the Australian context). Thus, as with other work (for example, Ristock, 2002a; Irwin, 2008; Hester et al, 2012), these authors point to the ways in which help-seeking for DVA in same sex relationships must be understood through intersectional lenses. The social-structural positioning of lesbians and of lesbian mothers were of crucial importance in shaping the extent to which victims/ survivors were able to, or believed they were able to, seek help, and these issues have also been found to be valid for gay men (Hester et al, 2012). Others (for example, Kanuha, 1990; Turell and Herrmann, 2008; Holmes, 2011) have also pointed to the ways in which 'race' intersects with sexuality and DVA to provide what Kanuha calls a 'triple jeopardy' of barriers to help-seeking. Hester et al (2012) indicate that such barriers can be even more intense where both help-seeker and agency staff are from the same or possibly different minority ethnic groups.

The insights of Hardesty et al (2011; see also Oswald et al, 2010) are extremely useful in bringing to the forefront the ways in which there are problems involved with separating out factors that have an impact on help-seeking. The focus on the individual might help them make sense of their own circumstances and recourse to help or change in their abusive relationship, yet it is also important that the individual is co-currently understood as a product of the society in which they live. Thus being out is not always or only just an individual's choice but is shaped and influenced by the local and wider socio-cultural context in which they live, including the social relationships they have established with their friendship, family and wider community networks. The distinction they make between the lesbian mothers in their study being open about their sexuality and being out about the DVA they were experiencing is also crucial to understanding how and in what ways help-seeking processes might be edited or partial in order to protect selves, abusive partners, children, families and communities from actual or perceived negative consequences.

In their work, St Pierre and Senn (2010) adopt the Barriers Model developed by Grigsby and Hartmann (in St Pierre and Senn, 2010). This is a four staged model arranged in concentric circles leading out from the most personal and individual (including prior experience of childhood abuse) through the psychological barriers that result from the abuse, through barriers resulting from family and socialisation to the outermost concentric circle which are the barriers in the environment. Grigsby and Hartmann have argued that it is the social and contextual factors that are of more importance in preventing help-seeking rather than individual-level determinants (in St Pierre and Senn, 2010). In their work, St Pierre and Senn found that outness was the only predictor of lesbians' help-seeking from formal sources.

We would argue that this further underlies the importance of the socio-cultural factors that can act as a barrier to help seeking for those in same sex relationships. The individual decision can again be interpreted as one that is embedded in the relationships, networks and communities with which individuals are involved and the extent to which they can trust help-providers to respond appropriately to their request for help. Placing the individual at the centre of their own story is of the utmost importance in order to identify what help and support might be the most appropriate. It is our argument, however, that in doing so the individual's circumstances and how they interpret them should also be understood as in large part the result of the wider socio-cultural context in which they live.

A common response to DVA both among the general public and across service providers is to ask why the victim/survivor does not leave the relationship. A corollary of this approach can also be the conception that providing help is futile since victims/survivors inevitably return to the abusive relationship. Yet the evidence is unequivocal that heterosexual female survivors not only seek help but continue to do so throughout their experiences of DVA (for example, Goodkind et al, 2003; Fugate et al, 2005; Hester et al, 2007). In their work which distinguished between those heterosexual women who had experienced situational couple violence and those who had experienced intimate terrorism, Leone et al (2007) found that the former were more likely to seek help from informal agencies while the latter sought help from formal agencies. The authors argue that this reflects the relative seriousness of experiences of those women. It was also the case in our study that the majority of survey participants had sought help and talked to somebody about their experiences (Donovan et al, 2006). Where they differ from their heterosexual counterparts is in their sources of help, and below we will explore these differences and discuss the implications of these differences for the provision of services for those in same sex relationships.

Recognising the problem

As others have argued, recognising and naming relationship experiences as DVA is not an easy process regardless of sexuality or gender. Here we argue that there are three interconnecting factors that have an impact on recognition: the public story about DVA, practices of love and self-reliance.

The public story of DVA

Others have discussed the ways in which heteronormative constructions of DVA impede recognition of DVA in lesbian and gay relationships by those involved in them, by LGBTQ communities (for example, Ristock, 2002a; Turell and Herrmann, 2008) and by service providers (for example, Island and Letellier, 1991; Renzetti, 1992; Ristock, 2002b; Helfrich and Simpson, 2006; Irwin, 2008; Walters, 2011). Here we focus on what we have called the public story to unpack the specific ways that this can be experienced by victims/survivors.

When and if a survivor decides to seek help, the form the help takes will be influenced by their understanding of what is happening to them. We have argued that a core difference that shapes the experiences of DVA in same sex as opposed to heterosexual relationships is not in the experiences of violence and abuse so much as in the relationship and societal contexts in which the violence and abuse takes place. As we have already indicated in Chapter Four in relation to identification and definition of DVA, the public story of DVA can delay recognition in same sex relationships because it construes the problem as one of heterosexual men for heterosexual women, as one of primarily physical violence and as one in which gender norms influence the understanding of what a victim/survivor and perpetrator looks like and how they might each behave. In the following excerpt, Audrey, a white lesbian, explains the difference between what she recognised as DVA in a previous heterosexual relationship (where there is a public story) and the difficulty of recognising DVA when it is in the context of the intersection between sexuality and a first same sex relationship (for which there is no public story):

> 'I just knew that if that had been a man – because my worst relationship was with a violent man and a man who was very psychologically abusing and I didn't stay there very long at all – I would not have put up with three years of that actually. I would not. So why was it any different? Because this was a relationship with a woman and it was my first one and I think that's the very reason why. I think I invested a lot more and I think I was also [pause] um, god! Because I was so disappointed in myself that I still couldn't even make a [starting to choke up with tears in her eyes] relationship with a woman work.' (Audrey, aged 55–60 at interview, 35/36 years old when she met her abusive

male partner and 53 when she began her first same sex relationship which was abusive)

The expectations some women have that relationships with other women might be free of abuse can also be a factor in not naming or taking longer to name experiences as DVA (see also Barnes, 2010; Walters, 2011).

For other interviewees who had experienced DVA in same sex relationships the public story constructing DVA primarily as a problem of physical violence acted to exclude recognition if a relationship was characterised by emotional, financial and emotionally coercive sexually abusive behaviours rather than physical violence. In the accounts given by those experiencing DVA in female same sex relationships this was typically the case. However, this was also evident in the accounts of some gay men, for example, Ted, a white gay man (see Chapter Four), had not realised his first same sex relationship had been abusive 'because it wasn't physical' until afterwards when he got involved with the local domestic violence forum.

As we have already argued, understanding DVA as coercive control in which physical violence may only be an occasional experience is crucial not only to facilitating recognition of DVA but also to understanding help-seeking and the provision of appropriate services. Prioritising physical violence in the public story makes it much harder to identify DVA. In addition, because emotional violence is often more difficult to identify as such, it can, as we argued in Chapter Five, enable relationship rules to be laid down incrementally such that it is often not until towards the end of the relationship or even after the relationship has ended that it is recognised for having been characterised by DVA; and this will apply to heterosexual relationships as well. In both our survey and interviews, women in same sex relationships typically experienced emotional abuse most persistently.

Another reason for why those in same sex relationships did not seek more formal sources of help, even when physical violence had been experienced, was because they did not feel that they would elicit a sympathetic response. The accounts of some women in same sex relationships whom we interviewed illustrates how the public story of DVA with its emphasis on a particular embodied gendered enactment of violence, that is, the bigger, stronger [man] partner being physically violent to the smaller, weaker [woman] partner, made them very distrustful that they would get an appropriate response. For example, Sarah, a white lesbian, was 22 when she met her abusive partner at a youth group. The relationship ended when Sarah started talking to another woman and they both realised that they were seeing the same abusive partner. Together they confronted the abusive partner and ended both relationships. As we have indicated in Chapter Five, a fortnight after she ended the relationship Sarah was abducted by her abusive ex-partner, physically assaulted and then dumped a long way from home without any money. When she was asked whether she had experienced domestic violence she first of all agreed that "Yeah, I'd probably stick it in as mild domestic violence." She then reflected on the abduction and called it a 'serious incident'. However, she did not report this incident to the police, partly because she feared making things worse, but also because she was concerned that her experience did not fit the public story of DVA and because she herself was physically bigger than her abusive partner:

> '[Y]eah, I'd put that in as a serious incident. But even then I didn't report it. You know, at the end of the day [laughing] I was sort of four or five inches taller than her. She was a tiny wee thing, and I thought people are never going to believe me. They're just gonna go, "Oh, look, she couldn't beat you up!"' (Sarah, a white lesbian, aged 30–34 years old at interview, and 25/26 when she began her first same sex relationship which was abusive)

Another white lesbian we interviewed, Cilla, also talked about not reporting her experiences because she did not think that she would be believed, again for the reason that she was bigger than her abuser:

> 'No, I wouldn't have thought of that. She was, she was smaller than I was [laughs] that's all I can tell you. She was, she was [indicating with her hand] down here somewhere.' (Cilla, aged 60–64 at interview, and 52/53 when she began an abusive same sex relationship)

Cilla's response suggests that not fitting the public story of DVA was a major reason why she did not even think about reporting her experiences of DVA. These accounts illustrate how the fears victims/ survivors in same sex relationships have about not being taken seriously is a factor preventing them from asking for help. Such a gap of trust, particularly with the police, had quite serious consequences for them. The laughter of these respondents seems to underline their sense of the ridiculous at the idea of reporting their experiences to the police.

Ted also explained that he would not have thought about reporting to the police. His experience was primarily emotional DVA but towards the end it also included a physical assault by his partner with a bottle. His account underscores the compelling nature of the public story about DVA that inhibits action in seeking formal help:

> INTERVIEWER: 'Did you consider phoning the police?'
> TED: 'You didn't then, it wasn't a thing you done…then, years
> ago it was two poufs having an argument. You know they
> just don't wanna know basically. I mean it's only recently
> the police are sort of getting their act together.' (Ted, a
> white gay man aged 55–59 at interview, and 28 when
> his first same sex relationship began which was abusive)

The public story about DVA is therefore an extremely powerful set of ideas and beliefs about what constitutes authentic DVA, an authentic victim/survivor, and an authentic perpetrator that has a material impact on how victims/survivors in same sex relationships are able to name their experiences as DVA and feel legitimised in seeking help.

Practices of love

Another set of factors shaping the help-seeking process is the impact of practices of love on how victims/survivors make sense of what is happening in their relationship and how they might address it. In Chapter Five we argued that relationship rules can become embedded in relationships across sexuality and gender that position one partner in a position of power and control over the other. A range of abusive behaviours can be used by abusive partners to assert the relationship rules and are often tailored by abusive partners' intimate knowledge about the vulnerabilities of their partner. These abusive behaviours introduce and/or remind victims/survivors about the relationship rules and/or punish them for their non-adherence to them. We also argued that this pattern of behaviours can be difficult to make sense of and/ or name as DVA when practices of love position the abusive partner as needy and the victim/survivor as responsible for the care of the abusive partner and the relationship. The impact of these practices on help-seeking is evidenced in many of the accounts of those we interviewed when they refer to wanting to protect and stay loyal to their abusive partner, the love their abusive partner had for them or that they felt for their abusive partner, and their self-blame for the abuse they were experiencing.

For example, Hazel, a white lesbian, had experienced DVA in both her first heterosexual relationship and in her first same sex relationship (in that order) yet she made no connections between the two experiences (see also Audrey in Chapters Four and Five). She had realised that something in her heterosexual relationship was wrong, but her abusive partner encouraged her to normalise his abuse as part of what love in heterosexual relationships meant:

> 'I just [pause] I just told myself to ignore it and that whatever he was doing he didn't mean because he told me he loved me and it was to do with the drugs or it was to do with the alcohol or…Yeah, that's how he would explain it, em. I believed it you know. I didn't have a clue about anything like this, I was so naïve, em, at that point and I just took it as that's what happens, you know – it was always, like, explained the way you see it happening on the TV, you know, people knock each other around and stay together because they love each other…even though that's not the…the role models I've been given, because it happens on TV it wasn't actually that abnormal and therefore it was ok, you know.' (Hazel, aged 20–24 at interview, 15 in her first relationship with a man which was abusive; and approximately 18 years old when she started her first same sex relationship which was also abusive)

While she knew that this relationship was problematic her route to help-seeking was to go to her GP, who she shared with her abusive partner. It may have been the fact that a public incident of physical violence was witnessed by the police and ignored by them, that led her to turn to her GP, but her account suggests that she had begun to feel responsible for her abusive partner and wanted to get help for him because she loved him. As we discussed in Chapter Five, even after the relationship Hazel had feelings of guilt that she had not done something sooner that might have prevented him from being sectioned as he was eventually. Hazel was eventually able to recognise her former male partner's behaviour as DVA, because it fitted the public story. Yet she had not thought her first same sex relationship was abusive at all, even though her female partner also used physical violence against her. On the contrary she had been flattered by the behaviour of her female partner:

'I think I put a very rosy view on it at the time. You know, people said to me "Why are you putting up with it?" "Oh, because she trusts me enough to come to me when she needs me," and that was what I – I think I must have convinced myself that that's what was happening rather than seeing now [that] she needed a bolt hole and I was very convenient in that I would let her in and, you know, look after her, kind of thing…[N]o I didn't really talk about it with anybody. Simply because again at the time I didn't, I didn't see it as anything other than she was really angry and, you know, she didn't mean to take it out on me…I don't know. I was very reluctant to admit to anybody that…it wasn't what I'd got in my head it was, do you know what I mean?' (Hazel)

Again, Hazel believed that she, Hazel, must be special if the partner felt able to come to her whenever she wished, even though this was often in the middle of the night when she was extremely angry and she became physically violent towards Hazel. Hazel, in common with other survivors, did not see the impact on herself as the defining feature of the relationship. Instead the needs of her abusive partner were more important, and she felt strong enough to address these, regardless of the costs to herself. In Hazel's account of her first same sex relationship there is evidence of the ways in which practices of love can result in a victim/survivor feeling that it is their responsibility to care for and look after an abusive partner, to protect them against other people's negative opinions, to explain away her partner's violence as the result of her need/neediness and to feel positively because Hazel herself felt needed by her abusive partner.

There is evidence that heterosexual women often do not recognise their experiences as DVA because they have come to understand them as normal for heterosexual relationships and the behaviours of their abusive partner as a normal heterosexual enactment of masculinity (for example, Wood, 2001). It is also the case that many victims/survivors of DVA, regardless of gender and sexuality, come to understand that they are, if not to blame, then in other ways deserving of, or responsible for, the violence and abuse they experience. This, we argue is another outcome of the practices of love that exist in abusive relationships that prevents victims/survivors from naming their experience as DVA. The account of Marcus, a white gay man we interviewed, illustrates these kinds of beliefs:

INTERVIEWER: 'So you would say that you've experienced
   domestic abuse?'
MARCUS: [pause] 'Yes. Yes.'
INTERVIEWER: 'Would you have said that at the time [two
   years previously]?'
MARCUS: 'No. And I'm still trying to struggle with that. And
   it's almost like there was a question for me thinking, I'd
   like to ask [the interviewer], "Do you think I've been in
   a domestic abuse [situation]?" – Do you know what I
   mean? Because, you know, I keep thinking – was I? Did
   I deserve it, you know, this is what, is all in my head, you
   know?' (Marcus, aged 35–39 at interview, and 35 when
   he began his abusive same sex relationship)

While the account of Marcus suggests that self-blame can be felt
across gender and sexuality by victims/survivors of DVA, in our study,
self-blame was more typical in the accounts of women regardless of
sexuality. Ada, for example, explained that it had taken a long time after
the end of her abusive relationship to realise that she had not been to
blame for what she had experienced:

> 'I've now come to realise and accept that it wasn't, it wasn't
> my problem and it wasn't my fault, and therefore, she's of
> an age where she's got to take responsibility for herself,
> and, and I can't, I can't do that.' (Ada, a white lesbian aged
> 45–49 at interview, and 33 when she began her abusive first
> same sex relationship)

Maxine, a white bisexual woman, blamed herself for remaining in an
abusive relationship, because she had been addicted to drugs and her
abusive partner at the time was a drug dealer. While she also explained
that her abusive ex-partner had 'got me hooked on drugs', she felt that
her addiction had been to blame for her remaining and returning to
the abusive relationship (Maxine said that she had left and returned to
him about ten times over an eighteen-month period):

MAXINE: 'I was in love with drugs; I was never in love with
   him. I didn't even fancy him.'
INTERVIEWER: 'Is this your analysis now or at the time…?'
MAXINE: 'At the time I knew exactly what was going on…
   Even at the time, yeah, but the drugs took over, yep.'
INTERVIEWER: 'Do you think, did he love you?'

MAXINE: 'Yeah…I mean I tried to get away from him a lot of times and he always tried, he, he would follow me, he would go to my house, my work. wherever he could get me. so I think it was more the idea of being in love. I don't think he really was in love with me. He took me to see his parents. it was all, you know, he took me to see his mum at Christmas. so I'ms not really sure. It's difficult to answer. He'd probably say – he'd probably say "Yeah."'
(Maxine, aged 30–34 at interview, and 24/25 when she began her abusive relationship)

In Maxine's account, her addiction and his practices of love combined to keep her in the abusive relationship.

In Chapter Five we explained how love and neediness expressed by perpetrators and care and responsibility expressed by victims/survivors often acted together to keep victims/survivors from recognising and naming their experience as DVA and from talking to and/or seeking help from others. Wanting to protect their abusive partner was also a barrier to help-seeking. Theresa, a white heterosexual woman, explains why she did not speak to her family about what she was experiencing:

'I would think, "Well, what's the point in telling them anything," because…they didn't like him and he didn't like them, it was like I was piggy in the middle. …So it was, like, quite difficult to like actually come out with, "Oh well, actually I'm living in a violent relationship."…Cos it was all the thing around your own feelings and what they would think and, like, I suppose part protecting him cos he didn't know any better, and, part, em, not wanting them to view you in a different light, it's, y'know, it's that stuff really.'
(Theresa, aged 40–44 at interview, and 16 when she began her first relationship which was abusive)

Theresa felt that it was her responsibility to protect and explain her abusive husband's behaviour because she felt sorry for him, and believed that he loved her. In Chapter Four we discussed the account of Kenneth, a white gay man whose practices of love resulted in him minimising or being 'in denial' about the abuse because he 'wanted that relationship, whatever'.

Another way in which practices of love are implicated in the help-seeking of victims/survivors of DVA across sexuality and gender are found in accounts of participants whose family (more often in accounts of heterosexual women) and friends reinforce and/or normalise the behaviours of an abusive partner as to be expected in a love relationship and/or reinforce the importance of staying in marriages and/or relationships. We return to this later in the chapter when we consider the unhelpful responses from the sources which victims/survivors of DVA turned to for support.

Self-reliance

Cindy Holmes has been involved in a Canadian project to provide programmes for building healthy relationships among lesbian, bisexual, queer and two-spirited communities. As a result of her analysis of the project, she has written of her concern that queer and/or feminist anti-violence movements are inadvertently colluding with neo-liberal state discourses to produce the idea of the responsible citizen acting rationally to self-help and protect the self against potential harm and risks in everyday personal lives (Holmes, 2011). The neo-liberal state has been variously defined as one in which government occurs at a distance (Rose, 2000), where the role of the state as interventionist or the 'nanny state' has been criticised for creating dependency and instead personal responsibility is emphasised as the route to staying safe, drawing on self-help, expert knowledge and expert assistance (Holmes, 2011). Garland (1996) has similarly argued that this trend can be seen in relation to how the state has been engaged in a re-formulation of its approach to deviance. He argues that the state is gradually abnegating responsibility for its citizenship: rather than retaining goals of rehabilitation and/or the elimination of deviant behaviours there has been a move to an acceptance of deviance and the need to manage and/or accommodate its risk within society. Thus, Garland (1996) argues, the state continues its commitment to increasingly severe penalties for the most serious offenders (what he calls the criminology of the other), but expects 'ordinary' citizens to be responsible for their own financial and personal security (the criminology of the self).

While others have agreed with the general thrust of Garland's argument, authors such as Moran et al (2003) have pointed out how for some groups in society – women, the most marginalised socio-economically, black and other minority ethnic groups and LGBTQ communities – this is business as usual and predates the emergence of neoliberal discourses. Women as victims/survivors of violence have historically struggled to get the state to recognise their experience as a public problem rather than a private trouble (Wright-Mills, 1959). We would agree with this argument saying that, similarly, those from

LGBTQ communities have a long history of being criminalised and/or pathologised by the state (Donovan and Hester, 2010) and have developed self-reliance as a default position either as individuals or by acting collectively within LGBTQ communities. In Chapter Three we discussed some of the successes LGBTQ communities have had across the world of using a human rights argument to secure citizenship rights and rights attached to couple and familial relationships. In this study, however, we found evidence of the ways in which self-reliance is still extremely common when it comes to addressing DVA in same sex relationships.

We also argue that the self-reliance encouraged by neo-liberalism coincides with the self-reliance promulgated by practices of love that construct norms through everyday expectations and practices to be private about intimate relationships. We have shown above how this can operate when loyalty, feelings of love and/or a sense of care is felt in response to an abusive partner expressing need or neediness, but there is another level at which this operates. This is in the various ways the accounts of victims/survivors across sexuality and gender reflect the shame and embarrassment they felt at the thought of needing help for an intimate relationship or for having got themselves into a DVA relationship. As we have mentioned in Chapter Four, the latter was especially the case for respondents who had experience of working with DVA professionally. Maxine, a white bisexual woman, explains:

> INTERVIEWER: 'So, did you not want to tell your friends?'
> MAXINE: 'No, I was too embarrassed, yeah...No, no because of the work I'm in. It's very difficult, because I might know somebody at Women's Aid or woman's...I do actually know quite a few people who work for them, so I just couldn't do it.' (Maxine, aged 30–34 at interview, and 24/25 when she began her abusive relationship)

Maxine's embarrassment stemmed both from the fact that she felt that she was in some way to blame for the abusive relationship, because of her addiction to drugs, but also that she should have known better and, having made a bad decision, should deal with it alone. In Kay's account she also talks about not having reported her experiences to the police, because she had not believed it to be a police matter and because she felt that she should be able to handle the situation herself. Kay also talked about having not spoken to friends:

'It was difficult because the friends that I'd made, I'd split up with her so many times, that it was just getting to that stage where it was embarrassing to talk about it [laughs]. So no, I didn't really talk to anybody about it.' (Kay, a white lesbian, aged 35–39 at interview, and 32/33 when she began her first same sex relationship which was abusive)

Such self-reliance is a feature of many accounts of DVA in our study across sexuality and gender. We argue, however, that it is particularly the case in same sex relationships where the public story also acts to interfere with recognition and naming of their experience of DVA and thus the abusive experiences are further individualised and characterised as a bad relationship from which the victim/survivor is responsible for extricating themselves.

Several respondents put geographical distance between themselves and their abusive relationship in an attempt (not always successfully) to end it. Five of our respondents either moved abroad (a heterosexual and a bisexual woman) or moved cities (two heterosexual women, a lesbian and a gay man) to get away from the abuser. Several others attempted to manage the abusive relationship and change it for the better. We have shown in Chapter Five how often through practices of love victims/survivors, especially women, believed they could 'fix' their abusive partner and enable them to change. Others told of how they attempted to manage the abusive situation. Ella, a black lesbian, recalled how she was a 'fixer' and had responded with potential solutions to each demand of her white, abusive partner for proof of love and commitment, yet never seemed able to satisfy her. Her abusive partner had four children from previous relationships with men and Ella found the experience of living with this family extremely difficult, especially when their behaviour as a group threatened to undermine her identity as a black woman:

'We got a cleaner because I couldn't bear…I wouldn't, I couldn't, wouldn't, lower myself to, to clean up after people who are quite capable of doing it themselves. And that's when the race thing really became an issue, because these were white people, English people, and I was a black person, and there was no [outraged laughter] way on this earth I'm going to skivvy after some, particularly male, children who could do it themselves. It was just, that was something there was no way I was going to do. And also to see another woman skivvying like that, and being given one,

no appreciation, and two, no help, I thought was appalling.'
(Ella, a black lesbian, aged 40–44 at interview, and 26/27
when her abusive relationship began)

Self-reliance then is a strong theme that runs throughout many of the
accounts of DVA relationships. Nonetheless, it is also the case that most
respondents in this study did seek help. We now turn to consider the
ways in which sexuality and, to some extent gender, intersects to shape
the type of help that is sought.

The decision to seek help

In the main, those in same sex relationships tend to seek more informal
and/or privatised sources of help. The findings from our survey showed
that most (58 per cent) of our respondents spoke to a friend as their
first source of support. Counselling or therapy was the second most
popular source of support (33 per cent) and the first formal source.
More than one in ten approached their GP (14 per cent), an LGBT
organisation (14 per cent) and/or talked to somebody at work (12 per
cent). Only 9 per cent indicated that they had sought help from the
police and they came last in the list of potential sources of support
(a similar proportion was found in a more recent UK survey of 134
victims/survivors of DVA where just under 10 per cent surveyed said
that they had called the police (LGBT DAF and Stonewall Housing,
2013). We compared our survey findings about help-seeking with those
provided by the Crime Survey England and Wales (CSEW) for the
years 2001 and 2011–12 (Walby and Allen, 2004; Smith et al, 2012).
These two surveys were chosen because the original analysis of our
data was carried out following and in comparison to the 2001 survey,
but the more recent CSEW has some different questions that allow us
to discuss other similarities and differences in help-seeking patterns
across sexuality and gender. An important caveat to this discussion is
that while the CSEW surveys are conducted with random samples, our
survey used a convenience sample (see Chapter Two). This means that
any conclusions we make based on comparisons are only suggestive.
Another caveat is that we made our comparisons based on our
understanding that the CSEW represents an ostensibly heterosexual
population.

In the 2001 CSEW survey friends and family were grouped together
as a potential source for help. In our survey, in recognition that those
in same sex relationships might be estranged from their families of
origin and/or may not speak to them about problems with a same sex

relationship, these two potential sources of help were separated. When we combined the figures for these groups we found that, as with the 2001 CSEW, informal sources were the most popular (58 per cent in the 2001 CSEW and 83 per cent in our survey). We were aware, however, first, that our figures showed a much greater proportion of respondents using these informal sources and second, that our findings showing friends as a source of support were much higher than the combined figure for friends and family in the CSEW (58 per cent in our survey said they had spoken to friends while 58 per cent said that they had spoken to either family or friends in the CSEW). Comparing our results with those of the 2011–12 CSEW, in which friends and neighbours are distinguished from a relative, the importance of friendships for those in same sex relationships is made even clearer. The majority of respondents in the 2011–12 CSEW (73 per cent in total, 58 per cent of women and 43 per cent of men) said that they had spoken to family or relatives while only 41 per cent (41 per cent of women and 39 per cent of men) had spoken to friends or neighbours. Clearly, for heterosexual women and men, family is a first port of call for help in a way that they are not for the majority of those in same sex relationships (see also Irwin, 2006). Conversely, friends seem to be of much more importance for those in same sex relationships than they are for those in heterosexual relationships (for example, Ristock, 2002a; Irwin, 2006).

Another difference that can only be seen by looking at the more recent CSEW data is in the prioritising of privatised sources of help by those experiencing DVA in same sex relationships (see also Turell, 1999; Ristock, 2001; Irwin, 2008; St Pierre and Senn, 2010; Hester et al, 2012) as opposed to those in heterosexual relationships. In our survey we included counselling and therapy as a possible source of help and this was chosen as the second most popular source out of the list provided (33 per cent of all of those responding said that they had used counselling or therapy, 34 per cent of the women and 30 per cent of the men). The CSEW 2001 did not include counselling and therapy as a choice, but the 2011–12 CSEW did and this showed that 18 per cent (21 per cent of women and 14 per cent of men) had used this as a source of help, making it the third 'agency' form of help chosen. Thus our research suggests that those in same sex relationships are more likely than those in heterosexual relationships to seek privatised and individualised forms of help. There is also, however, a gender difference in the findings from the CSEW 2011–12, which is the opposite to that found in our survey findings. In the CSEW more men chose counselling/therapy as their first source of formal help while women were more likely to choose the police or health professionals, ahead of a counsellor/therapist. As indicated earlier, in our survey, 14 per cent of the respondents had sought help from their GP and only 9 per cent had sought help from the police. In both of the CSEW surveys the police emerge as the most often used source of formal help by women (24 per cent in 2001 and 29 per cent in 2011–12). The CSEW data reflects the severity of experience of DVA by heterosexual women, which is greater than that of heterosexual men's, and, consequently, heterosexual women's increased need for protection and/or healthcare as a result of the violence they have experienced. By contrast, in our survey, gay men were more likely to access the police (11 per cent) than lesbians (7 per cent) and the police were the least often identified source of support. This is also echoed in police data, for instance, Hester and Westmarland (2006) found that in a police sample of 692 DVA cases in the North East of England, only seven involved male same sex partners and two involved female same sex partners. Similarly in a more recent survey of 134 survivors of DVA, 10 per cent had reported to the police (LGBT DAF and Stonewall Housing, 2013).

Contacting GPs or medical services were only asked about in the 2001 CSEW if injury had been sustained. Here, the pattern of help-seeking was very different to our survey, with women in the 2001 CSEW most likely to contact GPs (30 per cent as opposed to 14 per cent of men). In the 2011–12 survey 19 per cent of women said that they had sought help from a health professional while only 4 per cent of men had, but since the question was asked of all respondents regardless of whether they had suffered an injury this difference in responses over time is explained. In our survey there was the opposite gender difference and men were much more likely than women to seek help from their GP (17 per cent of men in same sex relationships reported to their GP while 12 per cent of women in same sex relationships sought help from their GP). The greater proportion of gay men accessing their GP might be explained by their increased use of health services in general since the advent of HIV and AIDS (as we discuss in Chapter One).

Overall the findings from our survey analysed alongside those from the CSEW suggest that survivors of DVA in same sex relationships are seeking help but mainly from informal and privatised or individualised sources. Only a minority seek support from mainstream and/or specialist domestic violence services. In the following sections we now consider the responses received from these sources in turn.

Sources of help

Informal sources of help

In Chapter Two we discussed how, in our survey the majority of respondents to the question responded that DVA in heterosexual and same sex relationships was the same. A substantial minority, however, also described how differences that exist result from the socio-cultural context in which abusive same sex relationships exist: because the abuse is invisible (ignored, denied, minimised) and/or because help providers are not able and/or willing to provide appropriate responses. We argue there is a cumulative impact for victims/survivors in same sex relationships – including bi and trans – of living in a society based on the heterosexual assumption out of which has emerged the public story of DVA. These impacts are at the level of the individual, LGBTQ communities and institutionally (in law, policy and practice).

As we stated earlier in this chapter, the research on heterosexual women's help-seeking often assumes that any contact made for support will be helpful from the point of view of the survivor (see Fugate et al, 2005). Yet this is not always the case. Friends and family have their own reactions to the information which they are asked to take in that might result in responses that are far from helpful, including colluding with the abusive partner by minimising or denying the DVA or by blaming the survivor for their experiences (for example, see Hanmer, 2000; Goodkind et al, 2003; Fugate et al, 2005). They may also be fearful of the abusive partner themselves, which may influence their responses to the survivors' requests for help (Goodkind et al, 2003; Fugate et al, 2005). While some of our interviewees across sexuality who experienced DVA spoke about supportive or helpful interventions from friends and family, there were also accounts of family and friends not being helpful. This was often unintentional, but nevertheless the damage done to respondents tended to stay with them long after the abusive relationships ended. As a result, contact was lost with family or friends because they were not able to accept why the survivor remained in the abusive relationship, and/or survivors backed away from family and friends whom they felt were making the situation worse with their interventions.

It is useful to use Plummer's (1995) concept of telling sexual stories here to explore the responses of friends and family to survivors of DVA. Plummer argues that telling stories depends on there being an audience willing to hear them. Audiences might be made up of those who share similar experiences, or the friends and relatives of those who have had similar experiences, or of those who have been able to hear and accept the stories being told. Willing audiences come about as a combination of social, cultural and political changes that facilitate the redefinition of social problems. This includes being able to identify and critically analyse power relationships that allow a different take on entitlement to speak and the new and challenging voices to be heard. Pioneers who make a breakthrough, gain legitimacy and give authenticity to the newly constructed experience are also crucial in making spaces for those who will follow with their own stories. This process of priming willing audiences takes time and in the process there are often those who are unwilling or unable to listen and those who are wary of telling their stories.

In the accounts of our respondents who had sought informal support or help from friends and family, four stories emerged: of edited or partial narratives, rejection of abuse narratives, willing but unhelpful audience narratives, and willing and helpful audience narratives. Even though the public story of DVA foregrounds the heterosexual relationship as the site for abuse, it is also the case that many of those in heterosexual relationships and their families and friends are unable to recognise and/or hear DVA stories. This is often because their concerns lie more with maintaining the heterosexual relationship for what it represents and symbolises and a belief in practices of love that include ideas about being together 'for better and worse', staying loyal and beliefs in the idea of commitment for life, particularly in heterosexual marriages, than with the individual experiences of any particular heterosexual relationship. Hence telling abuse stories in many heterosexual family networks and communities can precipitate a process of denial and anger shown towards the victim/survivor for disrupting social norms and reneging on the loyalty expected to be shown to heterosexuality. For those experiencing DVA in same sex relationships the public story about DVA means that abuse stories are not necessarily told or heard as such, because they are not known or are not recognised by either the teller or the told. Nevertheless, concern may be shown by friends and, to a lesser extent, by family members that might or might not ultimately be helpful (see Irwin, 2006). We suggest that one of the influences here will also be practices of love held as strongly and applied to behaviours and expectations about same sex relationships as well as heterosexual relationships.

Edited or partial narratives

Our interviewees described how they 'edited' their narratives in at least two ways. First by those in same sex relationships who believed that their sexuality got in the way of friends being able to hear their relationship story. Another kind of edited narrative was that given by survivors across sexuality who felt protective of and/or loyal toward their abusive partner which we have discussed earlier in this chapter. With regard to the first, when interviewees told or when they were asked about signs of abuse, they were unable to 'tell the story' because of their fear that the response would be motivated (albeit unintentionally) by the heterosexual assumption. Sarah's was one such account:

> INTERVIEW: '[W]ere you able to talk to anyone about what was going on?'
>
> SARAH: 'No, not really.'
>
> INTERVIEW: 'Not even to Maureen [her heterosexual best friend]?'
>
> SARAH: 'Well Maureen would…spot bruises and she'd say, "What's happened?" and I'd say, "Oh, I had a fight with Carly." And she would always just say, "I don't know why you're still with her." I said, "Cos she always apologises and I think I love her," and she went, "How can you love someone that does that to you?" I think Maureen didn't quite understand about me being gay anyway, so. I'm not saying she's homophobic but, she would just be like, "Well, I just think you should just leave her alone and not have anything to do with her."' (Sarah, a white lesbian aged 35–39 at interview, and 25/26 when she began her first same sex relationship which was abusive)

Sarah believed that Maureen's objections to Carly's abusive behaviour were the result of her not understanding the nature of Sarah's lesbian sexuality/relationship. This meant that what might have been a useful intervention challenging Sarah's acceptance of abusive behaviour from her girlfriend was instead seen as a misguided heterosexual friend who did not understand how lesbian relationships worked or, perhaps, was not comfortable with her friend's lesbian sexuality.

Edward, a white gay man, also edited his story when his abusive partner, who was also his manager started ringing him at home under the guise of employment related queries. Edward was not able to tell his family about his relationship and was not out to his father, so he was left only with an edited narrative that he felt gave him a reason to refuse to speak to his abusive partner when he rang:

> 'I don't remember speaking about it very much. And I was also put into this, sort of, difficult situation because obviously my family didn't know what I was going through with [his abusive partner], and, you know, if he wanted to speak to me he would call up on the house phone and, say to my mum or my dad that I'm needed at work, "Can he come in for a shift?", and…I was just sitting round at the dinner table at this one incident. Um, of course they would say, "Yeah, yeah, course he can come in." Then I would end up having a terrible argument with my family about, "No I don't wanna go to work!" and they were saying…"You've got to work, you've got to earn some money!" [laughs] "But I don't want to!" So…I kept on saying, "I don't like working for him!" So, and of course I couldn't say anything else.' (Edward, aged 35–39 at interview, and 16 when he started his first same sex relationship with his male manager which was abusive)

Ella, a black lesbian, told of friends who, towards the end of the abusive relationship had helped mediate between her and her abusive partner when they were splitting up so that they could come to an agreement about how to deal with their shared property. Ella had only given a partial narrative, however, and her friends did not know that the relationship was abusive even though they knew that it was a seriously troubled relationship. In her explanation about talking to her friends what also becomes clear is that friends often have a sense that there is something wrong with a relationship but, because of practices of love protecting the privacy of intimate relationship, they are wary of interfering:

> 'I had a group of very close friends who, [pause] when things were going wrong, seriously wrong, I opened up to. And, so yeah, there were people I could explain what was going on, but when it didn't appear to be going wrong, or I didn't express my doubts to people particularly because I just felt that that was a bit disloyal, so I didn't, you know, express any of my doubts, really, up until when it really started going wrong and I was, you know, desperate really, to get out of it. Um, but what I discovered when I did start

opening up to my friends was that they knew anyway that it was a terrible mess. They knew and were just waiting for me to say so, really. And, um, they'd also felt that they didn't want to push the fact that they knew that it was not right, because they felt they were interfering…so they didn't, I mean, one or two of them did kind of try to suggest things at certain times and I just didn't entertain, I didn't take any notice.' (Ella, a black lesbian, aged 40–44 at interview, and 26/27 when her abusive relationship began)

Narratives of rejection from informal sources of help

Rejection of the abuse story occurred because family or friends believed the abusive partner's version of events, because they normalised the abusive behaviours as practices of love or, in the accounts of heterosexual women, because the heterosexual relationship was valued more highly than the experience of the survivor herself. The account of Bruce, a gay man, illustrates how friends rejected his abuse narrative because they sided with his abusive partner:

'[H]e became quite pally with some of my friends and they, it got to the point where they basically said that, that I deserved what I got. And that is a very, that for me was probably one of the most rudest awakenings that I've ever had in my life and I've never gotten away from it. So trust was destroyed on all sorts of different levels, all sorts of different levels.' (Bruce, a white gay man aged 30–34, and 19 when his first same sex relationship began which was abusive)

Clearly, the impact of being told that the abuse one has received is deserved goes to the heart of a survivor's self-concept in making sense of an abusive relationship. Its impact is shattering as it can reinforce an existing sense of isolation and self-blame, strengthen the power the abusive partner has in presenting their version of the relationship as 'the truth' and undermine the survivor's attempts at telling the relationship story as an abusive one. For Marcus, too, the response of his friend to his abusive relationship story was devastating:

'I'd went down to under nine stone, you know, and er [sighs], and [I] texted [partner] and said "Look the relationship's over, I'm not going to talk to you and I'm not going to see [you]. Do not contact me again." And then a, a few weeks later, another phone message – I was getting these anonymous calls and stuff, you know, another message "Please listen to this Marcus"…being pleasant down the phone…and then…"If you don't contact me and talk to me I promise you I will never stop doing this, I will never stop contacting you"…[This post-separation abuse went on for six months and Marcus didn't report it.] No, no, no I, I just, you know, a friend of mine, Ollie…said, "That's not harassment, he just wants to talk to you," you know. And I'd, I've lost some friends over this kind of stuff, because I've actually felt really angry and I felt like they weren't friends. They didn't support me, ok, I was hard work but, you know, I nearly fucking topped myself over this, do you know what I mean?' (Marcus, aged 35–39 at interview, and 35 when he began his abusive same sex relationship)

Marcus's friend, Ollie, normalised the post-separation abuse Marcus was experiencing as practices of love: something to be expected when a relationship breaks down. Thus Marcus's attempts to seek reinforcement for problematising the ex-partner's behaviour were rejected. For some heterosexual women, informal reporting to their family of the abuse to which they had been subjected could result in rejection narratives with extremely dangerous instructions to stay with an abusive partner, as April, a white heterosexual woman explains:

'[F]ollowing an incident where he, in drink, he [pause] raped me, basically, and I went home to my mother that very night with a case of clothes and said, "I want to stay here," and she turned me around and said "You've made this mess you go back and face it"… So I lived in a car for a week and I went [back to husband].' (April, aged 45–49 at interview, and 20 when her abusive relationship began)

In April's account the concerns of her mother were to reinforce the importance of the heterosexual relationship regardless of the experiences her daughter was having in that relationship.

Narratives of willing but unhelpful audiences

Some respondents in same sex relationships had friends, who were willing audiences for abuse narratives and who, as a consequence, became extremely concerned about or angry with either the survivor or the abusive partner about what was happening. This, however, could also prove unhelpful ultimately as victims/survivors then felt torn between their loyalty and love for their abusive partner and the concern their friends were showing them. Marcus, a white gay man, explained what happened to him as a result of another one of his friends becoming angry with his abusive partner:

> 'And then it started to come out, you know – the stuff around the sex and being tied up and, you know, other bits and pieces. And…I just remember this "Marcus! What are you doing?"…and then…he got angry and he started treating George differently…we were in the [gay bar] one night and [Ryan]…kissed all my friends apart from George and then George, of course, played that off on me. You know, and I got loads of shit. You know, really, you know, he was fucking horrible, "Ryan's trying to split us up, I don't want you seeing him again," you know, rah, rah, rah, "He's really jealous of us," and rah, rah, "Let him go," and Ryan, Ryan tried to do me a service, but it was to my disservice basically.' (Marcus, aged 35–39 at interview, and 35 when he began his abusive same sex relationship)

In a similar vein, Bruce's friends became very angry with him because he did not do as they wanted him to do. This left Bruce feeling he was punished by friends withdrawing from him, which ironically pushed him back towards his abusive partner:

> 'People are notoriously intolerant of people who are in situations where there's violence going on and then they don't leave, erm. And intellectually I can understand all the reasons why they would say that and think that, but it is the worst and most awful situation to be in when people effectively write you off because you're not doing what they think you should do…Because obviously the reaction is: something awful happens to you, you turn to people for support. You get that support initially, but then if you don't kind of go along with what they will perceive as the appropriate and more sensible way of doing it then that support disappears very quickly. It really does and actually what you've got is another, another level of judgement and rejection which drives you back to the person!' (Bruce, aged

30–34 at interview, and 19 when he began his first same
sex relationship which was abusive)

Maxine's (a bisexual, white woman) flatmate refused to let Maxine's
abusive partner stay at the flat which resulted in Maxine staying 'six
out of seven nights at his'. Similarly, the actions of friends and family
could, unwittingly sometimes, push the victim/survivor further into
the relationship and make them feel that they had nobody to turn to
for help and support. This reinforced many respondents' sense that
they had to rely on themselves to deal with the abusive relationship.

Just as heterosexual women's families might reject pleas for help
because of their beliefs in practices of love, marriage and commitment
for life, so some lesbian, gay and queer respondents report that they
felt unable to approach friends who were also lesbian, gay or queer
because of the local LGBT cultural norms that made speaking out
about an abusive partner impossible. In Chapter Three Kay's account
of gay women's subcultures, where manipulation and game playing
were the norm, made it feel difficult for her to make sense of her own
abusive relationship experiences. Tess, too, talked about how difficult it
felt to speak to friends about the abuse she was experiencing, because
her friends were shared with her abusive partner and she felt unsure
about what could be spoken about:

> 'I think there was something in, you know, being in my first,
> kind of, significant same sex relationship and not knowing
> really what was ok to talk to other people about?' (Tess, a
> white lesbian aged 40–44 at interview, and 24 when she
> began her first same sex relationship which was abusive)

Others have talked about the ways in which lesbian, bi and trans women
victims/survivors have felt pressure from within their own communities
of identity to stay silent about the DVA they are experiencing and not
'wash the dirty laundry in public' (for example, Ristock, 2002a; Irwin,
2008; Turell and Herrmann, 2008; Duke and Davidson, 2009). The fact
that our respondents did not refer to these barriers to seeking help is
probably due to the nature of the sample because in the main they had
not recognised or named their experiences as DVA at the time that
they had been in the abusive relationship. In addition, as we argued in
Chapter Three, they normalised their experiences as to be expected if
they were in their first same sex relationship.

Narratives of willing and helpful audiences

Finally, some accounts of willing audiences demonstrated how by speaking to friends and/or family a different perspective might be engendered that challenged victims/survivors' previous understandings of their experiences as ordinary or acceptable. In parallel with other's work with heterosexual women's experiences (for example, Liang et al, 2005) the impact was not necessarily in the immediate moment, but more organic, helping build a momentum that, in the longer-term, led to leaving the abusive relationship. William talks about how his friends challenged his thinking about his first same sex relationship a couple of years before he finally ended it:

> WILLIAM: 'I think my feelings had started to change, had started to grow up a little bit. I don't know whether I categorised the violence with being part of loving, but I suppose I just accepted that it was part of the relationship and I was in a relationship where I liked the person but the love had sort of stopped, and when Lonnie and Nigel told me that they thought I was in love with being in love, and I remember sort of thinking really long and hard about that and it sort of, I thought, "Wow yes. They could be right actually."'
>
> INTERVIEWER: 'Yeah. And what point did those two friends say that to you?'
>
> WILLIAM: 'Ooh. [pause]. Um [pause]. Gosh. Perhaps half way through, two thirds of the way through the relationship. I'm just trying to think, because they left to go and live [elsewhere] after that. So I suppose year three stroke four?'
>
> INTERVIEWER: 'Yeah. But that was an important conversation?'
>
> WILLIAM: 'Yeah. I can remember, I can, I can see it in my head. I can see the pub. I can even see the table we were sitting at. Because it was a real kick in the nuts type conversation [laughs].'
>
> (William, a white gay man aged 40–44 at interview, and 22/23 when he began his first same sex relationship which was abusive)

Arlene, a white bisexual woman could also recall her mother and friends asking critical questions about why she remained in her abusive relationship with a man. Her account demonstrates how, while such questions can be rejected by the victim/survivor when first asked, they can have a cumulative effect of encouraging the victim/survivor to reflect on the opinions of family and friends whom they care for and respect:

> 'I think there were, there were elements, um, at the time that I thought well "Yeah, maybe that's not quite right," and I think, sort of, friends and family trying to not say "What the hell are you doing?" but trying to put that element of thought into it cos they know I can be stubborn you know. It's difficult for other people to say what they really think without them sounding…sort of nosey.' (Arlene, aged 25–29 at interview, and 21 when the abusive relationship began)

Very few of those experiencing DVA in same sex relationships referred to speaking to family members about their experiences, but Ted's account illustrates the rare occasions when family members were integral to a victim/survivor's support system. Ted's brother-in-law worked for Relate, a UK national counselling service originally intended to provide counselling to heterosexual couples. Ted explained that his sister and brother-in-law would come and try to mediate between Ted and his abusive partner. In addition, his brother-in-law also raised the issue of providing counselling for lesbian and gay couples with Relate which Ted explained was not responded to very positively (though more recently things have changed and Relate do provide services to those in same sex relationships).

Telling and hearing abusive relationship stories is difficult. Conversely, like heterosexuals, lesbians, gay men, bisexual, queer, as well as trans, people value relationship practices of loyalty and privacy and resist hearing stories that tell of betrayal and abuse. In addition, the combined impact of the heterosexual assumption and the public story of DVA make it difficult to identify and name DVA in same sex relationships and/or to betray the LGBTQ community/identity (for example, Pattavina et al, 2007). As with heterosexual families, there can be resistance from small, shared lesbian and/or gay and/or bisexual friendship networks who fear that the breakdown of an albeit abusive relationship, could have a profound impact felt in ripples beyond the immediate couple relationship to friends and their own relationships. These accounts caution us to consider more carefully assumptions that because victims/survivors are seeking help, they are receiving appropriate support in response (see also Turell and Herrmann, 2008).

Privatised support

As has been outlined earlier, over a third of our survey respondents had consulted with counsellors and/or therapists as a result of experiencing DVA. This individualised response to DVA suggests at least two overlapping explanations. First that LGBTQ people are still suspicious of mainstream services (Wilde, 2012), do not expect a respectful response that takes their account of DVA seriously and are self-reliant (Turell, 1999; Brown, 2008; Roch et al, 2010; Hewitt and Macredie, 2012). In addition, the impact of the public story is such that DVA is not identified by survivors in same sex relationships and instead what might be called DVA is re-cast as relationship problems for which survivors believe themselves responsible. Both explanations lead to self-reliance and underpin the gap of trust (Donovan and Hester, 2010) between those in same sex relationships and mainstream support services (see also Ristock, 2001; Irwin, 2006). Wariness about using mainstream services for fear of their inability to respond appropriately to their sexuality, gender and experiences is exacerbated by mainstream agencies perpetuating the public story about DVA in their literature, websites, images in waiting rooms and in their language.

While there may be some reassurance to be had from the numbers of survivors employing counselling and therapeutic solutions insofar as they are therefore receiving some support in coming to terms with their experiences of DVA, it is not clear whether the responses they get are appropriate. Indeed it is not clear how far the heterosexual assumption also suffuses counselling and therapeutic paradigms and results in responses to DVA in same sex relationships that are quite inappropriate (for example, Grove and Blasby, 2009). In our research there were a small number of interviewees who referred to their use of therapists/counsellors in dealing with the DVA they had experienced. While there were no direct questions about this aspect of help seeking, the few that offered accounts of their experiences suggested two potential problems with therapeutic paradigms: first, the heterosexual assumption results in counsellors/therapists applying heteronormative assumptions to same sex relationships; and second, that DVA is conceptualised as an individualistic problem requiring the survivor to manage the abusive partner and take responsibility for their own safety. Bob's experience illustrates the latter problem:

> 'Following the advice of my therapist I just ignored everything. I didn't get in the game. He says, "Don't even, just don't even cut him off when he phones. If you see

his number, so, if you see it's his number, do nothing. You know, put it on silent. Don't cut off. Don't even cut him off, because that's an act of engagement with him. Just don't engage in any way whatsoever." And it went on for eight months. And eventually…I just went upstairs and I phoned him and said, "Look. Do not phone me. Do not call me…I want nothing to do with [you]"…My therapist wasn't happy about it. But it worked…I mean one e-mail he sent me, he said, "I've got a job in Edinburgh. I'm coming up. And I'm going to move in with you."…So I went to a solicitor to get an injunction against him to keep him away from me, but…my therapist talked me out of it. He said, "It's what he wants." He says "He's engaging you, it's, it's getting you into the game." He said, "I wouldn't do it if I were you. Because he will ignore it anyway." He said…"Ok, then the police can lift him, but again you're just back in the game."' (Bob, a white gay man, aged 40–44 at interview, and in his late thirties when his abusive relationship began)

There have been debates in the literature about the utility of different therapeutic approaches to addressing DVA, one of which has resulted in Relate, the UK-wide counselling service that provides support for adult and familial relationships, agreeing not to undertake couple's counselling when DVA is indicated. This approach is not universally agreed with, however (see Harris, 2006, for an overview of this debate), and the provision of counselling and therapy for those who have experienced DVA in same sex and/or trans relationships is an area that needs further research in the UK context. For many survivors of DVA in same sex relationships, seeking help from mainstream agencies does not feel like an option, and it is possible that counselling and therapeutic sources of support will continue to be their first choice rather than more formal support.

Ted, a white gay man, was also referred to a counsellor by his sympathetic GP. When, however, Ted complained to the doctor about the counsellor because, "I just got the impression he didn't really want to be talking to gay people, if you like," the GP said "Well, we can't really pick and choose. It's what we've got."

Formal sources of help: the police

As we will discuss later, it was only when the DVA experienced had escalated, either in its physical severity or the fear it elicited in survivors, that the police might be involved. In the main, there was a common understanding among those who had not sought help that theirs was a relationship problem that should be resolved privately. Most of the respondents who had experienced DVA had only recognised it as such after the relationship was over; and had rarely reported it to any agency and/or talked to anybody about it at the time. We discussed earlier the responses of some lesbians who felt that their experiences of physical violence would not be taken seriously because they were physically bigger than their abusive partner. There is evidence that the fears embedded in these accounts have some wider validity. In North America research has concluded that help providers for survivors of DVA, including the police, perceive the circumstances of the survivor in a same sex relationship to be less serious than that of heterosexual women survivors (for example, Pattavina et al, 2007). This perception seems to be shaped by assumptions about gender such that violence between men is normalised and thus considered not to be as serious as when a man is violent towards a women; and women are constructed as more fragile and thus are perceived to be more in need of help, especially if their abusive partner is a heterosexual man. In their study of DVA crisis centre staff, Brown and Groscup (2009) also found that, although participants recognised the vignettes given of same sex and heterosexual relationships as DVA, their confidence in their judgement was influenced by the sexuality of the couple and the gender of the perpetrator and/or survivor. Thus they were most confident when the couple was heterosexual and least when the couple were gay male. Participants were also more likely to believe that DVA in same sex relationships was less likely to recur, did not escalate as much or be as serious as in heterosexual relationships and they believed that it was easier for survivors in same sex relationships to be able to leave the relationship. In their research of how gender stereotyping had an impact on psychology students' assessments of DVA in lesbian relationships, Little and Terrance (2010) found that the heterosexual assumption influenced the ways in which perceptions of both sexuality and gender had an impact on the blameworthiness of the survivor of DVA: the more masculine-looking survivor was blamed more for the DVA she had experienced and the more feminine-looking survivor was blamed less. These studies taken together suggest that victims/survivors in same sex relationships are right to be concerned that they will not receive an appropriate response from mainstream agencies.

A small number of our respondents had a more general distrust of the police, fearing that the latter were too homophobic to be expected to respond appropriately. Ted, a white gay man, whose abusive 15-year relationship had finished eight years before the interview explained how it had not occurred to him to report his experiences to the police and drew on community knowledges to explain why:

> 'I'd heard too many bad reports from other people that the police didn't want to know and, I mean, at the time they didn't even want to know about [laughing] ordinary domestic violence, if you like. It was just put down as a domestic, ignore it and drive away, sort of thing. I mean that's how it was handled then.' (Ted)

In Ted's allusion to 'ordinary domestic violence' he reveals the extent of his lack of confidence that he could have received an appropriate response from the police by comparing his experience with 'ordinary', that is heterosexual, domestic violence – if heterosexual women did not receive a suitable response, why would he?

There is also evidence that the police are influenced by the heterosexual assumption in their response to DVA in same sex relationships. Pattavina et al (2007) found that gender was the most influential factor shaping police responses in areas where mandatory arrest policies were in place. So while the severity of the offence did not affect whether an arrest was made when the same sex couple was female, when the couple were males the severity of the offence became crucial in the officers' decision to arrest. The authors suggest that this could reflect police officers' perception that female victims are more in need of protection and/or that male same sex couple violence is perceived as not as serious as when a female is a victim. Alternatively they argue that because the severity of the offence was more influential in decisions about arrest in male same sex couples, this might be because gay men are more likely only to report when a serious physical offence has been committed. They conclude that gender should be considered as a separate factor in studies of same sex DVA in order to elucidate the different experiences of women and men in same sex and heterosexual relationships.

The gap of trust between survivors and the police was also evident in our study (see Donovan and Hester, 2010) and illustrated by those who wished to protect their abusive partner from inappropriate responses. Typically, a response from female interviewees, the belief that intimacy elicits loyalty and privacy emerged in several accounts of those who had not discussed their experiences with anybody, but especially, the police. Zoe, an African lesbian explains:

'[S]ome of the things she was saying were things like, uhm, you know, black women needing to be supportive of each other and, and her reluctance to go and talk to someone outside of the relationship was linked to, if I wanted that then it was an unsupportive act, and so I listened to that and thought about that, even though in my own way I was suffering in the relationship.' (Zoe, aged 45–49 at interview, and in her early thirties when her first abusive relationship began)

Zoe's account illustrates how intersecting social positions related to 'race', gender and sexuality can act to shape how trustworthy mainstream agencies are perceived; and conversely how loyalty to an abusive partner and, by extension, a community of black women and lesbians can be called upon to keep survivors silent. Survivors were often successfully convinced by abusive partners to remain loyal to them by keeping silent about what went on in their abusive relationship. In other research in the UK, it has been clear that those with intersecting sexuality, gender, 'race' and other minority ethnic identities have particular concerns about inappropriate services that are unable and/or unwilling to understand their specific needs (see Hester et al, 2012). Here the responses of BME participants, including gay men, suggest that existing services are set up to respond to the public story in which the victim/survivor is also assumed to be white.

Those living as sexual minorities, with intersecting identities such as gender and 'race' have been schooled in self-reliance by living in a society that has historically positioned them as outsiders. This can result in not perceiving their experience as criminal, but instead as their own problem to be dealt with at a private, informal level. Others have written about the specific impacts of being positioned as a minority group for refugees and asylum seekers, black and indigenous peoples, travellers, disabled people and the homeless (for example, Kanuha, 1990; Irwin, 2008; Turell and Herrmann, 2008; Cramer and Plummer, 2009; Lehavot et al, 2010). While the research suggests that members of these groups experience much higher levels of interpersonal violence in general, it also suggests that they come to believe that mainstream services are not for them. A privatised, individualised response is not one explicitly promoted by the UK state to deal with DVA in same sex relationships as evidenced in the 2004 Domestic Violence and Victims Act, yet we argue that this response is the culmination of community knowledges and experiences about the world settling around three core assumptions: that DVA is a problem for white, heterosexual able-bodied women; that public agencies will either not be sympathetic or not be able to appropriately respond to those who do not fit the public story; and that membership of intersecting communities of identity compounds the isolation and distance individuals feel from accessing and receiving appropriate help and support. For those in our study who had experienced behaviours they knew should have resulted in intervention from the police the gap of trust between the latter and themselves meant that they were suspicious of receiving a sympathetic response. These respondents perceived their relationships, safety and security as being better served by a reliance on self.

Escalation in fear and/or violence: accessing police support

Only four interviewees in our study of same sex relationships reported DVA experiences to the police and each time their decision to do so had been precipitated by an escalation both in the violence and the fear experienced. Reporting to the police, however, was part of a range of precautionary tactics undertaken, partly because doing so typically did not result in a satisfactory outcome, and partly to prevent further violence. Marie's account of an abusive relationship that ended seven years before the interview, illustrates this kind of strategy and how profound precautionary tactics can be in their implications for the lives of victim/survivors. As with many respondents, Marie experienced post-separation abuse from a same sex partner, but for her this culminated in the ex-partner breaking into the accommodation of Marie's new partner and physically assaulting her (see Chapter Five). Although the police were called, Marie's new partner subsequently dropped any charges and together they moved away from the area. When asked why the charges had been dropped, Marie explained:

> 'Oh, it would make things worse…when they let her out, she was straight on the phone to me for hours and saying, "How could you leave me there?" And make me feel so guilty about it…And…I don't know if the children will ever forgive me for that either, to press charging [*sic*] against their Mum, and…I don't think it would have made any difference…she would just do what she wants all the time, and the police, the law, that, that didn't make any difference. When we went to see a solicitor to try to get an injunction, he sent a letter to her, she went berserk. She left an hour-long message on his ansaphone and he just – he didn't want to have anything to do with us after that…So [laughs],

she just didn't care…She's evil. She'd be on the phone to [Marie's new partner's] mum saying that, "She, you know, just loves gang shagging," and stuff like that to her mum and things, awful things. She'd tell the children that I'm a paedophile, or any, any, anything that you can think, she would come out with.' (Marie, a white European lesbian, aged 35–39 at interview, and 21 when her first same sex relationship began which was abusive)

The response from the police and solicitors did not elicit confidence in Marie that she and her partner would be made safer. Their decision-making also had to include the possible consequences for Marie's abusive ex-partner's three children (whom Marie had co-parented for 12 years).

Bruce, whose abusive relationship had ended about 15 years before his interview used the police for help on two occasions when he was being physically chased by his abusive partner and was in fear of what might happen. On both occasions, the police did nothing. On the second occasion, a stranger helped Bruce, took him to the police station and offered to be a witness. Yet the police response was indifference:

'[The witness] took me to the police station and they just said "What happened?" and I told them what happened and they said "Oh well, what do you want us to do?" and I said "Well, I don't know. I just wanna go home." And so, they let me ring my mother and my mother came and picked me up. Didn't offer me a cup of tea, didn't offer me somewhere to go wash my face, didn't say to me, "Do you want to make a statement? Do you want to make a complaint about this?" Nothing.' (Bruce, aged 30–34 at interview, and 19 when he began his first same sex relationship which was abusive)

Bob, whose abusive relationship ended about three years before his interview also spoke to the police after being held captive by his abusive partner for 12 hours and subjected to a serious assault. Bob spoke to a police LGBT liaison officer and believed that he had reported the assault, but later when he wanted to pursue charges he was informed that the officer, who had a record of Bob's appointment, reported that Bob had not asked him to arrest and charge the abusive partner, had believed that Bob only wanted advice and had not recorded any of his injuries even though Bob had stitches in his face as a result of his injuries.

Ella's abusive relationship had ended approximately two years prior to the interview, but she was still experiencing post-separation abuse. The post-separation abuse came from her ex-partner and her ex-partner's brother. Ella reported these experiences to the police, but not her ex-partner's albeit occasional physical or more ongoing emotional abuse while in the relationship. The police arrested and cautioned the brother but did nothing to the ex-partner saying that they did not have enough evidence. Ella said that her experience of the police was mixed:

> 'I think actually the women who I spoke to at the Domestic Violence Unit were spot on and on the ball. But the PC Plod down at the station who I had to make a statement to, I bet he had a laugh with his mates [laugh]. Once I'd disappeared out the station I don't think for a minute they were serious about it.' (Ella)

As we have discussed in Chapter Five, post-separation abuse was quite common yet only two respondents reported any experience of post-separation abuse to the police. Ella and Marie's experiences have been discussed above. Marie explained how the police response changed once she and her partner decided to drop charges:

> 'With the police, once you don't press charges, they're quite reluctant afterwards to do anything…They had a right laugh about it, I'm sure, but – so I didn't press charges at that time when she was really trying to – she wanted to kill… my partner…She was quite violent that night. After that, they were not really hugely interested about all the things that she did, and, even when we went to see a solicitor to try and get an injunction, and that costs so much money that we had to leave that, so we just left the place.' (Marie)

Both Marie and Ella said that they had felt that the police had 'laughed' at them, indicating the extent to which they felt that their experiences had not been taken seriously. Most other respondents had not considered reporting the post-separation abuse to the police. Rather, they adopted self-reliant, protective behaviours: changing their mobile phone contract, entering counselling, meeting up to appease the abusive partner, or in other ways making contact with them to stop their harassment.

Thus a small number of interviewees reported experiences of DVA to the police and or solicitors either because the violence/abuse was escalating or because there was an increase in fear. More recent research has also suggested that victims/survivors from LGBTQ relationships might be at a higher risk than their heterosexual counterparts when they report reflecting their reluctance to report until they feel more at risk and suggesting that practitioners should be aware that even one call to the police from an LGBT victim/survivor might signify that they are at very high risk (Donovan, 2010; CAADA, 2013). Their accounts reflect the criminology of other (Garland, 1996) in that they reported the extraordinary (usually physical) violence which they experienced in the belief that they could legitimately expect help. The response of the police, however, was usually inappropriate even in times of acute danger, risk or fear. Of course, as we have said earlier, all of the respondents' accounts of DVA had occurred in relationships that ended before their interview, sometimes, as in Bruce's case, over a decade before. More recent research, however, suggests that there has been little change and that those embodying intersecting identities experience an increased sense of the impossibility of approaching mainstream agencies (Hester et al, 2012).

Summary

• While help-seeking models are useful to break down the processes individuals might go through in seeking help and support for DVA, it is important to keep in mind that individuals are the product of the socio-cultural context in which they live.

• Socio-cultural factors are crucially important in making sense of help-seeking behaviours, and while living in a heterosexist and homophobic society results in individuals believing themselves to be excluded from mainstream support or unlikely to receive an appropriate response, other socio-cultural factors are also important in understanding why so many LGBTQ people do not seek formal sources of help. These are:
   − the public story of DVA which can be understood to only involve white, able-bodied heterosexual women experiencing predominantly physical violence from men;
   − practices of love that encourage victims/survivors to prioritise the perceived needs of the perpetrators, to remain loyal and to protect them.

    – self reliance which is the result of the cumulative impact of a neoliberal state producing the responsible citizen and the legacy of LGBTQ people being criminalised and pathologised by the state.

- There were some important differences in the help-seeking behaviours of victims/survivors of same sex and heterosexual DVA:
  - Victims/survivors in same sex relationships were far more likely to seek support from friends than family. The reverse was true for heterosexual victims/survivors.
  - Counsellors and therapists were the most popular formal source of support for victims/survivors in same sex relationships. This reflects two further findings:
    » those in same sex relationships often do not recognise their experiences as DVA but rather a relationship problem for which they need individualised, privatised support;
    » there is a gap of trust between victims/survivors of DVA and mainstream agencies.
  - The police are the least likely source of formal support for those in same sex relationships but the first source of support for those in heterosexual relationships.

- Existing evidence suggests that victims/survivors are correct to be wary of approaching mainstream agencies for support.

- The police were reported to by a minority of interviewees and usually because they had experienced an escalation either in the violence or their fear of their abusive partner.

- The gap of trust is the result of the heterosexual assumption and the public story about DVA:
  - Victims/survivors are fearful of receiving an unsympathetic or hostile response because of homophobia.
  - Victims/survivors are wary that they will not be believed or that their experiences of DVA will not be taken seriously because they do not 'fit' the public story of DVA.

SEVEN

Key findings and implications for practice

In this book we set out to address the following questions:

- What is domestic violence and abuse in the context of same sex relationships?
- Are the domestic violence and abuse experiences of lesbians and gay men similar and/or different to those in heterosexual relationships?
- What about gender if individuals are the same sex?
- What has love got to do with it?

In this concluding chapter we revisit our main findings and themes and discuss how they can help in developing best practice in the provision of services for those experiencing DVA in both same-sex and heterosexual relationships. Some of our previous research has shown that the Power and Control Wheel (Pence and Shephard, 1999) can be very effective in enabling individuals to identify and name the DVA they are experiencing, whether as an early intervention tool or as risk increases (Hester and Westmarland, 2006/7); however this approach has shortcomings in relation to same sex DVA and in recognising the impact of practices of love on DVA across sexuality and gender. In this chapter we therefore outline a new version of the Wheel, the COHSAR Power and Control Wheel, which can be used in practice with all victims/survivors of DVA regardless of sexuality or gender. Where appropriate, we highlight when findings also have relevance for those in trans relationships.

Domestic violence and abuse in same sex relationships: similarities, differences and the role of gender

Our findings show that DVA, as a wide range of behaviours that make up intimate terrorism and coercive control, can be a feature of same sex relationships and that it can be experienced in very similar ways across same sex sexualities, whether lesbian, gay male, bisexual, or male or female homosexual. The limited research that exists suggest the same is true for trans people (Roch et al, 2010; Bornstein et al, 2006). Severity and impact of DVA increases with the frequency of violent and abusive events and especially where a combination of more than one form of abuse (emotional, physical and/or sexual) is used by the perpetrator. Only a small number (less than one in five in the previous 12 months) appeared to have experienced intimate terrorism or coercive control, and half that (one in ten) experienced the most severe combined forms of DVA. 'Mutual' abuse and situational couple violence did not characterise the violence and abuse being reported by our survey respondents, and our findings provide a strong rejection of the myths that characterise DVA in same sex relationships as a 'fair fight' or as not as serious as DVA in heterosexual relationships. The survey showed some clear differences by gender: physical violence and physically coercive sexual violence was more typically used by male perpetrators, whether their partners were female or male. Men in same sex relationships were significantly more likely than women in same sex relationships to experience forced sex, refusal to comply with requests for safer sex and/or safe words in sexual role play and/or sadomasochistic sex. They were also significantly more likely to experience financial abuse. Men were less often in relationships of dependency, being more likely not to live with abusive partners and thus, typically, having shorter abusive relationships. In contrast, abusive partners in female same sex relationships more typically used emotional violence and emotionally coercive sexual violence. The survey also showed that women in same sex relationships were significantly more likely to want to try harder to please a partner as a result of experiencing abusive behaviours. Women were more likely to be parents and for that to be used as part of the abuse against them. Women were more likely to live with an abusive partner regardless of sexuality and have a longer abusive relationship than were men. Women thus appeared more willing to use emotionally abusive ways of behaving and speaking that undermined and established an abusive power dynamic in a same sex relationship. Women were also more likely to enact gendered behaviours that reinforce situations of structured dependency, for example, by living with abusive partners and/or having children and/or getting married. Gendered norms are therefore important in understanding both heterosexual and same sex DVA. Clearly, gender must be understood as being constructed, reconstructed and reinforced through and operating at the individual, interrelational, communal, institutional (including legislative) and societal levels, all of which have historically positioned heterosexual women as subordinate and dependent, and heterosexual men as dominant and entitled to particular privileges in their intimate and family lives. These socially and culturally produced ways of normalising gendered inequalities have no doubt produced a context that has supported DVA occurring in heterosexual relationships. Other factors, however, are at least as important for understanding same sex DVA.

In a similar way, we argue that the existence of homophobia and heterosexism in a society based on the heterosexual assumption provides a supporting factor for DVA in same sex and trans relationships. In Chapter Three we argued that minority stress as a causal factor for DVA in same sex relationships is problematic, mainly for methodological reasons and its individualised focus. We have, however, shown how living in a society based on the heterosexual assumption, where homophobia, discrimination and hate crime are still expected, feared, and/or experienced does have an impact on the ways in which victims/survivors: are able to recognise and name their experiences as DVA, particularly in first same sex relationships; experience particular abuses based on their sexuality and/or gender identity; and make their help-seeking decisions. Thus, as the wider socio-cultural context, which results in gender inequalities and misogyny, supports DVA in heterosexual relationships, so the wider socio-cultural context, which results in homophobia and heterosexism, supports DVA in same sex relationships.

As we highlighted in Chapter Four, intersectional factors linked to socio-cultural context were important in creating circumstances with increased risk for DVA. Differences and inequalities between partners in terms of age, income, community knowledge, class and education were especially prominent in such contexts, with these features intersecting and mutually shaping in a variety of ways that fed into the power and control exerted by abusers. The survey highlighted that young age, low income and low educational attainment were particular indicators of risk of DVA, and also significantly correlated with individuals self-defining as having experienced such abuse. Interviews illustrated how young age is an indicator of risk for DVA, often because these individuals are in first same sex relationships and lack an obvious 'script' of what constitutes a good relationship. At the same time, as we have argued in Chapter Four, in same sex relationships 'age' is a fluid rather than chronological concept. In other words, regardless of chronological age, in a first same sex relationship with somebody who is already out and has experience of being in same sex relationships, there is the potential for the less experienced, 'younger' partner to be exploited by the more experienced 'older' partner because of the former being naïve both about how same sex relationships might work and also about what it is to be LGBQ. This could also have implications for somebody who has recently transitioned. We also suggested that the intersections and contexts for abuse are not necessarily obvious from survey data. For instance, where having a low income intersects with becoming a mother, it may be that being a mother rather than the low income could position women in same sex relationships as vulnerable to abuse. This is something that would benefit from further research.

Recognition of the intersecting identities of both victims/survivors and abusive partners may help us to understand DVA in a number of ways. First, in the degree to which abusive experiences are perceived and/or understood as such by victims/survivors or are normalised as part of everyday life. Second, in relation to the willingness of abusive partners to utilise fears about existing stereotypes and discrimination against members of those social groups to further control victims/survivors and prevent them from seeking help. Third, in the role of family, friendship and community (including faith and virtual) networks, as often the first source of support, in either (often unwittingly) colluding with the abusive partner, by advising or expecting the survivor to remain in the abusive relationship, or encouraging the survivor to identify their needs and prioritise their safety. Fourth, regarding the gap of trust that exists between victims/survivors and potential formal sources of help and their belief that services will be inclusive, appropriate, confidential and respectful.

In Chapter Five we argued, that there is yet another lens through which violent and abusive relationships must be analysed, which is that of practices of love and relationship rules. Love for an abusive partner is among the reasons most often given for staying in or returning to a violent and abusive relationship, although it has remained the least researched aspect of DVA (for notable exceptions, see Lloyd and Emery, 2000; Wood, 2001; Fraser, 2008). In our study we began from the premise that most DVA relationships begin consensually and with feelings of potential or actual love and we explored the role of love in how interviewees made sense of their abusive relationships. We have shown that there are similar beliefs held about love whatever the sexuality or gender of the individuals involved, and that these beliefs act to keep victims/survivors in abusive relationships. These include wanting to stay loyal to an abusive partner, to protect them from the expected hostility of those outside the relationship, believing in commitments to stay with a relationship through bad times as well as good and, women particularly, wanting to try to make changes that will prevent the violence and abuse. Being told that they are loved elicits strong feelings that mitigate the violent and abusive behaviours enacted by abusive partners and reminds us how powerful love is as a supportive factor for DVA. We have shown that positive feelings elicited by declarations of love from their abusive partner, their declarations and acts of contrition and apparent commitments to change can act as a powerful glue keeping victims/survivors in abusive relationships. We have argued therefore that practices of love are implicated as factors supporting DVA and should be explored more explicitly with victims/ survivors in the process of their being able to recognise and name their experiences as DVA. We have also argued that practices of love can be understood as gendered, but in ways that can confuse a victim/survivor about how to make sense of their experiences.

As we showed in Chapter Five, practices of love include declarations of love by abusive partners, often in critical moments when survivors are considering or threatening to leave the relationship; expressions of need or neediness, when abusive partners give explanations or excuses for their abusive behaviours that elicit concern or care from survivors and take the focus away from the abuse and its impact on them; and emotion and care work when survivors feel that they are emotionally stronger than the abusive partner and responsible for taking care of them and keeping the relationship together. In the latter circumstances, we found that survivors resisted the idea that they had been victims of DVA because they had not felt passive or weak in the relationship. Practices of love can also include the positive experiences which victims/survivors might associate with the abusive relationship and their abusive partner that confuse their being able to make sense of the abuse which they are experiencing and engenders a way of coping that isolates abusive experiences as exceptional rather than connected to each other.

Further, we have argued that practices of love enable abusive partners to establish and maintain relationship rules that underpin abusive relationships. The relationship rules can be seen to characterise the gender norms of heterosexual love in so far as the abusive partner is the key decision-maker, setting the terms for the relationship (traditionally associated with masculinity in men) and the survivor is positioned as responsible for the emotional life and care of the abusive partner and the relationship (traditionally associated with femininity in women). By unhooking these behaviours from embodied women and men, however, it becomes clearer how abusive partners exhibit both stereotypically feminine and masculine behaviours. Expressions of need by abusive partners, that is, their willingness to reveal and share apparently painful memories and experiences to explain their violence and abuse, together with their expressed and perceived neediness for and dependency on the victim/survivor can be understood as more reflective of femininity. These behaviours may thus be experienced by victims/survivors as confirmation of love, commitment, trust, as well as neediness from the abusive partner. Conversely, the care and emotion work expected of victims/survivors may be enacted by them through a self-perception of emotional strength and a sense of responsibility to manage the abusive partner to meet their needs and sustain the relationship. Such self-perception does not fit with the public story of DVA that constructs victims as weak and powerless in the face of the bigger, stronger abusive (male) partner. Thus care and emotion work rather than being understood as traditionally feminine, and as such passive and expressive, can be seen as active and agential leading to a sense of being responsible for the abusive partner and the relationship. These are characteristics more often associated with masculinity. We have argued that relationship rules exist in abusive relationships whether these are heterosexual or same sex. The first rule is that the relationship is for the abusive partner and on their terms. Key decision making, which can include the decision to abnegate any responsibility for children, the relationship or the maintenance of a household, creates a dynamic that positions the abusive partner in charge. We have argued that this dynamic can be embedded incrementally over time, as the abusive partner deploys different ways of establishing the first relationship rule (for example, by over hours, days, weeks, or months, continually sulking, withdrawing affection, being moody, shouting, coming back to an argument, and so on). Male abusive partners might also more quickly establish this dynamic by using physical and/or sexual violence. The second relationship rule decrees that the victim/survivor is responsible for the care of the abusive partner and the relationship. Again, this can reinforce the self-perception of the survivor as being emotionally stronger than the abusive partner and has a negative impact on their sense of being able to leave and/or remain away from the relationship. Post-separation abuse and anticipation of separation abuse is often enacted and experienced to remind survivors of, and/or punish survivors who have 'forgotten', their responsibility for the abusive partner.

Practices of love and relationship rules enable abusive partners to position victims/survivors as responsible for the violence and abuse they experience and remain loyal to and responsible for abusive partners. The impact of practices of love and relationship rules suggests that these should be more explicitly implicated in understandings of how DVA operates and how victims/survivors might be supported to recognise their experiences as DVA. They also provide a way of speaking about DVA in ways that recognise the importance of gender and other aspects of intersectionality, but also foreground the importance of understandings about love and relationships that permeate and provide further context for how abusive relationships operate and are sustained. It is with this in mind that we now turn to our re-imagining of the Duluth Power and Control Wheel.

Re-imagining the Duluth Power and Control Wheel: The COHSAR Wheel

By building on all our findings we have been able to develop a new 'Power and control' wheel for practitioners to use with victims/ survivors in both same sex and heterosexual relationships. The Power and Control Wheel was originally developed by the Domestic Abuse Intervention Project in Duluth in the United States, originally as a tool for working with heterosexual women as survivors and heterosexual men as abusive partners in DVA relationships (Pence and Shephard, 1999). The tool was intended to assist practitioners in their work with victims/survivors to enable them to recognise their experiences holistically, challenge perceptions of violence and abuse as isolated experiences and encourage an understanding of the impacts of DVA on their sense of self. It was also intended to assist work with abusive men to challenge them to recognise and understand the connectivity of their behaviours and the impact of them on their partners (and children) and to encourage behaviour change. While its use has been global, there has been recognition that the wheel is problematic, not only because of its exclusive focus on the experiences of heterosexual women, but also because of its tendency to universalise heterosexual experiences. This means that the diversity of experiences and meaning-making by those living with other identities tend to be rendered invisible.

The original wheel (see Figure 7.1) has at its hub the power and control abusive partners exert over their partners. From the hub, eight spokes radiate outwards, each of which represents a particular set of behaviours that can be used to control and/or punish a partner: male privilege, economic abuse, coercion and threats, intimidation, emotion abuse, isolation, minimising, denying and blaming, and the use of children. Under each of these headings examples are given to aid discussion with victims/survivors and abusive partners. The spokes all meet the rim of the wheel, which represents the physical and sexual violence that are understood to support the eight sets of behaviours (or tactics of power and control). The wheel has been adapted in different

Figure 7.1: Duluth Power and Control Wheel

Source: Domestic Abuse Intervention Project, 202 East Superior Street, Duluth, MN 55802, 218-722-2781 (www.theduluthmodel.org)

ways either to include different kinds of behaviours or different social groups, and there have been previous attempts to incorporate LGBTQ victims/survivors (see Figure 7.2, Roe and Jagodinsky, undated). More recently, Chavis and Hill (2009) have developed what they call the Multicultural Power and Control Wheel. This is their attempt to embed in the tool awareness of the impact of intersecting identities on the experiences of DVA survivors. The authors recognise how by enlarging the wheel outwards it becomes difficult to include examples of each group of power and control tactics. Instead they provide a separate table that gives examples of what each power and control tactic might look like from the perspective of each intersectional identity.

These attempts to promote more inclusive understandings of DVA in practical tools are valuable in encouraging more inclusive services that recognise the diversity of experiences as well as the commonalities

Figure 7.2: Power and Control Wheel for lesbian, gay, bisexual and trans relationships

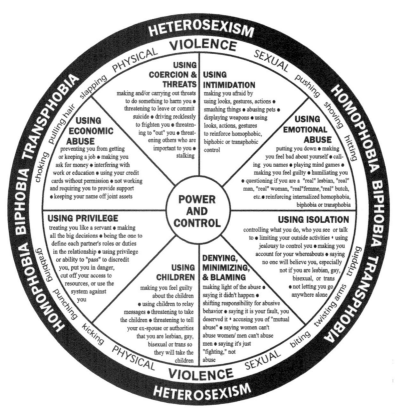

Source: Roe and Jagodinsky, undated

of experiences across complex and intersecting identities. The multicultural wheel, however, still only speaks to the experiences of women as victims/survivors. Moreover, the practices of love and relationship rules we have identified as important factors in DVA relationships are also missing. Here it is our intention to suggest a new way of conceptualising the Power and Control Wheel that incorporates the findings from our research with respect to the wider context of abuse and relationship rules.

In doing this we acknowledge two caveats. First, we are wary about how information embedded in tools such as the power and control wheel become rarified such that they come to define what DVA is and who can experience it. This is a critique that Stark (2007) also makes in the US context, and has happened to some extent with the use of risk assessment tools in the UK (see, for example, Donovan

(2013) and discussion below) This can lead to practitioners using the wheel as a list of items to tick rather than as an interactive process whereby individuals can identify and reflect on their experiences and needs. The wheel should therefore be understood as indicative rather than exhaustive and as a live tool that should be regularly reviewed, amended, tested and adapted. The second, and related, caveat is our recognition of the importance of listening to the accounts of victims/survivors of their experiences. By prioritising their stories of abuse rather than attempting to fit their stories to templates (whether that be the wheel or risk assessment check lists) we argue that it should be possible to be inclusive of the heterogeneity of survivors' experiences and needs and to respond accordingly.

A new COHSAR DVA wheel

At the hub of our new COHSAR wheel we place the relationship rules (see Figure 7.3): that the DVA relationship has to be on the abuser's terms and the victim/survivor has to look after the abusive partner and their needs. A focus on self and the meeting of their own needs (and whims) are at the core of abusive partners' behaviours along with the willingness to enact violence and abuse (using a repertoire of behaviours related to social location and positionality) to get what they want and assert the relationship rules or to punish a partner for apparent disobedience. A further ring surrounding the hub identifies power and control as the means by which the relationship rules will be achieved.

From the double-rimmed hub, eleven spokes radiate out to meet the outer rim. These spokes represent the repertoire of behaviours on which the abuser may draw, and include seven from the original wheel: economic abuse, coercion and threats, intimidation, emotional abuse, isolation, minimising, denying and blaming, and the use of children. The spoke of 'male privilege' in the original Duluth wheel we have replaced with two spokes: 'identity abuse' and 'entitlement abuse'. In Table 7.1 we list each of these spokes and give lists of indicative examples of each. These are drawn from our findings (see Chapters Four and Five) as well as the original Duluth model and that of the Texas Council on Family Violence (Roe and Jagodinsky, undated) to show how the COHSAR model incorporates and expands on those models. 'Identity abuse' is intended to bring to the fore the different ways that sexist, misogynistic, heterosexist, homophobic, biphobic, transphobic, racist, classist, ablest, ageist and anti-faith insults, slurs, stereotyping and assumptions might be used to further undermine,

Figure 7.3: COHSAR Power and Control Wheel

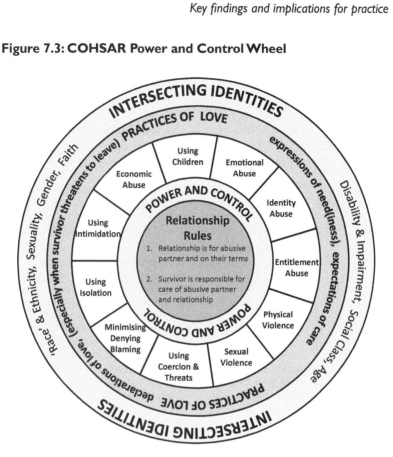

threaten, isolate or punish a partner. Examples of these would include: withdrawing medications from a gay male partner who is HIV+ or the hormone treatments from a partner who is gender transitioning, undermining a person's sense of themselves as a 'real woman' or 'man', a 'real lesbian' or 'gay man'; withdrawing physical care from a disabled partner and leaving them in situations of physical danger; and controlling what kinds of clothes an individual might wear or how they style their hair.

Entitlement abuse facilitates exploration of the ways in which gender, chronological age, age through experience, 'race' and ethnicity, (dis)ability, social class, education and immigration status can be used to impose power and control and thus enact relationship rules. Examples of this include heterosexual men expecting their partners to maintain the household and take responsibility for children while expecting that they can take leisure time outside the home with their friends whenever they wish; or an older and/or more experienced gay man or lesbian expecting that their partner will not engage with the local LGBTQ scene and/or make LGBTQ friends.

Physical and sexual violence are included as the ninth and tenth spokes. Positioning these as separate spokes alongside other tactics

Table 7.1: Indicative behaviours in the COHSAR Power and Control Wheel

Concentric circles	Explanations
Relationship rules	In most abusive relationships, regardless of gender or sexuality, there are two key relationships rules that emerge as a result of the abusive behaviour and expectations of the abusive partner.
	1. That the relationship is for them and on their terms. This means that they expect, or the impact of their behaviour is that they are able, to set the terms for the relationship and see it as a vehicle for meeting their own needs. They expect their partner to accept and comply with the terms and are prepared to use a range of abusive behaviours (see the spokes of the COHSAR Wheel) which both alert their partner to the rules and can be used to punish their partner when they do not comply. Being able to set the terms also means that the abusive partner is able to change their mind, be unpredictable or to state that they do not want to take any responsibility for anything in the relationship (so for example, they might not do paid work, they might refuse to take a share of the household duties, childcare etc, or they may explain they have a fear of commitment).
	2. The victim/survivor is responsible for the relationship and for the abusive partner. This means that the victim/survivor is blamed when things go wrong, including when violence/abuse occurs; that they are responsible for 'managing' the abusive partners' relationships with family of origin, other friends, etc, including protecting them from others' negative criticism about their behaviour; provide support and care for the abusive partner when they are upset by the outside world, their employer, their difficulties coping with life, and even after they have been violent and/or abusive. Because the victim/survivor is held responsible for the relationship, abusive partners are often extremely reluctant to let go and employ different ways of persuading victim/survivors to stay or return to the abusive relationship or to punish them for leaving/staying away. Conversely, it is also the case that victim/survivors might experience themselves as emotionally 'stronger' than their abusive partner and often believe that they should take care of them (see practices of love).
Power and control	The range of behaviours that are employed by abusive partners are all intended to exert power and control over the victim/survivor so that the relationship rules are understood and complied with; including punishment for breaking the rules.

(continued)

Table 7.1: Indicative behaviours in the COHSAR Power and Control Wheel (continued)

Concentric circles	Explanations
Practices of love	Abusive partners might engage in many practices of love which act to confuse the victim/survivor about what is happening in the relationship, how to understand it and how to recognise and name their experience as DVA. Many abusive relationships are not experienced negatively all of the time. Very often abusive relationships can have 'happy' periods or times when victim/survivors feel that they are loved and needed by an abusive partner. In this way expressions of love can in themselves form part of the violence/abuse as they confuse, manipulate and act to glue victim/survivors into abusive relationships.
	1. Declarations of love: abusive partners might declare their love for a partner especially when their partner is thinking about/threatening to and/or actually leaving.
	This kind of declaration is often accompanied by:
	2. Expressions of need/neediness: abusive partners talk about why they behave the way they do in an effort to elicit forgiveness, care and support and love from their partner; and to persuade them to stay in the abusive relationship.
	These revelations often lead to:
	3. Expectations of care: abusive partners often elicit feelings in victim/survivors that obligate them to respond to the declarations of love and expressions of need/neediness their abusive partners reveal. This compounds their sense that they are responsible for looking after their abusive partner and that they are the emotionally 'stronger' partner who should protect and remain loyal to their partner.
Intersecting identities	Abusive partners and victim/survivors rarely identify in simple ways. Most experience their world in ways that are shaped by how their identity is assumed to be by those around them in their family/friendship networks as well as by professionals in more formal contexts; and by how they identify themselves. This can include their 'race' and/or ethnicity, their age, their social class, their gender, their faith and whether they are able bodied or not. When working with victim/survivors and/or abusive partners being aware of what intersecting identities they inhabit will help understand:
	1. how they perceive their behaviours, including their moral code and/or whether they normalise their behaviours
	2. their likely support networks and whether these might reinforce abusive relationships or support non-abusive relationships
	3. their readiness to seek help and degree of trust they might place in different sources of help.

(continued)

Table 7.1 (continued)

Indicative behaviours for spokes in COHSAR Power and Control Wheel

Spokes in COHSAR P&C Wheel	Indicative examples
Coercion and threats	Making and/or carrying out threats to hurt a partner; threatening to leave her/him, to commit suicide, driving recklessly to frighten her/him, making her/him drop charges, making her/him do illegal things.
Intimidation	Making her/him afraid with looks, actions, gestures, weapons; destroying her/his property/things; abusing pets.
Emotional abuse	Putting her/him down; making her/him feel bad about her/himself; calling her/him names; making her/him think she/he's crazy; playing mind games; humiliating her/him; making her/him feel guilty; undermining her/his sense of self so that she/he believes that she/he is incompetent, stupid, 'wrong', to blame; claiming that nobody will take her/him seriously if she/he speaks to anybody; making her/him believe she/he is lucky they are in a relationship with her/him.
Using isolation	Controlling what she/he does, whom they see and/or talk to, what she/he reads or watches on the television, looks at on the computer, and where she/he goes; limiting their contacts with the outside world; using jealousy to justify your own actions.
Minimising, denying and blaming	Making light of the abuse and not taking their concerns about it seriously; saying the abuse didn't happen, shifting the responsibility for the abuse onto her/him, other external factors, or on your own problems (your substance use, own unhappy, abusive childhoods etc).
Using children	Making her/him feel guilty about their children; undermining their parenting; using the children to relay messages; using visitation to harass her/him; threatening to take children away; telling lies to the children about her/him.
Economic abuse	Preventing her/him from getting or keeping a job; making her/him ask for money; giving her/him an allowance; taking their money; not letting her/him know about/ have access to the household income; running up debts without their knowledge, (eg by not paying bills, taking out loans); making all big decisions about how money will be spent; refusing to get paid work and/or expecting her/him to support him/her.
Physical abuse	Slapping/pushing/shoving; physically threatening them; kicking/punching; restraining/holding them down/tying them up; stalking/following them; beating up; choking/ strangling/suffocating; locking them out of the house/ room; hitting them with an object/weapon; biting; abducting them and keeping them somewhere against their will.

(continued)

**Indicative behaviours for spokes in COHSAR Power and
Control Wheel (continued)**

Spokes in COHSAR P&C Wheel	Indicative examples
Sexual abuse	Persuading them to have sex for sake of peace; touched them in ways that causes fear/alarm/distress; forcing into sexual activity, including rape, forcing them to watch or enact pornography; hurting during sex; disrespecting 'safe' words/boundaries; sexually assaulting/abusing; refusing requests for safer sex.
Entitlement abuse	Treating her/him like a servant; making all the big decisions; being the one to define roles in the relationship (of women and men; or how partners in same sex relationships should act); using religious faith as a justification for inequalities in the relationship; claiming that their behaviour is normal and that 'everyone else' would agree.
Identity abuse	Threatening to out or actually outing their sexuality, gender (or birth gender) identity or HIV status to their employer/colleagues, faith community, family of origin, children's services; undermining their sense of self as a women, man, lesbian, gay man, bisexual women or man, a trans women or man; controlling what she/he looks like, what clothes she/he wears, what hair style she/he has, her/his 'look' and behaviours; threatening to or withdrawing their medication, hormones, physical care supports; refusing her/him money for the costs of their gender transition.

of power and control addresses the often inappropriate prioritising these have had, and which have helped reinforce the public story of DVA. This also allows exploration of a range of physical and sexual violence that might elicit a more comprehensive understanding of how these abuses have been experienced by survivors. For example, listing physical violences that might have been trivialised, isolated as one-off incidents, 'forgotten' or normalised might encourage a deeper understanding of their experiences as DVA. Similarly, naming the different ways that sexual violence might be experienced (for example, being touched in ways that elicit fear, being forced to watch and/or enact pornographic images, having photographs of sexual acts made public without permission, as well as having sex to keep the peace, or being expected to 'make up' after an argument, or being forced to have sex or be raped) can provide opportunities to acknowledge and recognise painful experiences in the context of other behaviours so that the overriding pattern of relationship rules can be realised.

The eleven spokes with the repertoire of abusive behaviours are enclosed in a thick rim that represents practices of love and care. These practices underpin most abusive relationships entered into consensually and include strategic declarations of love, expressions of need or neediness (abusive partners' reasons for their abusive behaviour that elicit concern and care from survivors), and expectations of care and loyalty. Practices of love are situated around the outer rim because they reflect wider social norms that are drawn on by abusers, and also because it is intended to convey that they influence how the other behaviours and tactics of power and control might be experienced and that they might not necessarily be experienced negatively, abusively or as controlling. For example, where an abusive partner is using jealousy this might be experienced not as an isolating tactic but positively as a sign of an abusive partner's love; and their threats to commit suicide might elicit concern and care in the victim/survivor that confuses any sense of guilt about the implied causal relationship between the victim/survivor's behaviour and the abusive partner's threats to take their life.

In the outermost rim of the wheel we place the different intersecting, structural factors that provide the social and cultural context for the relationship. Understanding the ways that love and relationships are perceived, constructed and experienced through the intersecting lenses and positioning of sexuality and gender, 'race' and ethnicity, social class, faith, age and disability and so on provide crucial knowledge about how survivors make sense of their experiences, their own role in the relationship, the likely support they might receive and from whom in their families (of choice), friendship networks and communities, and their strengths, fears and resources. Rather than placing these structural factors in concentric circles, as do Chavis and Hill (2009), we place them in one circle to convey the ways in which survivors have multiple and overlapping identities that require recognition holistically rather than in any sequence.

In offering this new wheel for consideration we are aware that criticism might be raised about the apparent lack of a gender analysis of DVA. This is not our intention. We have maintained that gender is central to understanding the ways in which DVA can be expressed and experienced across gender and sexuality. Our focus in the wheel is on practice at the individual level of a victim/survivor (or abusive partner). We fully expect that heterosexual women will continue to constitute the biggest group of survivors accessing services for DVA; and that their experiences will be shaped by their relative social positioning as women in relation to that of men in society. The wheel allows for the particular ways that gender shapes experience of DVA to be explored, recognised and named. In addition, the wheel prompts consideration of how other, intersecting identities of heterosexual women might also shape their understanding both of their experiences and their potential to make the changes they wish. The wheel, however, is also intended to provide a way of reminding practitioners that they should start anew with each victim/survivor rather than take for granted what might be known about any particular relationship context, individuals' identities or the trajectories of DVA relationships.

Challenging the public story of DVA to improve recognition of DVA and help-seeking

In this book we have argued that recognition of DVA among those in same sex relationships is affected negatively by the public story about DVA. This depicts DVA as a problem of heterosexual men abusing heterosexual women, focused primarily on men's physical violence and that portrays gender as being enacted through embodied men who are bigger and stronger than embodied women who are smaller and weaker (both physically and emotionally). We have argued that non-recognition of DVA in same sex relationships has implications in at least three ways. First, as we showed in Chapter Three with accounts from those in first same sex relationships, abusive behaviours, experiences and relationships can be normalised so that they become expected. A lack of community knowledges about practices in same sex relationships exacerbates this as the negative impact of the heterosexual assumption leads some to expect and consider as normal negative (abusive) relationships that are not named as DVA. The societal context which is based on the heterosexual assumption is a supporting factor for DVA here. Second, as we showed in Chapter Four, non-recognition of DVA as understood in the public story can confuse survivors about whether or not their experiences 'count' as DVA. Not having a language that is inclusive of the kinds of abusive relationships and practices they have experienced can act to make DVA invisible not only to survivors but also to those they go to for support. In the case of those in same sex relationships this is likely to be friends, who will also be ill-equipped to assist in the naming of DVA for similar reasons. Third, non-recognition of DVA in same sex relationships results in relatively few survivors reporting their experiences to the police or other mainstream and specialist DVA services. We have highlighted (in Chapter Six) the gap of trust that exists between LGBTQ communities and those agencies, particularly the police, which can be exacerbated by intersecting identities, for example, being of a young age, from a minoritised ethnicity and/or particular faith. Fears about reporting arise from fears about not being believed because they do not 'fit' the model conveyed in the public story. Thus, some lesbian women we interviewed were conscious that they were bigger and looked stronger than their abusive female partner and therefore would not be believed. Others in same sex relationships feared or expected not to be taken seriously, expected hostility and/or discrimination from mainstream agencies. The very few who did report did not have positive experiences, which in turn reinforces these fears.

The formal source of support most often identified in our survey by those experiencing DVA in same sex relationships was counselling or therapy. This choice of privatised sources of support raises three major concerns. First, that DVA in same sex relationships has not achieved the status of it being a public problem in the way that this has begun to happen in relation to heterosexual women. Second, that the gap of trust between LGBTQ communities and mainstream agencies has resulted in survivors engaging in self-reliance and self-care that reinforces the individualisation of their experiences and the private nature of 'the problem'. Third, that more research is needed in the UK on the responses survivors actually receive from counsellors and therapists to their abusive relationship experiences.

In Chapter Six we also pointed to the impact that practices of love and self-reliance have on non-reporting. Victims/survivors in same sex relationships most often seek help from informal sources, particularly friends. We pointed to the ways in which friends' beliefs about practices of love could reinforce the sense of isolation a victim/survivor might feel about their experiences as behaviours such as post-separation abuse – harassment and/or stalking – were re-interpreted as normal behaviours of an ex-partner attempting to re-establish contact in order to talk about the relationship. In addition, we argued that self-reliance, argued to be a consequence of neoliberal discourses of the rational citizen are exacerbated by the experiences of being part of a minoritised community historically pathologised and criminalised by mainstream society. These factors support the enactment of DVA and also lead to victims/survivors individualising their experiences and seeking more private means of support through counselling and therapy.

Our findings suggest the following recommendations for practice: the need for awareness-raising within LGBTQ communities about the ways in which DVA is experienced and perpetrated, including the impact of practices of love and relationship rules more widely in normalising abusive behaviours; awareness-raising and training for practitioners about how they might respond to individual survivors of DVA in same sex relationships; and more generalised awareness-raising across mainstream and DVA specialist support services to challenge the public story, recognise the impact of practices of love and relationships rules across sexuality and gender and to encourage the provision of more inclusive services.

Awareness raising within LGBTQ communities

Awareness raising within LGBTQ communities about DVA is crucial for several reasons: to facilitate recognition of the wide repertoire of abusive behaviours, mechanisms of power and control, and naming of DVA and help-seeking in survivors; to encourage a culture change within LGBTQ communities and friendship networks to talk about relationships and to challenge the normalisation of violence and abuse through practices of love; to target those coming out or questioning their sexuality at any age, but particularly among young people; to challenge the influence of the heterosexual assumption that might lead survivors to normalise their experience of abuse as 'to be expected' in a same sex relationship; to empower those entering their first same sex relationships, particularly young people to recognise and name signs of abuse and negotiate relationships of respect that are enjoyable, loving and mutually supportive; and to challenge the individualistic interpretations that minimise and/or deny DVA or result in self-blame, guilt and shame.

Awareness raising and training for practitioners

Awareness raising and training for frontline practitioners is also crucial for the following reasons: to introduce the COHSAR power and control wheel and introduce the new aspects to DVA, particularly practices of love and relationship rules; to remind practitioners that much of the experience they have built up through working with heterosexual women will be useful in making sense of the experiences of those in same sex and trans relationships. As we have shown in this research, the range of behaviours of power and control used by abusive partners and the impacts on survivors are very similar across sexuality and gender. The differences in experiences of DVA most often emerge in relation to identity and entitlement abuses. Training and awareness-raising will enable practitioners to explore and learn about these to enhance their skills in relation to responding to survivors across sexuality and gender and in relation to other intersecting identities and positioning.

Awareness-raising and training is also needed to facilitate practitioners to understand how membership of different social groups arising from a variety of social locations and intersecting identities might have an impact on how abusive behaviours are made sense of, how the role of the survivor might be understood as implicated in the abuse and what resources (material, financial as well as in terms of support from friends, family and communities) the survivor has available to them. Such awareness will also enable more holistic risk assessments that encourage the use of professional judgement when risk assessment criteria appear inadequate to capture the risk a practitioner believes a victim/survivor faces. Such training would also go some way to ensuring that DVA accounts of survivors across sexuality and gender are heard and responded to in ways that promote their safety and meet their needs.

It is essential that practitioners' assumptions based on the public story of DVA are challenged so that when they first encounter a referral about, or report from, a survivor of DVA they are enabled to listen and react to the victim/survivor's account rather than the public story about DVA. This will also equip practitioners with the professional confidence to identify the victim/survivor and the abusive partner in the case of DVA in same sex relationships.

Inclusive services

More needs to be done to facilitate the development of more inclusive services for those experiencing DVA in same sex relationships. This requires that policies need to be redrawn to include those in same sex and/or trans relationships; and that they are monitored and regularly evaluated to ensure that they are fit for purpose. In addition, publicity about services, including websites, flyers, posters and leaflets should be written and designed to be inclusive of DVA in same sex relationships. This does not mean, however, that they should just be rewritten in gender neutral language. Instead we argue that agencies' literature should, where appropriate, specifically state that they provide services to LGBTQ survivors. To ensure that changes in practices are bedded down in each agency it is essential that training and awareness-raising about LGBT relationships and DVA in same sex and/or trans relationships should be provided and attended on a regular and mandatory basis. In addition, management and supervisory processes should include opportunities to reflect on the needs of minoritised groups, for the development of skills, knowledge and confidence in responding to LGBTQ service users, the creation of reach-out strategies to engage with local LGBTQ communities, including the use of the internet (see also, Duke and Davidson, 2009) and the embedding of a monitoring and evaluation process to record progress and identify gaps (see also, Helfrich and Simpson, 2006; Duke and Davidson, 2009).

It is also important to create new and more positive community knowledges about local services that challenge assumptions of them as homo-, bi-, or trans- phobic and instead reassure potential service users that they will be treated with respect, that their confidentiality will be protected and that they will not suffer discrimination or hate crime. This can be done in many ways, but requires agencies to engage in reach-out to their local LGBTQ communities; and perhaps securing the permission of LGBTQ victims/survivors to make public their positive experience of accessing a mainstream and/or specialist DVA service.

A final word

In this book we have presented the findings of our research that compared love and violence in same sex and heterosexual relationships. In doing so we have outlined our approach to utilise feminist, and intersectional methods of thinking about and explaining those findings. We have focused on how DVA occurs in same sex and heterosexual relationships, and have pointed to what we consider some of the key factors are that support it occurring across different sexualities and genders. Rather than concentrating on individual and/or psychological factors we have considered the impact of societal and cultural beliefs, expectations and norms that shape our understandings of gender, love, DVA, how and when help is sought and from whom; and how those social and cultural beliefs can also support DVA occurring across sexuality and gender. We have argued that the experiences and impact of DVA are extraordinarily similar across sexuality and gender, but that it is in the broader socio-cultural context in which heterosexual and same sex relationships are lived that differences are to be found and have an impact on whether and how DVA is recognised and named as such; and in the help-seeking engaged in or not. We have also, however, argued that it is in practices of love and relationship rules that we can find another factor that supports the enactment of DVA. We argue that in this research feelings of love were often at odds with relationship practices: what abusive partners said they felt for their partner did not match up with how they behaved towards them (see hooks, 2000). In making this case we consider the extent to which we are all implicated in re-creating norms about love that, left unquestioned, leave victims/ survivors trapped and/or isolated in violent and abusive relationships. We need to have public and/or societal conversations about love that resist normalising feelings such as of jealousy and possessiveness as rationales for controlling, cruel and/or abusive behaviour; of unconditional love and belief in a commitment to 'forever', through the good times and bad; that persuades us to forgive the unforgiveable and that love conquers all so that we believe that redemption is possible in the face of mounting evidence against this being possible; that renounces the idea that leaving an abusive relationship is shaming or a personal failing, or embarrassing or that it brings shame on relatives; that prioritises feelings over actions. We would argue that opportunities should be opened up for such discussions to take place in order to create and construct new norms about love and how it is practised and evidenced in relationships free from violence and abuse. We need to move towards a society where we valorise and eroticise equality rather than power over someone (Hester, 1992), and where we celebrate equal and respectful relationships whatever our sexuality or gender.

References

Aguinaldo, JP, 2004, Rethinking validity in qualitative research from a social constructionist perspective: From 'is this valid research?' to 'what is this research valid for?, *Qualitative Report* 9, 127–36

Archer, J, 2000a, Sex differences in aggression between heterosexual partners: A meta-analytic review, *Psychological Bulletin* 126, 651–80

Archer, J, 2000b, Sex difference in physical aggression to partners: A reply to Frieze et al, 2000, *Psychological Bulletin* 126, 697–702

Archer, J, 2002, Sex differences in physically aggressive acts between heterosexual partners: A meta-analysis review, *Aggression and Violent Behaviour* 7, 313–51

Baker, H, 2008, Constructing women who experience male violence: Criminal legal discourse and individual experiences, *Liverpool Law Review* 29, 123–42

Balsam, K, 2001, Nowhere to hide: Lesbian battering, homophobia, and minority stress, in E Kaschak (ed) *Intimate betrayal: Domestic violence in lesbian relationships*, Philadelphia, PA: Haworth Press

Balsam, KF, Szymanski, DM, 2005, Relationship quality and domestic violence in women's same-sex relationships: The role of minority stress, *Psychology of Women Quarterly* 29, 258–69

Barnes, R, 2008, 'I still sort of flounder in a sea of non-language': The constraints of language and labels in women's accounts of woman-to-woman partner abuse, in K Throsby, F Alexander (eds) *Gender and interpersonal violence: Language, action and representation*, Basingstoke: Palgrave Macmillan

Barnes, R, 2010, 'Suffering in a silent vacuum': Woman-to-woman partner abuse as a challenge to the lesbian feminist vision, *Feminism and Psychology* 21, 233–9

Barter, C, McCarry, M, Berridge, D, Evan, K, 2009, *Partner exploitation and violence in teenage intimate relationships: Executive summary*, London: NSPCC

Bauman, Z, 2003, *Liquid love*, Cambridge: Polity Press

Beck, U, 1992, *Risk and society: Towards a new modernity*, London: Sage

Beck, U, Beck-Gernsheim, E, 1995, *The normal chaos of love*, Cambridge: Polity Press

Blassius, M, 1994, *Gay and lesbian politics: Sexuality and the emergence of a new ethic*, Philadelphia, PA: Temple University Press

Bograd, M, 2005, Strengthening domestic violence theories: Intersections of race, class, sexual orientation, and gender, in NJ Sokoloff, C Pratt (eds) *Domestic violence at the margins: Readings on race, class, gender and culture*, New York: Rutgers University Press

Bornstein, D, Fawcett, J, Sullivan, M, Senturia, K, Shiu-Thornton, S, 2006, Understanding the experiences of lesbian, bisexual and trans survivors of domestic violence: A qualitative study, *Journal of Homosexuality* 51, 159–81

Broken Rainbow, 2002, *Conference report*, 5 December, London

Brown, C, 2008, Gender-role implications of same-sex intimate partner abuse, *Journal of Family Violence* 23, 457–62

Brown, MJ, Groscup, J, 2009, Perceptions of same-sex domestic violence among crisis center staff, *Journal of Family Violence* 24, 87–93

CAADA (Co-ordinated Action Against Domestic Abuse), 2012a, *A place of greater safety: Insights into domestic violence*, Bristol: CAADA

CAADA (Co-ordinated Action Against Domestic Abuse), 2012b, *Risk identification checklist (RIC) and quick start guidance for domestic abuse, stalking and 'honour'-based violence*, Bristol: CAADA

CAADA (Co-ordinated Action Against Domestic Abuse), 2013, Practice briefing for IDVAs: Engaging and working with lesbian, gay, bisexual and transgender (LGBT) clients, www.caada.org.uk/documents/LGBT_practice_briefing.pdf, Bristol: CAADA

Campbell, JC, Soeken, K, 1999, Women's responses to battering over time: An analysis of change, *Journal of Interpersonal Violence* 14, 21–40

Campbell, JC, Rose, L, Kub, J, 1998, Voices of strength and resistance: A contextual and longitudinal analysis of women's responses to battering, *Journal of Interpersonal Violence* 13, 743–62

Cancian, F, 1990, *Love in America*, Cambridge: Cambridge University Press

Carabine, J, 1996, Heterosexuality and social policy, in D Richardson (ed) *Theorising heterosexuality*, Milton Keynes: Open University Press

Carvalho, AF, Lewis, RJ, Derlega, VJ, Winstead, BA, Viggiano, C, 2011, Internalized sexual minority stressors and same sex intimate partner violence, *Journal of Family Violence* 26, 501–9

Chantler, K, Gangoli, G, 2012, Violence against women in minoritised communities: Cultural norm or cultural anomaly?, in RK Thiara, SA Condon, M Schrottle (eds) *Violence against women and ethnicity: Commonalities and differences across Europe*, Leverkusen: Barbara Budrich Publishers

Chavis, A, Hill, M, 2009, Integrating multiple intersecting identities: A multicultural conceptualization of the power and control wheel, *Women and Therapy* 32, 121–49

Cockburn, C, 2007, *From where we stand: War, women's activism and feminist analysis*, London: Zed Books

Connell, R, 2000, *The men and the boys*, Cambridge: Polity Press

Coy, M, Kelly, L, 2011, *Islands in the stream: An evaluation of four London independent domestic violence advocacy schemes*, London: London Metropolitan University

Cramer, E, Plummer, S, 2009, People of color with disabilities: Intersectionality as a framework for analyzing intimate partner violence in social, historical, and political contexts, *Journal of Aggression, Maltreatment and Trauma* 18, 162–81

Crenshaw, K, 1989, *Demarginalizing the intersection of race and sex: A black feminist critique of antidiscrimation doctrine, feminist theory and antiracist politics*, Chicago, IL: University of Chicago Legal Forum

Crenshaw, KW, 1994, *Mapping the margins: Intersectionality, identity politics, and violence against women of color*, in MA, Fineman, R, Mykitiuk (eds) *The public nature of private violence*, New York: Routledge

Cruz, J, 2003, 'Why doesn't he just leave?': Gay male violence and the reasons victims stay, *Journal of Men's Studies* 11, 309–23

De Beauvoir, S, 1972, *The second sex*, Middlesex: Penguin Books

Dennis, N, Erdos, G, 1992, *Families without fatherhood*, London: IEA Health and Welfare Unit

DfEE (Department for Education Employment), 2000, *Sex and relationship education guidance*, London: DfEE

Dobash, RE, Dobash, RP, 1992, *Women, violence and social change*, London: Routledge

Dobash, R, Dobash, R, 2000, *The politics and policies of responding to violence against women: Home truths about domestic violence*, London: Routledge

Donovan, C, 2004, Why reach for the moon? Because the stars aren't enough, *Feminism Psychology* 14, 24–9

Donovan, C, 2010, *Barriers to making referrals of lesbian, gay, bisexual and transgendered (LGBT) victim/survivors to the MARAC and recommendations for improvement: A study of IDVAs, MARAC coordinators and PPU detective inspectors within the Northumbria police force area*, Sunderland: University of Sunderland/Gateshead Council

Donovan, C, 2013, Redefining domestic violence and abuse: Unintended consequences of risk assessment, in J Kearney, C Donovan (eds) *Constructing risky identities in policy and practice*, Basingstoke: Palgrave Macmillan

Donovan, C, Griffiths, S, Groves, N with Johnson, H, Douglass, J (2010) *Making connections count: An evaluation of early intervention models for change in domestic violence, 2004-2009*, http://www.nr-foundation. org.uk/publications_domabuse.html.pdf

Donovan, C, Hester, M, 2008, 'Because she was my first girlfriend, I didn't know any different': Making the case for mainstreaming same-sex sex/relationship education, *Sex Education* 8, 277–87

Donovan, C, Hester, M, 2010, 'I hate the word "victim"': An exploration of recognition of domestic violence in same sex relationships, *Social Policy and Society* 9, 279–89

Donovan, C, Hester, M, 2011, Exploring emotion work in domestically abusive relationships, in J Ristock (ed) *Intimate partner violence in LGBTQ lives*, New York and Abingdon: Routledge

Donovan, C, Rowlands, J, 2011, Barriers to making referrals of lesbian, gay, bisexual and transgendered (LGBT) victim/survivors to the MARAC and recommendations for improvements, *Safe, The Domestic Abuse Quarterly* 36, Winter, 22–5

Donovan, C, Heaphy, B, Weeks, J, 1999, Citzenship and same sex relationships, *Journal of Social Policy* 28, 689–709

Donovan, C, Hester, M, Holmes, J, McCarry, M, 2006, *Comparing domestic abuse in same sex and heterosexual relationships: Initial report from a study funded by the Economic and Social Research Council*, Sunderland: University of Sunderland/University of Bristol

Duffy, K, 2011, There's no pride in domestic violence: The same sex domestic violence interagency, Sydney, Australia, in J Ristock (ed) *Intimate partner violence in LGBTQ lives*, New York and Abingdon: Routledge

Duke, A, Davidson, M, 2009, Same sex intimate partner violence: Lesbian, gay and bisexual affirmative outreach and advocacy, *Journal of Aggression, Maltreatment and Trauma* 18, 795–816

Duncombe, J, Marsden, D, 1993, Love and intimacy: The gender division of emotion and 'emotion work' a neglected aspect of sociological discussion of heterosexual relationships, *Sociology* 27, 221–41

Duncombe, J, Marsden, D, 1995, 'Workaholics' and 'whingeing women': Theorising intimacy and emotion work – the last frontier of gender equality?, *Sociology Review* 43, 150–69

Duncombe, J, Marsden, D, 1996, Can we research the private sphere? Methodology and ethical problems in the study of the role of intimate emotion in personal relationships, in L Morris, ES Lyon (eds) *Gender relations in public and private: New research perspectives*, London: Macmillan

Dunne, G, 1999, A passion for 'sameness'?: Sexuality and gender accountability, in EB Silva, C Smart (eds) *The new family?*, London: Sage

Elliott, P, 1996, Shattering illusions: Same-sex domestic violence, *Journal of Gay and Lesbian Social Services* 4, 1–8

Equal Love, nd, http://equallove.org.uk

Eriksson, M, 2008, Revolutionary mothers? Interacting power relations, agency, and social change, *Nordic Journal of Feminist and Gender Research* 16, 96–13

Evans, M, 2003, *Love: An unromantic discussion*, Cambridge: Polity Press

Finch, J, 2007, Displaying families, *Sociology* 41, 65–81

Finch, J, Mason, J, 1993, *Negotiating family responsibilities*, London: Routledge

Formby, E, 2011, Sex and relationships education, sexual health, and lesbian, gay and bisexual sexual cultures: Views from young people, *Sex Education* 11, 255–66

Fraser, H, 2008, *In the name of love: Women's narratives of love and abuse*, Toronto: Canada

Fugate, M, Landis, L, Riordan, K, Naurecks, S, Engle, B, 2005, Barriers to domestic violence help seeking: Implications for interventions, *Violence Against Women* 11, 290–310

Gabb, J, 2008, *Researching intimacy in families*, Basingstoke: Palgrave Macmillan

Gamson, J, 1994, Must identity movements self-destruct? A queer dilemma, *Social Problems* 42, 390–407

Gangoli, G, Razak, A, McCarry, M, 2006, *Forced marriage and domestic violence among South Asian communities in North East England*, University of Bristol/Northern Rock Foundation

Gangoli, G, Chantler, K, Hester, M, Singleton, A, 2011, Understanding forced marriage: Definitions and realities, in A Gill, A Sundhari (eds) *Forced marriage: Introducing a social justice and human rights perspective*, London: Zed Books

Garland, D, 1996, The limits of the sovereign state, *British Journal of Criminology* 36, 445–71

Giddens, A, 1992, *The transformation of intimacy: Sexuality, love and eroticism in modern societies*, Cambridge: Polity Press

Giorgio, G, 2002, Speaking silence: Definitional dialogues in abusive lesbian relationships, *Violence Against Women* 8, 1233–59

Goodkind, JR, Gillum, TL, Bybee, DI, Sullivan, CM, 2003, The impact on family and friends' reactions on wellbeing of women with abusive partners, *Violence Against Women* 9, 347–73

Greenwood, GL, Reif, MV, Huang, B, Pollack, LM, Canchofa, JA, Catania, JA, 2002, Battering victimization among a probability-based sample of men who have sex with men, *American Journal of Public Health* 92, 1964–9

Grossi, R, 2012, The meaning of love in the debate for legal recognition of same-sex marriage in Australia, *International Journal of Law in Context* 8, 487–505

Grove, J, Blasby, S, 2009, Counselling and psychotherapy research: Linking research with practice, *Counselling and Psychotherapy Research* 9, 257–65

Guasp, A, 2012, *Gay and bisexual men's health survey*, London: Stonewall

Hall, A, 1992, Abuse by lesbians, *Trouble and Strife: The Radical Feminist Magazine* 23, 38

Hanmer, J, 2000, Domestic violence and gender relations, contexts and connections, in J Hanmer, C Itzin with S Quaid, D Wrigglesworth (eds) *Home truths about domestic violence: Feminist influences on policy and practice. A reader*, London: Routledge

Hanmer, J, Griffiths, S, Jerwood, D, 1999, Arresting evidence: Domestic violence and repeat victimisation, *Police Research Series Paper* 104, London: Home Office

Hardesty, JL, Oswald, RF, Khaw, L, Fonseca, C, 2011, Lesbian/bisexual mothers and intimate partner violence: Help seeking in the context of social and legal vulnerability, *Violence Against Women* 17, 28–46

Hardesty, JL, Oswald, RF, Khaw, L, Fonseca, C, Chung, GH, 2008, Lesbian mothering in the context of intimate partner violence, *Journal of Lesbian Studies* 12, 191-210

Harris, GE, 2006, Conjoint therapy and domestic violence: Treating the individuals and the relationship, *Counselling Psychology Quarterly* 19, 373–79

Harrison, J, MacGibbon, L, Morton, M, 2001, Regimes of trustworthiness in qualitative research: The rigors of reciprocity, *Qualitative Inquiry* 7, 323–45

Hart, B, 1986, Lesbian battering: An examination, in K Lobel (ed) *Naming the violence: Speaking out about lesbian battering*, Washington, DC: Seal Press

Hassouneh, D, Glass, N, 2008, The influence of gender role stereotyping on women's experiences of female same-sex intimate partner violence, *Violence Against Women* 14, 310–25

Heaphy, B, Weeks, J, Donovan, C, 1998, 'That's like my life': Researching stories of non-heterosexual relationships, *Sexualities* 1, 453–70

Heaphy, B, Weeks, J Donovan, C, 1999, Sex, money and the kitchen sink: Power in same-sex couple relationships, in J Seymour, P Bagguley (eds) *Relating intimacies: Power and resistance*, London: Macmillan

Hearn, J, 1996a, Men's violence to known women: Historical, everyday and theoretical constructions by men, in B Fawcett, B Featherstone, J Hearn, C Toft (eds) *Violence and gender relations: Theories and interventions*, London: Sage

Hearn, J, 1996b, Men's violence to known women: Men's accounts and men's policy development, in B Fawcett, B Featherstone, J Hearn, C Toft (eds) *Violence and gender relations: Theories and interventions*, London: Sage

Heintz, AJ, Melendez, RM, 2006, Intimate partner violence and HIV/STD risk among lesbian, gay, bisexual and transgender individuals, *Journal of Interpersonal Violence* 21, 193–208

Helfrich, C, Simpson, E, 2006, Improving services for lesbian clients: What do domestic violence agencies need to do?, *Health Care for Women International* 27, 344–61

Henderson, L, 2003, *Prevalence of domestic violence among lesbians and gay men: Data report to Flame TV*, London: Sigma Research

Hester, M, 1992, *Lewd women and wicked witches: A study of the dynamics of male domination*, Abingdon: Routledge

Hester, M, 2004, Future trends and developments: Violence against women in Europe and East Asia, *Violence Against Women* 10, 1431–48

Hester, M, 2006, Making it through the criminal justice system: Attrition and domestic violence, *Social Policy and Society* 5, 79–90

Hester, M, 2009, *Who does what to whom? Gender and domestic violence perpetrators*, Bristol: University of Bristol in association with Northern Rock Foundation

Hester, M, 2010, Gender and sexuality, in C Itzin, A Taket, S Barter-Godfrey (eds) *Domestic and sexual violence and abuse: Tackling the health and mental health effects*, London: Routledge

Hester, M, 2012, Portrayal of women as intimate partner domestic violence perpetrators, *Violence Against Women* 18, 1–16

Hester, M, 2013, Who does what to whom? Gender and domestic violence perpetrators in English police reports, *European Journal of Criminology* 10, 5, 623–37

Hester, M, Donovan, C, 2009, Researching domestic violence in same-sex relationships: A feminist epistemological approach to survey development, *Journal of Lesbian Studies* 13, 161–73

Hester, M, Westmarland, N, 2006, *Service provision for perpetrators of domestic violence,* Bristol: University of Bristol in association with Northern Rock Foundation

Hester, M, Westmarland, N, 2006/07, Domestic violence perpetrators, *Crime Justice Matters* Winter, 66, 34–5

Hester, M, Westmarland, N, Gangoli, G et al, 2006, *Domestic violence perpetrators: Identifying needs to inform early intervention*, Bristol: Northern Rock Foundation/Home Office, University of Bristol

Hester, M, Pearson, C, Harwin, N, Abrahams, H, 2007, *Making an impact: Children and domestic violence. A reader*, London: Jessica Kingsley Publishers

Hester, M, Donovan, C, Fahmy, E, 2010, Feminist epistemology and the politics of method: surveying same sex domestic violence, *International Journal of Social Research Methodology* 13, 251–63

Hester, H, Williamson, E, Regan, L et al, 2012, *Exploring the service and support needs of male, lesbian, gay, bisexual and transgendered and black and other minority ethnic victims of domestic and sexual violence*, Bristol: School for Policy Studies

Hewitt, R, Macredie, S, 2012, *I count! Wakefield district same sex relationships and domestic abuse needs assessment. Report of findings: Equity partnership*, NHS Calderdale, Kirklees and Wakefield District Cluster Partnership, Bradford Equity Partnership

Hochschild, AR, 1979, Emotion work, feeling rules and social structure, *American Journal of Sociology* 85, 551–75

Hochschild, A, 2003, *The managed heart: Commercialization of human feeling*, London: University of California Press

Holmes, C, 2011, Troubling normalcy: Examining 'healthy relationships' discourses in lesbian domestic violence prevention, in J Ristock (ed) *Intimate partner violence in LGBTQ lives*, New York and Abingdon: Routledge

Home Office Affairs Select Committee, 2008, *Domestic violence, forced marriage and 'honour'-based violence*, London: House of Commons

Home Office, 2007, *National domestic violence delivery plan: Annual progress report 2006/07*, London: Home Office

Home Office, 2008, *National domestic violence delivery plan: Annual progress report 2007/08*, London: Home Office

Home Office, 2009a, Together we can end violence against women and girls: A consultation paper, https://www.gov.uk/government/uploads/system/uploads/attachment_data/file/97905/vawg-paper.pdf

Home Office, 2009b, *National domestic violence delivery plan: Annual progress report 2008/09*, London: Home Office

Home Office, 2010, *Call to end violence against women and girls. Taking Action – the next chapter*, London: Home Office, www.gov.uk/government/publications/call-to-end-violence-against-women-and-girls (accessed 7 February 2014)

Home Office, 2011, *Call to end violence against woman and girls: Action plan*, London: HM Government

hooks, b, 2000, *All about love*, New York: William Morrow Company

Howarth, E, Stimpson, L, Barran, D, Robinson, A, 2009, *Safety in numbers: Multi-site evaluation of IDVA (independent domestic violence advisor) services*, London: Hestia Fund/Sigrid Rausing Trust/Henry Smith Charity

Hunt, R, Fish, J, 2008, *Prescription for change: Lesbian and bisexual women's health check*, London: Stonewall

Illouz, E, 2011, Romantic love, in S Seidman, N Fischer, C Meeks (eds) *Introducing the new sexuality studies* (2nd edn), London: Routledge

Irwin, J, 2006, Lesbians and domestic violence: stories of seeking support, *Women in Welfare Education* 8, 28–36

Irwin, J, 2008, (Dis)counted stories: Domestic violence and lesbians, *Qualitative Social Work* 7, 199–215

Irwin, K, Chesney-Lind, M, 2008, Girls' violence: Beyond dangerous masculinity, *Sociology Compass* 2, 837–55

Island, D, Letellier, P, 1991, *Men who beat the men who love them: Battered gay men and domestic violence*, Abingdon: Routledge

Jackson, S, 1993, Even sociologists fall in love: An exploration in the sociology of emotions, *Sociology* 23, 201–20

Jamieson, L, 1998, *Intimacy and personal relationships in modern society*, Cambridge: Polity Press

Johnson, MP, 1995, Patriarchal terrorism and common couple violence: Two forms of violence against women, *Journal of Marriage and the Family* 57, 283–94

Johnson, MP, 2006, Conflict and control: Gender symmetry and asymmetry in domestic violence, *Violence Against Women* 12, 1003–18

Johnson, M, Ferraro, K, 2000, Research on domestic violence in the 1990s: Making distinctions, *Journal of Marriage and Family* 62, 948–63

Johnston, L, Valentine, G, 1995, Wherever I lay my girlfriend, that's my home: The performance and surveillance of lesbian identities in domestic environments, in D Bell, G Valentine (eds) *Mapping desire: Geographies of sexualities*, London: Routledge

Kanuha, K, 1990, Compounding the triple jeopardy: Battering in lesbian of colour relationships, *Women and Therapy* 9, 169–84

Kelly, B, Izienicki, H, Bimbi, DS, Parsons, J, 2011, The intersection of mutual partner violence and substance abuse among urban gays, lesbians, and bisexuals, *Deviant Behaviour* 32, 379–404

Kelly, L, 1988, *Surviving sexual violence*, Cambridge: Polity Press

Kelly, L, 1991, Unspeakable acts: Women who abuse, *Trouble and Strife: The Radical Feminist Magazine* 21, 13–20

Kelly, L, 1996, When does the speaking profit us? Reflections on the challenges of developing feminist perspectives on abuse and violence by women, in M Hester, L Kelly, J Radford (eds) *Women, violence and male power*, Milton Keynes: Open University Press

King, M, McKeown, E, 2003, Mental health and social well-being of gay men, lesbians and bisexuals in England and Wales, London: Mind

Kwong-Lai Poon, M, 2011, Beyond good and evil: The social construction of violence in intimate gay relationships, in J Ristock (ed) *Intimate partner violence in LGBTQ lives*, New York and Abingdon: Routledge

Lehavot, K, Walters, KL, Simoni, JM, 2010, Abuse, mastery, and health among lesbian, bisexual and two-spirit American Indian and Alaska native women, *Psychology of Violence* 1, 53–67

Leone, JM, Johnson, MP, Cohan, CL, 2007, Victim help seeking: Differences between intimate terrorism and situational couple violence, *Family Relations* 56, 427–39

Lewis, R, Milletich, R, Kelley, M, Woody, A, 2012, Minority stress, substance use and intimate partner violence among sexual minority women, *Aggression and Violent Behaviour* 17, 247–56

LGBT DAF (LGBT Domestic Abuse Forum), Stonewall Housing, 2013, *Roar: Because silence is deadly*, London: LGBT DAF and Stonewall Housing

Liang, B, Goodman, L, Tummala-Narra, P, Weintraub, S, 2005, A theoretical framework for understanding help-seeking processes among survivors of intimate partner violence, *American Journal of Community Psychology* 36, 71–84

Lie, G, Gentlewarrier, S, 1991, Intimate violence in lesbian relationships: Discussion of survey findings and practice implications, *Journal of Social Service Research* 15, 41–59

Little, B, Terrance, C, 2010, Perceptions of domestic violence in lesbian relationships: Stereotypes and gender role expectations, *Journal of Homosexuality* 57, 429–40

Lloyd, S, Emery, B, 2000, *The dark side of courtship: Physical and sexual aggression*, London: Sage

Lobel, K, 1986, *Naming the violence: Speaking out about lesbian battering*, Seattle, WA: Seal Press

Lockhart, LL, White, BW, Causby, V, Isaac, A, 1994, Letting out the secret: Violence in lesbian relationships, *Journal of Interpersonal Violence* 9, 469–92

McCall, L, 2005, The complexity of intersectionality, *Signs* 3, 1771–800

McCarry, M, Hester, M, Donovan, C, 2008, Researching same sex domestic violence: Constructing a comprehensive survey methodology, *Sociological Research Online*, 13

McClennen, JC, 2005, Domestic violence between same-gender partners: Recent findings and future research, *Journal of Interpersonal Violence* 20, 149–54

McLaughlin, E, Rozee, P, 2001, Knowledge about heterosexual versus lesbian battering among lesbians, in E Kaschak (ed) *Intimate betrayal: Domestic violence in lesbian relationships*, Philadelphia, PA: Haworth Press

Mendoza, J, 2011, The impact of minority stress on gay male partner abuse, in J Ristock (ed) *Intimate partner violence in LGBTQ lives*, New York and Abingdon: Routledge

Merlis, S, Linville, D, 2006, Exploring a community's response to lesbian domestic violence through the voices of providers: A qualitative study, *Journal of Feminist Family Therapy*, 18, 97–136

Merrill, GM, 1996, Ruling the exceptions: Same-sex battering and domestic violence theory, in C Renzetti, C Miley (eds) *Violence in gay and lesbian domestic partnerships*, New York: Harrington Park Press

Merrill, GM, Wolfe, VA, 2000, Battered gay men: An exploration of abuse, help seeking and why they stay, *Journal of Homosexuality*, 39, 1–30

Miller, DH, Greene, K, Causby, V, White, B, Lockhart, L, 2001, Domestic violence in lesbian relationships, in E Kaschak (ed) *Intimate betrayal: Domestic violence in lesbian relationships*, Philadelphia, PA: Haworth Press

Moran, J, 2001, Childhood sexuality and education: The case of section 28, *Sexualities* 4, 73–89

Moran, LJ, Skeggs, B, Tyrer, P, Corteen, K, 2003, The constitution of fear in gay space, in EA Stanko (ed) *The meanings of violence*, Abingdon: Routledge

Morgan, D, 1999, Risk and family practice: Accounting for change and fluidity in family life, in E Silva, C Smart (eds) *The new family*, London: Sage

Morris, L, 1999, The household and the labour market, in G Allen (ed) *The sociology of the family: A reader*, Oxford: Blackwell Publishers

Morris, M, with Bunjun, B, 2007, *Using intersectional feminist frameworks in research: A resource for embracing the complexities of women's lives*, Ontario: Canada, CRIAW/ICREF (Canadian Research Institute for the Advancement of Women, Ottawa)

Morris, N, 2013, The return of Section 28: Schools and academies practising homophobic policy that was outlawed under Tony Blair, 20 August, www.independent.co.uk/news/uk/politics/the-return-of-section-28-schools-and-academies-practising-homophobic-policy-that-was-outlawed-under-tony-blair-8775249.html

Mullender, A, Hague, G, Imam, U, Kelly, L, Malos, E, Regan, L, 2002, *Children's perspectives on domestic violence*, London: Sage

Murray, C, 1996a, The emerging British underclass, in R Lister (ed) *Charles Murray and the underclass: The developing debate*, London: IEA in Association with The Sunday Times, IEA Health and Welfare Unit, Choice in Welfare

Murray, C, 1996b, Underclass: The crisis deepens, in R Lister (ed) *Charles Murray and the underclass: The developing debate*, London: IEA in Association with *The Sunday Times*, IEA Health and Welfare Unit, Choice in Welfare

Murray, CE, Mobley, AK, 2009, Empirical research about same-sex intimate partner violence: A methodological review, *Journal of Homosexuality* 56, 361–86

National Statistics, 2006, *Annual survey of hours and earnings*, London: National Statistics

Nowinski, SN, Bowen, E, 2012, Partner violence against heterosexual and gay men: Prevalence and correlates, *Aggression and Violent Behavior* 17, 36–52

Oakley, A, 2000, *Experiments in knowing: Gender and method in the social sciences*, New York: The New Press

Obama, B, 2013, Inauguration Address, www.whitehouse.gov/the-press-office/2013/01/21/inaugural-address-president-barack-obama

Osterlund, K, 2009, Love, freedom and governance: Same-sex marriage in Canada, *Social and Legal Studies* 18, 93–109

Oswald, RF, Fonseca, CA, Hardesty, JL, 2010, Lesbian mothers' counselling experiences in the context of intimate partner violence, *Psychology of Women Quarterly* 34, 286–96

Pattavina, A, Hirschel, D, Buzawa, E, Faggiani, D, Bentley, H, 2007, A comparison of the police response to heterosexual versus same-sex intimate partner violence, *Violence Against Women* 13, 374–94

Pence, EL, Shephard, MF, (1999) An introduction: Developing a coordinated community response, in MF Shephard, EL Pence (eds) *Coordinating community responses to domestic violence: Lessons from Duluth and beyond*, London: Sage

Peplua, LA, Fingerhut, AW, 2007, The close relationships of lesbians and gay men, *Annual Review of Psychology* 58, 405–24

Pierce, A, 2012, How Mr Cameron's obsession with gay marriage is killing the Tory party, *Daily Mail*, 9 January

Plummer, K, 1995, *Telling sexual stories: Power, change and social worlds*, London: Routledge

Poorman, P, Seelau, SM, 2001, Lesbians who abuse their partners: Using the FIRO-B to assess interpersonal characteristics, in E Kaschak (ed) *Intimate betrayal: Domestic violence in lesbian relationships*, Philadelphia, PA: Haworth Press

Povey, D, Coleman, K, Kaiza, P, Hoare, J, Jansson, K, 2008, *Homicides, firearm offences and intimate violence 2006/07* (Supplementary Volume 2 to *Crime in England and Wales 06/07*), London: Home Office Statistical Bulletin

Pullella, P, 2012, Gay marriage a threat to humanity's future, Reuters, www.reuters.com/article/2012/01/09/us-pope-gay-idUSTRE8081RM20120109

Radford, J, Kelly, L, Hester, M, 1996, Introduction, in M Hester, L Kelly, J Radford (eds) *Women, violence and male power: Feminist activism, research and practice*, Buckingham: Open University Press

Radford, L, Hester, M, 2006, *Mothering through domestic violence*, London: Jessica Kingsley Publishers

Ramazanoğlu, C with Holland, J, 2002, *Feminist methodology: Challenges and choices*, London: Sage

Renzetti, CM, 1992, *Violent betrayal: Partner abuse in lesbian relationships*, London: Sage

Rich, A, 1980, Compulsory heterosexuality and lesbian existence, *Signs* 5, 631–60

Richardson, D, 2004, Locating sexualities: From here to normality, *Sexualities* 7, 391–411

Richardson, D, 2005, Desiring sameness? The rise of a neoliberal politics of normalisation, *Sexualities* 7, 515–35

Richardson, D, 2007, Patterned fluidities: (Re)imagining the relationship between gender and sexuality, *Sociology* 41, 457–74

Richardson, D, Monro, S, 2012, *Sexuality, diversity and equality*, Basingstoke: Palgrave Macmillan

Ristock, J, 1997, 'Kiss and kill': Some impacts of cultural representations of women's sexualities, in P Greenhill, D Tye (eds) *Undisciplined women: Tradition and culture in Canada*, Quebec, Canada: McGill-Queen's University Press

Ristock, J, 2001, Decentering heterosexuality: Responses of feminist counsellors to abuse in lesbian relationships, *Women and Therapy* 23, 59–72

Ristock, J, 2002a, *No more secrets: Violence in lesbian relationships*, London and New York: Routledge

Ristock, J, 2002b, Responding to lesbian relationship violence: An ethical challenge, in LM Tutty, C Goard (eds) *Reclaiming self: Issues and resources for women abused by intimate partners*, Halifax: Fernwood Publishing

Ristock, J, 2002c, *The politics of responding to violence in lesbian relationships*, Abingdon: Taylor and Francis

Ristock, J, 2003, Exploring dynamics of abusive lesbian relationships: Preliminary analysis of a multisite, qualitative study, *American Journal of Community Psychology* 31(3/4), 329–41

Ristock, J, 2011, Introduction: Intimate partner violence in LGBTQ lives, in J Ristock (ed) *Intimate partner violence in LGBTQ lives*, New York and Abingdon: Routledge

Robinson, A, 2006, *Advice, support, safety and information services together (ASSIST): The benefits of providing assistance to victims of domestic abuse in Glasgow*, Final Evaluation Report, Cardiff: Cardiff University

Robinson, A, 2009, *Independent sexual violence advisors: A process evaluation*, Final Evaluation Report, Cardiff: Cardiff University

Robinson, A, Rowlands, J, 2009, Assessing and managing risk among different victims of domestic abuse: Limits of a generic model of risk assessment?, *Security Journal* 22, 190–204

Roch, A, Morton, J, Ritchie, G, 2010, *Out of sight, out of mind? Transgender people's experience of domestic abuse*, Edinburgh: Stop Domestic Abuse, Scottish Trans Alliance and Equality Network

Roe, Jagodinsky (undated) *Power and Control Wheel for lesbian, gay, bisexual and trans relationships*, Texas Council on Family Violence, http://tcfv.org/pdf/Updated_wheels/LGBT.pdf

Rohrbaugh, JR, 2006, Domestic violence in same-gender relationships, *Family Court Review* 44, 287–99

Rose, N, 2000, Government and control, *British Journal of Criminology* 40, 321–9

Russell, S, Ryan, C, Toomey, R, Diaz, R, Sanchez, J, 2011, Lesbian, gay, bisexual, and transgender adolescent school victimization: Implications for young adult health and adjustment, *Journal of School Health* 81, 223–30

Saalsfield, C, 1993, Lesbian marriage…(K)not, in A Stein (ed) *Sisters, sexperts, queers: Beyond the lesbian nation*, London: Penguin Books

Savage, M, Burrows, R, 2007, The coming crisis of empirical sociology, *Sociology* 41, 885–99

Seidman, S, Meeks, C, Traschsen, F, 1999, Beyond the closet? The changing social meaning of homosexuality in the United States, *Sexualities* 2, 9–34

Skinner, T, Hester, M, Malos, E, 2005, *Researching gender violence: Feminist methodology in action*, Abingdon: Willan

Smith, D, 1988, *The everyday world as problematic: A feminist sociology*, Milton Keynes: Open University Press

Smith, K, Flatley, J, Coleman, K, Osborne, S, Kaiza, P, Roe, S, 2010, *Homicides, firearm offences and intimate violence 2008/09* (Supplementary Volume 2 to *Crime in England and Wales*), 3rd edn, London: Home Office Statistical Bulletin

Smith, K, Osborne, S, Lau, I, Britton, A, 2012, *Homicides, Firearm Offences and Intimate Violence 2010/11* (Supplementary Volume 2 to *Crime in England and Wales*), London: Home Office Statistical Bulletin

Sokoloff, N, Dupont, I, 2005, Domestic violence at the intersections of race, class and gender: Challenges and contributions to understanding violence against marginalized women in diverse communities, *Violence Against Women* 11, 38–64

Stanley, JL, Bartholomew, K, 2006, Intimate violence in male same-sex relationships, *Journal of Family Violence* 21, 31–42

Stanley, JL, Bartholomew, K, Taylor, T, Oram, D, Landolt, M, 2006, Intimate violence in male same-sex relationships, *Journal of Family Violence* 21, 31–42

Stark, E, 2007, *Coercive control: How men entrap women in personal life*, Oxford: Oxford University Press

Steel, N, Blakeborough, L, Nicholas, S, 2011, *Supporting high risk victims of domestic violence: A review of multi-agency risk assessment conferences (MARACs). Research Report 55: Summary*, London: Home Office

Stovold, A, Mitchell, S, Permjit, C, 2005, *What do you think? 2004 LGBT experiences of domestic violence and homophobic crime,* London: London Borough of Hounslow

St Pierre, M, Senn, CY, 2010, External barriers to help-seeking encountered by Canadian gay and lesbian victims of intimate partner abuse: An application of the barriers model, *Violence and Victims* 25, 536–52

Straus, MA, Gelles, RJ, Steinmetz, SK, 1980, *Behind closed doors: Violence in the American family*, Piscataway, NJ: Transaction Publishers

Straus, MA, 1999, The controversy over domestic violence by women: A methodological, theoretical, and sociology of science analysis, in X Arriaga, S Oskamp (eds) *Violence in intimate relationships*, Thousand Oaks, CA: Sage

Taylor, J, Chandler, T, 1995, *Lesbians talk violent relationships*, London: Scarlet Press

Tellez Santaya, P, Walters, A, 2011, Intimate partner violence within gay couples: Dimensionalizing partner violence among Cuban gay men, *Sexuality and Culture* 15, 153–78

Tesch, B, Bekerian, D, English, P, Harrington, E, 2010, Same-sex domestic violence: Why victims are more at risk, *International Journal of Police Science and Management* 12, 526–35

Thiara, R, Hague, G, Bashall, R, Ellis, R, Mullender, A, 2011, *Disabled women and domestic violence: Responding to the experiences of survivors*, London: Jessica Kingsley Publishers

Tigert, L, 2001, The power of shame: Lesbian battering as a manifestation of homophobia, *Women and Therapy* 23, 73–85

Tjaden, P, Thoennes, N, 2000, *Full report of the prevalence, incidence, and consequences of violence against women: Findings from the National Violence Against Women survey*, Washington DC: US Department of Justice

Tjaden, P, Thoennes, N, Allison, CJ, 1999, Comparing violence over the life span in samples of same-sex and opposite-sex cohabitants, *Violence and Victims* 14, 413–25

Towers, J, Walby, S, 2012, *Measuring the impact of cuts in public expenditure on provision of services to prevent violence against women and girls*, Newcastle: Northern Rock Foundation. www.nr-foundation.org.uk/wp-content/uploads/2012/03/Measuring-the-impact-of-cuts-in-public-expenditure-on-the-provision-of-services-to-prevent-violence-against-women-and-girls- Full-report-3.pdf

Turell, S, 1999, Seeking help for same-sex relationship abuses, *Journal of Gay and Lesbian Social Services* 10, 35–9

Turell, SC, 2000, A descriptive analysis of same-sex relationship violence for a diverse sample, *Journal of Family Violence* 15, 281–93

Turell, SC, Herrmann, MM, 2008, 'Family' support for family violence: Exploring community support systems for lesbian and bisexual women who have experienced abuse, *Journal of Lesbian Studies* 12, 211–24

Urquhart, C, 2013, How did your MP vote on the gay marriage bill?, *Guardian*, 5 February, www.theguardian.com/society/2013/feb/05/gay-marriage-gay-rights

Vogler, C, Pahl, J, 1999, Money, power and inequality in marriage, in G Allen (ed) *The sociology of the family: A reader*, Oxford: Blackwell Publishers

Walby, S, Allen, J, 2004, *Domestic violence, sexual assault and stalking: Findings from the British Crime Survey*, London: Home Office

Walby, S, Armstrong, J, Strid, S, 2012, Intersectionality: Multiple inequalities in social theory, *Sociology* 46, 224–40

Waldner-Haugrud, LK, Gratch, LV, Magruder, B, 1997, Victimization and perpetration rates of violence in gay and lesbian relationships: Gender issues explored, *Violence and Victims* 12, 173–84

Walklate, S, Mythen, G, 2011, Beyond risk theory: Experiential knowledge and 'knowing otherwise', *Criminology and Criminal Justice* 11, 99–113

Walters, ML, 2011, Straighten up and act like a lady: A qualitative study of lesbian survivors of intimate partner violence, *Journal of Gay and Lesbian Social Services* 23, 250–70

Walters, ML, Chen J, Breiding, MJ, 2013, *The National Intimate Partner and Sexual Violence Survey (NISVS): 2010 findings on victimization by sexual orientation*, Atlanta, GA: National Center for Injury Prevention and Control, Centers for Disease Control and Prevention

Warwick, I, Chase, E, Aggleton, P, with Sanders, S, 2004, *Homophobia, sexual orientation and schools: A review and implications for action, Research report RR594*, London: Department of Education and Skills

Watson, D, Parsons, S, 2005, *Domestic abuse of women and men in Ireland: Report on the National Study of Domestic Abuse*, Dublin: The National Crime Council in Association with the Economic and Social Research Institute

Weeks, J, 2007, *The world we have won*, Abingdon: Routledge

Weeks, J, Heaphy, B, Donovan, C, 2001, *Same sex intimacies: Families of choice and other life experiments*, London/New York: Routledge

West, C, 1998, Lifting the 'political gag order': Breaking the silence around partner violence in ethnic minority families, in JL Jasinski, LM Williams (eds) *Partner violence: A comprehensive review of 20 years of research*, Thousand Oaks, CA: Sage

Weston, K, 1991, *Families we choose: Lesbians, gays, kinship*, New York: Columbia University Press

Whittle, S, Turner, L, Al-Alami, M, 2007, *Engendered penalties: Transgender and transsexual people's experiences of inequality and discrimination*, Manchester: The Equalities Review, Manchester Metropolitan University

Wight, D, 1994, Boys' thoughts and talk about sex in a working class locality of Glasgow, *Sociological Review* 42, 702–37

Wilcox, P, 2006, *Surviving domestic violence*, Basingstoke: Palgrave MacMillan.

Wilde, B, 2012, *'Delivering equality': Executive summary. Somerset lesbian, gay, bisexual and trans health and social care report*, Wellington: The Diversity Trust, NHS Somerset and Somerset Link

Williams, F, 2004, *Rethinking families*, London: Calouste Gulbenkian Foundation

Wood, JT, 2001, The normalization of violence in heterosexual romantic relationships: Women's narratives of love and violence, *Journal of Social and Personal Relationships* 18, 239–61

Worcester, N, 2002, Women's use of force: Complexities and challenges of taking the issue seriously, *Violence Against Women* 8, 1390–14

Wright-Mills, C, 1959, *The sociological imagination*, Oxford: Oxford University Press

Index

Note: Italic page numbers indicate figures and tables.

A

abuse scales 44, 105–6, 112–18
adoption 61
age
  of consent 62
  risk factor for DVA 26, 101, 102–3,
    106, 197–8
  of survey respondents 45, 51
Archer, J 30
assimilationist approaches 66–73
awareness raising 212–13
  for practitioners 213–14
  within LGBTQ communities 213

B

Baker, H 10
Balsam, K 74–6
Barriers Model 159
Bauman, Z 123–4
Blassius, M, 'heterosexual panorama' 59
Bograd, M 11
British Humanist Society survey 64–5
Brown, MJ 187

C

CAADA (Coordinated Action Against
    Domestic Abuse) 7, 8
Campbell, JC 10
Cancian, F 19
care expectations/obligations 147–52
  indicative behaviour, Power and
    Control Wheel 207
Carvalho, AF 76
Causby, V 2
CCR see Coordinated Community
    Response
Chavis, A 202, 210
Children Adoption Act (2004) 61
civil partnerships 6, 23, 68
closet metaphor 72, 74, 75, 77
Cockburn, C 15–16
coercive behaviour, defined 6

coercive control 12, 37, 76, 113, 119,
    123, 195–6
  not recognised as an offence 90
COHSAR Power and Control Wheel
    204–6, 209–11
  indicative behaviours 206–9
COHSAR research approach 35–8
COHSAR survey 38
  comparison with previous surveys
    41–2
  covert vs. overt approach 39–41
  findings 97–105, 195–201
  incorporating impact 43–4
  interviews 48–53
  obtaining the survey sample 38–9
  participants 44–8
  summary 53–5
'combined abused' 105–6, 114–15, 118
coming out 60–1, 75, 85, 86
  gay women 81–3
  and help-seeking ability 77–8
  stress associated with 77
community knowledges, lack of 78, 81,
    82, 83, 103, 211
Conflict Tactics Scale (CTS) 30–1, 43,
    76, 90
confluent love 20–1
control 11–12
  in relationships 94–5, 103–5
  see also coercive control; COHSAR
    Power and Control Wheel
controlling behaviour, defined 5
Coordinated Action Against Domestic
    Abuse (CAADA) 7, 8, 142
Coordinated Community Response
    (CCR) 6, 7
  failure in responding to LGBTQ
    victims/survivors 7–8
Coy, M 7
Crenshaw, K 16
Crime Survey for England and Wales
    (CSEW) 26–7, 31, 38, 41–2, 54, 100
and help-seeking 172–4

Criminal Justice (Scotland) Act (2003) 6–7
criminal justice system 5–7, 60
Cruz, J 91, 95
CSEW *see* Crime Survey for England and Wales
CTS (Conflict Tactics Scale) 30–1, 43, 76, 90

D

dating relationships 130–1
decision-making within relationships 132–8
deconstruction, feminist project 35–6
'defensive' strategies 116
definitions of DVA 4–6, 8, 90
dependency
  of abusive partners 127, 141, 152
  of mothers 123
  'nanny' state creating 169
  of women, construct of 125–6
disability 47, 52
Domestic Abuse National Strategy for Scotland 6
Domestic Violence Crime and Victims Act (2004) 4, 6, 7, 189–90
Donovan, Catherine 2, 8, 123
Duluth Power and Control Wheel 201–2
  for LGBTQ relationships 202, *203*
  multicultural wheel 202, 203
  new COHSAR wheeel 204–11
  SHOULD BE 'wheel'
Duncombe, J 125
Dunne, G 69
DVA (domestic violence and abuse)
  background 2–4
  challenging public story of 211–15
  definitions of 4–6, 8, 90
  experiences of 97–105
  identifying as a problem 160–72
  identifying and recognising 90–7
  impact of 15, 105–12
  potentially abusive behaviour against partners 115–18
  previous research 25–31
  severity-impact relationship 112–15

E

earnings *see* income
economic abuse *205, 208*
edited narratives 177–8
education
  guidance on sex and relationships 63–5
  of survey respondents 46–7
  used as a weapon of control 103–4
  see also low educational attainers

Emery, B 22, 125–7
emotional abuse
  difficulty identifying 92–3
  impact of 105–12
  incidence of *98*
  perpetration of 115–18
  severity and impact 112–15
emotional strength in victims/survivors 152–5
Employment Act (2008) 61
entitlement abuse 205–6, 209
epistemological approach 31–2, 35, 36, 38
Equal Love 68
equal rights 63, 64–5, 66, 69–70
Equality Act (2010) 61, 62
Eriksson, M 103
ethnicity 46, 51–2
Evans, M 123–4

F

family
  LGBTQ communities 68–9
  relationship practices 131
  responses of 175–6
  as source of help 172–3
  as willing and helpful audience 183–4
fear
  and accessing police support 190–3
  as control weapon 111–12
femininities, expectations about 60
feminism/feminist discourse 3, 9, 19, 20–1
  important feminist principle 90
  and love 123–4
  power and control notion 11–15
feminist research
  epistemological approach 31–2, 35, 36, 38
  importance of ethics 40
  quantitative vs. qualitative methods 25, 31, 35–6
financial abuse 83–4, 103–4, 111, 208
Finch, J 131
first same sex relationships 77–86
formal sources of help *see* police
freedom, loss of 78–9
friends
  difficulty talking to 170–1, 182
  importance of 173
  isolation from 81, 99–100, 122
  potential source of help 172–3
  responses of 175–6, 179–80
  as willing and helpful audience 183–4

G

Gabb, J 50
Garland, D 169
gender-based definition of DVA 4–5
gender differences 15, 53, 90–1, 119, 196–7
  emotional abuse 108
  in sexual abuse 100–1
  in type of abuse used 122–3
gender(ed) norms 22–3, 24, 46, 122, 124–5, 155, 196–7
Gender Reassignment Act (2004) 61–2
Gender Recognition Certificate (GRC) 61–2
gendered assumptions, relationship roles 121–2
Giddens, A 20–1, 124
government policy and definitions 4–8
Greenwood, GL 29
Grigsby, Nancy 159
Groscup, J 187
guidance, sex and relationship 63–5
Sex and Relationship Guidance (2000) 63–4
guilt 136, 142, 150, 165, 190, 208

H

Hardesty, JL 158–9
Hart, B 24
Hartmann, Brenda 159
hate crime 68, 74, 86, 197
help-seeking barriers 157
  decision to seek help 172–4
  edited/partial narratives 177–9
  models of help-seeking 157–60
  police support 190–3
  problem recognition 160–72
  rejection from informal sources of help 179–80
  sources of help 175–6
  willing and helpful audiences 183–90
  willing but unhelpful audiences 180–2
Hester, Marianne 1–2, 125–6, 154–5, 159, 174
heterosexism 12, 13, 58–9, 61, 73, 75–6, 197
heterosexual assumption 19, 21, 24, 59–61, 69–72, 187, 188
  consequences of living under 73–7
  impact on LGBTQ people 77–86, 87
hidden nature of DVA in same sex relationships 70, 71–2
Hill, M 202, 210
HIV 2, 3
  abuse related to 41–2, 205, 209
  and dependency relationships 140–1
  risk of contracting 110
Holmes, Cindy 169
homophobia, internalised 73, 74, 75–6
homophobic bullying 22, 64, 74, 86
homosexuality 'promotion' 3, 64–5
'honour'-based violence 6, 123
human rights 57, 70, 150

I

identity abuse 122, 204–5, *209*
impact scales 43–4, 112–13
incidence 29, 30, *98–9*, 113–14
inclusion 62
inclusive services 214–15
income
  of COHSAR respondents 46
  see also low income respondents
Independent Sexual Violence Advisers (ISVAs) 7
inequalities 16–17, 37, 53, 57–8
  between partners 197
  in heterosexual relationships 125
  and minority stress 74
informal sources of help 173, 175–6
  rejection from 179–80
  see also family; friends
intersectionality 10–11, 13, 15–16, 17, 22, 102–3
interventionist state 169
interviews 48–53
intimate partner violence, US surveys 27–8, 29, 41, 100
intimate terrorism 12, 13, 113, 119, 195–6
isolation 85–6, 205
  from families of origin 78, 82, 84
  and help-seeking 122, 179, 190
Issac, A 2

J

Jackson, S 124
Jamieson, L 9, 19–20, 21, 125
jealousy 127, 148–9, 210
Johnson, MP 12 13

K

Kanuha, K 159
Kelly, B 211
Kelly, Liz 7, 90, 96, 108
Kwong-Lai Poon, M 10, 14

L

legislation 3–4, 6–8, 61–2
Leone, JM 160
lesbian relationships
  minimisation of DVA in 2–3
  research on DVA 13–14, 25–31
Letellier, P 14

Lewis, R 75–6
LGBTR community SHOULD BE
    LGBTQ community
  awareness raising within 213
  greater acceptance of 4
  Power and Control Wheel 203–4
Liang, B 157
literature reviews 2–4, 29, 49–50,
    157–8
Little, B 187
Lloyd, S 22, 125–7
Local Government Act (1988), Section
    28# 3
Lockhart, LL 2
love 121–2, 198–200
  declarations of 144, 145, 199, *207*
  and emotion work 18–25
  and help-seeking behaviour 164–9
  importance of 122–31
  see also relationship rules
low educational attainers
  heightened impact of abuse 110
  and material exploitation 103–4
  and risk of DVA 102, 106, 197
low income respondents
  at greater risk of DVA 101–2, 104,
    197, 198
  impacts of abuse 110–11
  and motherhood 104–5
loyalty 83, 86, 127, 139, 141, 176, 181,
    188–9, 198

M

mainstream services, wariness about
    using 185
MARACs (multi-agency risk assessment
    conferences) 7, 8
marriage
  beliefs about 128, 182
  educational guidance 63
  feminist critiques of 68–9, 123
marriage, same sex 62
  arguments in favour of 68
  campaigns for 65–6
  legalisation of 4, 23, 62
  rejection of 69–70
Marriage (Same Sex Couples) Bill 65
Marsden, D 125
masculinities 20, 22, 60, 137, 155, 156,
    200
Mendoza, J 75–6
Merrill, GM 11–12
Miller, DH 75–6
minority groups 74, 159, 189
minority stress 73–7, 86–7
Mobley, AK 44
Moran, LJ 169
Morgan, D 131

multi-agency risk assessment
  conferences (MARACs) 7, 8
Multicultural Power and Control Wheel
    202
Murray, CE 44
mutual abuse 76, 77, 116, 196
'mutual shaping' 17
mutual violent control 12
'mutually abusive' 118

N

naïvety 81–2, 165, 197–8
'nanny' state 169
National Intimate Partner and Sexual
    Violence survey (NISVS) 28
National Violence Against Women
    (NVAW) survey, US 27, 28
neediness in abusive partners 138–47
  and care obligation 151–2
  eliciting emotional strength 152–3
  excusing abuse 149–50
  indicative behaviour, Power and
    Control Wheel *207*
neo-liberal state 169–70
NISVS survey 28
normalisation agenda 67
NVAW survey, US 27, 28

O

Oakley, Ann 36
Obama, Barack 66
obligation of care 140, 147–52
oppression sickness, lesbian abuse as
    74–5

P

Parental Order Register 61
parents, same sex partners as 47–8, 61,
    104–5
partial narratives 177–9
Pattavina, A 184, 188
perpetration of abuse 115–18
perpetrators, presentation of 154–5
pervasive public stories 9–10
physical abuse
  impact of 105–12
  incidence of *99*
  perpetration of 115–18
  public story of DVA 9–10
  severity and impact 112–15
Plummer, K 66, 175–6
police
  non-reporting to 8, 163–4, 170–1,
    211–12
  as source of help 172, 174, 186–90
  support, accessing 190–3
policy 4–8, 25, 63–5

the Pope, views on marriage 65
positionality 11, 15–16, 22, 74, 97, 102
post-separation abuse 143, 145, 146–7, 180, 190, 192, 200
postmodern approaches 36–7
power and control, feminist notion of 11–14
Power and Control Wheels
  COHSAR Wheel 204–11
  Duluth 201–3
  multicultural 202, 203
practices of love 164–9
prevalence 26–30
privatised support 185–6
problem recognition 160–72
protected characteristics, Equality Act 62
Protection from Abuse (Scotland) Act (2001) 6
public story of DVA 161–4
  challenging 211–15
  focusing on physical violence 9–10, 152
pure relationship 20–1

Q

qualitative vs. quantitative research 35–6
queer respondents 45–6, 51, 55

R

racial identity 171–2
Ramazanoglu, C 38
rape
  definition 42
  by gay men 109
  negative impact 28
  prevalence 28
recognition of DVA 160, ADD 90-96
OR ADD identifying 90-96
  improving 211–14
  practices of love 164–9
  public story of DVA 161–4
  self reliance 169–72
relationship education/guidance 63–5
relationship length 47
relationship rules 121, 164, 199, 200
care expectations/obligations 147–52
  decision-making setting relationship terms 132–8
  and emotional strength in victims/survivors 152–5
  establishing 131–2
  need and/or neediness expressions 138–47
  new COHSAR wheel 204, *205, 206*

relationship type by abuse scale *118*
Renzetti, CM 13
reporting of DVA
  to family 180
  to police 8, 163–4, 190, 211–12
responsibility for the relationship 147–55, 206
Rich, A, 'compulsory heterosexuality' 59
Richardson, D 67
risk assessment 7, 8, 203–4, 214
risk factors for potential abuse 111, 119
  gender 109
  low educational attainment 102
  low income 101–2, 104–5
  relative age/experience 26, 101, 102–3, 106, 197–8
Ristock, J 9, 13–15, 27, 90–1, 100
romance 126, 127
  feminist critique 123–4
Rowlands, J 8

S

safer sex 100, 110
same gender vs. same sex, terminology 1
same sex marriage, campaigns for 65–6
same sex partners
  emotional, physical and sexual behaviours from *98*
  impact of emotional, physical and sexual behaviours from *107*
same sex relationships
  research on DVA in 25–31
sampling 38–9
Scottish Partnership on Domestic Violence 6
Section 28, Local Government Act (1988) 3–4, 62
  legacy of 63–5
security, lack of 81–2
Seidman, S 67, 75
self-blame 127, 164–5, 167, 170, 179
self-defence 31, 44, 44, 76, 116
  violent resistance 12
self-defined abuse 114–15, 118–19
self-identification, COHSAR survey participants 45–6
self-reliance 169–72
Senn, CY 159
service providers, expectations of 60
services, wariness about using 185
sex and relationship guidance 63–5
sexual abuse
  crime survey questions on 42
  gender differences 100
  impact of 105–12
  incidence of *99*

perpetration of 115–18
severity and impact 112–15
sexual inequality 12, 15, 37
Sexual Offences Act (2003) 42
sexual orientation, educational advice
    on 63–4
Sigma surveys 25, 30
situational couple violence 12–13, 38,
    160, 196
socio-cultural positioning, barrier to
    help-seeking 158–60
Soeken, K 10
SSDVA (same sex domestic violence
    and abuse) 4, 5, 11–15
current research 31–2
previous research 25–31
see also COHSAR survey
St Pierre, M 159
standpoint approaches 36, 37
Stanley, JL 14
Stark, E 12, 37, 89, 203–4
state, neoliberal discourses 169–70
Stonewall survey 25–6, 30–1
Strategy on Violence Against Women
    and Girls (2010) 4
Straus, MA 30
structural intersectionality 11, 16–17
structured dependency 53, 123, 196
suicide threats 127, 142–3, 210
Szymanski, DM 75

T

Terrance, C 187
therapeutic support 185–7
Tigert, L 74–5
training for practitioners 213–14
trans people, legal recognition 61–2
trust, gap of 157, 162–4, 185, 188, 194,
    198
see also help-seeking barriers
Turell, S 29

U

United Nations (UN) Convention
    on Elimination of Discrimination
    against Women (CEDAW) 4–5

V

'victim', construction of 9–10
victims/survivors, emotional strength
    in 152–5
violence, reporting to police 190–3
violent resistance 12

W

Walby, S 16–17
Waldner-Haugrud, LK 29, 91
Weeks, J 59, 64, 68–9

West, C 72
Westmarland, N 174
Weston, K 69
White, B 2
women
    definitions of violence against 6
    surveys on violence against 27–8
    use of violence 2–3
    see also gender differences

Y

younger respondents, greater risk of
    DVA 26, 101, 102–3, 106, 197–8